D1241367

LANDMARK
ARCHITECTURE
OF
ALLEGHENY COUNTY
PENNSYLVANIA

by
James D. Van Trump
&
Arthur P. Ziegler, Jr.

THE STONES OF PITTSBURGH, NUMBER V

Published by

Pittsburgh History & Landmarks Foundation

Pittsburgh, Pennsylvania

1967

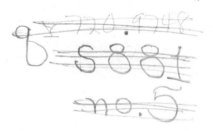

Incorporators

Pittsburgh History & Landmarks Foundation

Hon. William W. Scranton

Hon. Joseph M. Barr

Charles Covert Arensberg

Rev. John Baiz

Stanton Belfour

Paul G. Benedum

James M. Bovard

Arthur E. Braun

Frank H. Briggs

John G. Buchanan

Mrs. J. Mabon Childs

David W. Craig

Russell O. Deeter

Charles Denby

Harmar D. Denny

Edward D. Eddy, Jr.

David C. Fahringer

Rabbi Solomon Freehof

Miss Helen Clay Frick

James G. Fulton

Ralph E. Griswold

Gustave von Groschwitz

Blair F. Gunther

Calvin S. Hamilton

Mrs. Leland Hazard

Leon E. Hickman

Henry L. Hillman

James F. Hillman

Mrs. Henry P. Hoffstot, Jr.

Alfred M. Hunt

Roy A. Hunt

B. Kenneth Johnstone

The Junior League of Pittsburgh

George E. Kelly

Mrs. Albert H. Kiefer

James W. Knox

Emil Limbach

Edward H. Litchfield

Edward J. Magee

Frank L. Magee

S. P. Marland, Jr.

Rev. Henry J. McAnulty

William D. McClelland

Rev. Frank Dixon McCloy

John E. McGrady

William S. Moorhead

Thomas E. Morgan

David Olbum

David McNeil Olds

William R. Oliver

Steven L. Osterweis

W. H. Rea

Dahlen K. Ritchey

Rev. R. Dixon Rollit

Rev. Howard C. Scharfe

A. W. Schmidt

Mrs. William E. Schroeder

Paul Schweikher

Mr. & Mrs. R. Jackson Seay, Jr.

Miss Jeannette Seneff

John O. Simonds

W. P. Snyder, III

S. K. Stevens

Nicholas R. Stone

Charles M. Stotz

Lawrence Thurman

James D. Van Trump

J. C. Warner

Anthony Wolfe

Lawrence Wolfe

Most Rev. John J. Wright

Arthur P. Ziegler, Jr.

Board of Directors

The Committee
for The Register

Charles Covert Arensberg, Chairman

Mrs. Robert E. Fulton

Ralph E. Griswold

Mrs. Henry P. Hoffstot, Jr.

David Lewis

William R. Oliver

S. K. Stevens

Charles M. Stotz

James D. Van Trump

Arthur P. Ziegler, Jr.

The Staff
for The Register

Project Director
 Arthur P. Ziegler, Jr.

Research Assistants
 Julie H. Grimstad
 Elizabeth Bell Hetherington
 Margaret Steck

Photographers
 Bern Keating
 Barbara D. Hoffstot
 Charles W. Shane
 Paul Harnagy

Director of Research and Writing
 James D. Van Trump

Designer
 A. H. Kiefer

Staff
 Gay M. Blair
 Jane Blair
 Creta Coulter
 Ruth C. Hunter
 Ruth Murphy
 Kathleen Smith
 David J. Speer

Table of Contents

Credits

Such a compendium as this entails the time and effort of many people. In all of our work we are forever beholden to Mrs. George Cunningham at the Pennsylvania Room of Carnegie Library and Miss Prudence B. Trimble at the Western Pennsylvania Historical Society, who proved to be of inexhaustible help and equal patience. Keith Doms, Director of Carnegie Library, and Professor John Pekruhn at the Department of Architecture, Carnegie Institute of Technology, assisted us in working out the depository of records and measured drawings while James Massey and John Poppeliers of the Historic American Buildings Survey were invaluable in giving us guidance. Our associate Charles W. Shane was indefatigable in proofreading and assisting with the promotion of this book, and A. H. Kiefer deserves tribute for its design.

Several photographers other than those listed under "Staff" on the preceding page provided photos including John Alexandrowicz, James H. Cook, Robert E. Dick, and George Hetrick.

We are deeply grateful to the A. W. Mellon Educational and Charitable Trust for making this endeavor possible and to its representatives A. W. Schmidt, who conceived the idea of the Survey, and Theodore L. Hazlett, Jr., who counseled us in our plans.

Our own Survey Committee members were untiring in their assistance and yet very generous in allowing us to pursue the work in our own way. The unflagging, warm interest of Charles C. Arensberg, the commitment and solicitude of Barbara Hoffstot, the studious reflections of Joan Fulton, the glowing friendliness of William Oliver, and the incisive, critical, but always considerate responses of Ralph Griswold, Charles Stotz, S. K. Stevens, and David Lewis made our eighteen months a sound and pleasurable educational experience.

But beyond these are the persons—as anonymous as many of the buildings in this register—who sent us leads and material, who offered to help, who admitted us to their homes unannounced, who followed us through the streets curious and eager to learn, and who provided us with abundant information and hospitality. It is all of these persons as well as those named above that have made this study possible, who have been loyal to the buildings about them, and who have infused these pages with a spirit of dedication. We in turn dedicate our book to all of them.

A. P. Z., Jr.

Foreword

What is it that the Pittsburgh History & Landmarks Foundation is trying to do? Why did our distinguished incorporators lend their names to our cause? Why have many Pittsburghers helped us in our work for the past two years and in the publication of this survey?

We are a charity, but we are not "controversial". We do not feed or clothe the poor or bring them a better life in the material sense. We are not engaged in a struggle for civil or constitutional rights. We do not even focus on the future primarily. But we do see the past as a way of providing a better future for Pittsburgh.

"Remove not the ancient landmark which thy fathers have set" says *Proverbs*. We believe in that. We also believe in a view such as an eminent visiting architect expressed recently. Pittsburgh he said is, in its dramatic setting, in its unique regional charm, one of the three most fascinating cities in North America, along with San Francisco and Quebec.

According to Marshall McLuhan, "the insolent chariot" which along with the industrial revolution has all but destroyed our cities, has at best only a decade or more to go until it will be supplanted in turn by the techniques of the electric age.

Thus there is hope again for a "human scale" in our cities when the carapace of the car will yield up its uniformity and standardization and our cities will again be casual and pleasant places to live in.

We hope this register gives some hint of the possibilities in such a future.

Charles Covert Arensberg
President

North Side Market House

Fourth Avenue Post Office

North Side Post Office: doomed

| 6000 Meade Street, Boston | Projected highway casualty: Allegheny at Ridge Avenues | Point Bridge, Pittsburgh: Living on borrowed time |

AN INTRODUCTION
Both Personal and Programmatic

by Arthur P. Ziegler, Jr.

THE PITTSBURGH HISTORY AND LANDMARKS FOUNDATION was organized in September 1964, to preserve significant architecture in Allegheny County and to educate the public about the historical heritage of the area. Our first problem was to determine what landmarks exist and then to record them as a basis for further action.

Between 1932 and 1936 the Western Pennsylvania Architectural Survey under the chairmanship of Charles M. Stotz, was conducted in twenty-seven counties, including Allegheny, and the findings were published in *The Early Architecture of Western Pennsylvania*. This remarkable survey had nevertheless three shortcomings for our requirements. At the time it was made so many good buildings still remained that the recorders included only representative examples; it stopped with 1860; and, needless to add, it is now thirty years old.

Since 1936 the City had experienced massive redevelopment, the countryside suffered suburban sprawl, the highway departments had been permitted to demolish buildings for new roads and road relocations at will, and a good many early houses had simply collapsed with age.

We therefore faced the necessity of completing anew a County-wide survey of existing buildings before we could proceed with the act of planning wisely for preservation, and for this purpose we made application to the A. W. Mellon Educational and Charitable Trust for a grant of $30,000. The money was given to us in July 1965, and we predicted that the work would be completed in the fall of 1966.

The program called for registering the structures in book form, ascertaining basic information (date of construction, architect, materials), defining their individual significance, photographing some of the most important of them and representative samples of the rest, and depositing the research materials at the Pennsylvania Room of Carnegie Library, where the public may have access to them.

In many cases, particularly those of the smaller anonymous structures in the County, it was not possible to research thoroughly all data pertaining to them due to the limitations of time. Much of this arduous labor must remain for local students of the future. We hope that our notice of these buildings, primarily for preservation purposes, will evoke information from sources unknown to us at the time of the Survey.

PERSONNEL

The Executive Committee of the Foundation constituted the nucleus of the Survey Committee. The members of the former were Charles Covert Arensberg, president;

1

Mrs. Henry P. Hoffstot, Jr., vice-president; James D. Van Trump, vice-president; Mrs. Robert E. Fulton, secretary; and William R. Oliver, treasurer. To this committee were added three members of the Board of Directors, Ralph E. Griswold, Charles M. Stotz, and David Lewis (who also serves as our consultant in urban planning), Dr. S. K. Stevens, Director of the Pennsylvania Historical and Museum Commission, and myself, the Executive Director of the Foundation.

Mr. Van Trump and I were appointed to implement the work of the survey. Mr. Van Trump, with his great knowledge of the architecture of the region, directed the research and wrote most of the primary entries in the register while I coordinated the work and assisted in the writing.

FINDING THE BUILDINGS

The task of searching out the candidates for inclusion in our register took us back over the WPAS survey research records at Carnegie Library and through the standard histories of the City and the County. We braced ourselves for the sentimental borough and township histories and also contacted all the current municipal leaders we could for leads. The city and local newspapers and magazines carried our requests for recommendations, and we adjusted ourselves to television lights and cameras to further disseminate the word. Our members returned several dozen suggestions in response to a mailing, and by the time the initial publicity was over in September 1965, we had about 250 buildings on the list to examine.

But the work was incomplete. What nuggets might be hidden in the gridiron of North Side or the green valleys of O'Hara Township? What rich vein might be mined in Glenshaw or lodestones found on the streets of Duquesne?

The demand was obvious; we had to sally forth, not without dust and heat, and search. From late September to early January we made our way through the County, almost every day, seven days a week. We walked the densely built areas of the City like The Hill, North Side, South Side, Downtown, and Lawrenceville, and we drove through the rest of the County. A Corvair, already at the ancient age of four years and 55,000 miles, bumped over the Belden bricks, the concrete, the gravel, the encrusted mud, and ultimately the caked snow throughout this period of intensive work. Our only misadventures were three flat tires. But as the hours of driving slackened in the late winter and spring, the car itself lost momentum and putted to its own final stop in March.

DISCOVERY AND EDUCATION

Charles M. Stotz speaks of his field explorations as the most "entertaining and colorful" part of the work because "the territory was far richer than had been supposed", and Van Trump speaks of our excursions with equal enthusiasm in his essay.

Although I embarked as a naive lad of 28, a youngster in the preservation field, I cannot equal their sense of lively adventure. Without doubt we uncovered a host of unknown structures and, more important I think, defined areas where neighborhoods of buildings, insignificant in themselves, together contribute to the architectural character of the City, where, in Christopher Tunnard's words, the "architectural whole is greater than the parts."

Detail of stable, Canal Street, North Side

We also discovered areas of the City where architectual historians and enthusiasts had not trod, and from the tops of Pittsburgh hills we saw views so startling, so dramatic, that we felt,

> . . . like stout Cortez, when with eagle eyes
> He stared at the Pacific—and all his men
> Look'd at each other with wild surmise—
> Silent, upon a peak in Darien.

We had the pleasure of driving through the countryside in the fall and of witnessing the changing

2

spectacle of color, and we enjoyed the sense of discovery and variety as we wound our way around the hills and valleys of the County.

But, as I say, I was naive; I expected more. All of the new experiences that quicken the senses and fire the mind were reduced, overshadowed, vitiated by the sight of the desecration that man had wrought. While it is no secret that much of the architecture of the County is unfortunate, it is demoralizing to be exposed to it so intensively. All too often buildings are cheap, unimaginative, poorly designed, and ugly. And it does not matter whether they are old or new, they stand as ironic monuments to our willingness to abide the expedient; the kind of housing that we endure, the wretched shopping districts (or shopping centers) we permit, the bad taste we flaunt should appall us.

Industrial architecture, Natrona

Land use is equally shocking. With the exception of a few limited stretches, our four river valleys are hideous infernos of mills, intermixed with a tangle of warehouses, railroads, and highways. Many times when we had strayed from our course, we relocated ourselves by looking for the smog from the river valleys. Except for a few blocks here and there like Water Street in Elizabeth or First Street in Tarentum, no one lives on the riverfronts; in fact the water is inaccessible, sealed off by a jumble of industry, railroads, and highways.

Workers' Housing, Natrona

The immediate hillsides above the rivers are frequently littered with cheap nineteenth century workers' housing that has now often become hopelessly decayed. Behind these march the ranks of Edwardian houses, dull and staid, and spreading ruthlessly over the back hills are the new suburbs with all their monotony and indifference to their sites.

The rural story is no different. Patches of miners' housing together with the mines themselves blight hundreds of acres of the countryside. The old roads frequently are dimly punctuated with sagging piles of indifferent frame houses and woe-begone shops, and the new ones sport meretricious modern stores.

Suburban monotony, Harrison Township

It is a tawdry spectacle, and saddest of all is the fact that we have learned nothing; we still despoil the landscape and defile our ideals.

A rural house in Collier Township

Even so, the architectural nuggets do gleam— albeit often tarnished—through the disarray. We did ferret out hundreds of structures worthy of note, and their existence and endurance redeems our building history a little. If ignorance is everywhere and invincible, so too are the banners of struggle against it. The marks of the sensitive and plucky dot this county, and our book is a testament to them.

ACTION

But this book is not meant to be their tombstone or their elegy; we hope it will in some small way help them achieve salvation, for this architecture of value must be saved. In the midst of so much bad site planning, a Chatham Village becomes even more impor-

Abandoned coal tipple, Collier Township

Derelict fruit stand, Route 48

tant; with so little left of the eighteenth century, the Neal Log House in Schenley Park deserves the more distinction; with almost no rural communities of architectural character, the town called Boston is paramount.

During the course of our work, however, buildings of tremendous significance were falling about us. Psychologically or perhaps spiritually speaking, the most important building in the County after the Court House and Jail was the 1863 Allegheny Market House. It was destroyed in the fall of 1965 to make way for an apartment high-rise in Allegheny Center, and at the same time down went some of North Side's last Greek Revival houses. One of the finest municipal structures in the County, the Fourth Avenue Post Office, was razed in 1966 for a park and parking lot, despite its own stubborn resistance.

One of the last great engine roundhouses, that of the Pennsylvania Railroad on Liberty Avenue at 28th Street was obliterated as were numerous houses in East End and North Side. The Phipps Apartments on General Robinson Street suffered the same fate as did the fine Brierly House in West Homestead, the Denny House in Harmarville, and the Five Mile House near West View. We arrived on the scene in time to retrieve the cornerstone of the Risher Springhouse (1838) in Hays, which had been knocked down only one week earlier to make parking room for two trucks. Worse, in a way, than demolition was the stripping of the terra cotta ornamental skin of the Farmers Bank Building to replace it with metal panels.

We faced the impending demolition of a number of structures living on borrowed time, scheduled for oblivion in the next two or three years, and we followed the general rule of excluding most of them from the register. Included among them are the Manchester and Point Bridges and fifty acres of buildings in the Avery-Nash-Lockhart Street area on the North Side, which must make way for a vast interchange of the North Side Expressway. Avery College (1849), an

The spectacle of the modern highway, Route 51

important Greek Revival structure prominent in local Negro history, is located here. This new road slices up the East Street Valley annihilating every building in its path, including St. Boniface Church (1925-26). Also to be lost to progress is that little gem, the North Side Post Office (1895-97). Redevelopment of the lower North Side will wipe out a large number of mid-nineteenth century brick houses while Penn Park will flatten everything between Tenth and Twentieth Streets on the Pittsburgh side of the Allegheny. It even lays claim to the rotunda of the Pennsylvania Railroad Station (1900) and the Fort Pitt Hotel (1905-1909) with its Norse Room, done entirely in Rookwood tiles.

The crash of the headache ball, the falling stones, the crumbling brick and rotting wood discourage everyone sensitive to our architectural heritage. Worse often than rampant demolition or collapse are the structures erected on the old sites. But the ravaging of the emblems of our past can spur us on.

Across this country an awareness of beauty, an interest in history, a commitment to preservation is developing. We present to the public this book as evidence that here in Allegheny County we can be dedicated to this cause and to know the cause to which we should be dedicated.

4

THE COUNTY JOURNEY:

the Back of the Hand and the Heart

by James D. Van Trump

WHEN THE FOUNDATION WAS ASKED TO MAKE an architectural survey of Allegheny County, so sure was I of the terrain that I felt that another look at the County would be like examining the back of my hand. Synonymous with the hand would be the rivers and the hills, something so totally known that I could start speaking or writing almost automatically like one who dreams or speaks in his sleep. From this land and all its western flowing waters I emerged. I have borne in my blood the burden of all its building, known its joys and its sorrows and its seasons. Across its echoing valleys I have by writing made my flesh a bridge; girders and hillside stairs and golden rod issue from my fingers. From whatever hill or hollow I look upon this place, I do but consult my heart or my hand.

So in my ignorance, I considered how easy would be my task. I had in very fact, however, to learn by much searching that one never does fully know the heart or the back of the hand, or the road one has traveled a thousand times, or the hill that one has looked upon night and morning for a score of years. This is as it should be. For the writer or the graphic artist, the thing most surely known must always have some newness in it. When wonder dies, death ensues for the beholder; life must, by its nature, be always something strange and novel, and whatever land we inhabit should remain, a little, far and foreign to the usual day.

The night breeds mysteries and sometimes I made nocturnal journeys to procure information or to see the interiors of houses. Lamplight and shadow may cause a room to rise superior to its diurnal furniture and, similarly, the city may become a well of visual adventure, of far-flung, fabulous vistas. Down the slope of Mt. Washington there is a Piranesian arch from under which the illuminated city bursts upon us like a near constellation. Nightly, wonder remains close to us, and the back of the hand becomes as spacious as an astronaut's orbit. I would not give the midnight prospect of the Point from Duquesne Heights for all the star lands of Orion.

By day and night the land will perpetually reveal itself, even when I have done writing here, but are its revelations in any way more splendid than the wider prospect of the world? My commission was limited; I was to make a quick journey about the County for the purposes of architectural preservation. But I came to Allegheny County from a long stay in Europe and I was saturated with its densities of civilization and the sheer delightful weight of its centuries of architectural accretion. Some of my friends suggested that it might be difficult for me to appreciate the minor pleasures of the local landscape after such splendors. Just off the plane, I was inclined to agree with them.

But again I did not properly reckon with my heart or the back of my hand or the land which contains them both. With my companion of the survey, I began a systematic visitation of the country about Pittsburgh. All in the fine autumn weather we traveled the outer roads of the County seeking the minor and little-known buildings, towns in valleys or beside the rivers, old bridges and half-forgotten churches. As the months deepened into winter, we moved farther in toward the city where, it is true, many of the buildings and areas described here were already known to me. However, these sometimes took on new aspects. Under the influence of the day or the hour, the weather in the streets, or tricks of sun or mist, familiar buildings be-

5

came something other than they usually appeared. Again, a road never traversed before, a hill never previously visited revealed something new about the city.

As day succeeded day and the journey proceeded, my interest in my own land revived and my fascination with the renewed life of the familiar became totally absorbing. The heart was justified, the back of the hand vindicated.

At Pittsburgh, the core of Allegheny County, the land seems to fold inward toward the Point, the apex of that mystical triangle of earth, where locally everything begins and ends. This salience and its attendant rivers was, in time past, the symbolic gateway to the west, as, in a sense, it still is. Here is the great dream-like gathering of towers (such a collection marks the center of all modern American cities) among which is the tower of the Allegheny County Court House and Jail—Pittsburgh's undoubted architectural masterpieces of national importance. Here the back of the hand was most apparent and most surely known. We had counted over these tall downtown structures many times, and our accounting here is merely a recapitulation of past encounters.

But the heart says again that regional architecture is much more than a collection of public landmarks, important as they are. There are also a myriad anonymous buildings—houses, shops, churches—lying in their various multitudes all across the heavy folds of the land. One could devote a whole book to that curious and totally admirable Pittsburgh phenomenon, the hillside house. Again, in the County there are small towns and boroughs, or, within the City, neighborhoods, areas, environments all with special characteristics and qualities of their own. Boston on the Youghiogheny River, Pittsburgh's South Side and Troy Hill, Thornburg, Braddock, Sewickley, each of them differs from the other, yet all exist within the unity of the land. Often I have only noted the architectural presence of minor structures. Further research in these byways must wait upon a further leisure.

Of the County and the City as living physical entities it is almost impossible here to speak. Could I but note a fragment of the impressions gathered on the journey through the County, I should have volumes more. The strange, unutterable beauty of faces, old and young, moving along a busy street, hands grasping endlessly the balustrade of a stair, a golden tree dancing in an October wind, bright streams flashing around old truck tires in a green, shale-hung ravine, streets of stone and cracked asphalt, patterns of steel girders and tree branches, a carnival of fire from a nocturnal mill—all help to preserve the City and the County, give them their essential character and life.

The past is part of the life of the land and we are interested only in preservation for life's sake. The human heart desires, as well as the back of the hand, the past which is, in the end, the anchor of man's dreams and his remembering.

6

STARS, STONE, AND STEEL:

Notes on the Building History of Allegheny County

by James D. Van Trump

MOST OF THE BUILDINGS PRESENTED HERE will tell their own stories as we meet them in the survey, in the descriptive lists of which this book is composed.

It would be pointless in this essay to tell the same story twice, but we will attempt here some general historical landscape, a calendar of humanity and time against which the structures built by man can be more vividly seen, more closely comprehended.

Architecture emerges always from the land, and no less is this true in the County and in the City of which we speak. In the stones and in the trees, in clay and shale, lay the materials that the builders must use, but for long centuries in the land around the Point where the rivers meet there were only the primitive shelters of the Indians under the heavy verdure and the endlessly repeated branches of the living forest. In this wide expanse of sky and water and the infinite leaf our story does not lie. Only when the expanding shadow of Europe began to move across the wilderness do we begin to speak.

THE FORTS

That moving and stirring, scarcely perceptible at first, grew like great clouds and strong winds, and all this turmoil was the voice of rivalry and war. Stars fell from the turbulent skies, and it was the grand geometry of the military engineers that formed the first important architectural contribution of the Europeans to the local landscape. So it was that under the aegis of the French there appeared in 1754 at the Point a star called Fort Duquesne—for surely the historians of fortification will allow us so poetically to speak. All around stretched the hills and the waters, and perhaps their ancient calm was disturbed by this portent of a larger destiny, the seal and sign of Europe that was manifested almost mystically in their midst. That star has continued to expand, unfurling outward over all the land we call our County and our City. Now the limits of its growth no chronicler can predict, and the brilliance of its light no man essentially can measure.

The little fort of earth and logs was the warrior's star—a stockade surrounded by a moat—but it was also for the French the star called Wormwood, which poisoned their hopes and portended their dispersal. Rudely and hastily constructed, it was blown up by the retreating garrison in November 1758 at the approach of the English forces under Forbes.

From that dispersal and that sudden fire there rose a much grander and several-pointed star—Fort Pitt. When first the English forces possessed the Point, they ran up, in case of necessity, a temporary fort that was given the name of Pitt, but the real fortification was not begun until September, 1759. Constructed in the shape of an irregular pentagon, this expansive structure with its bastions, revetments, redoubts, and barracks, was a major military installation in the European manner and, for a time, a strategic star of the first magnitude on the western frontier.

After 1760 the installations were augmented even further; the Fort experienced a disastrous flood in 1762, and in 1763 it withstood a ten weeks siege during Pontiac's Rebellion. From 1764 dates the only surviving building of Fort Pitt—the redoubt of Colonel Bouquet, now known as the Block House, which may still be seen in the Point State Park.

After 1765 the importance of Fort Pitt as star of the western frontier began to wane, the fortifications were neglected, and in 1772 it was abandoned and its building material ordered sold. However, it still remained a fort until 1797, when the installations belonging to the United States were ordered to be put up for sale. So disappeared the military Star of the West.

Another fortification, Fort Fayette or La Fayette, was constructed in the vicinity of Penn Avenue and Ninth Street, but it did not remain useful beyond the War of 1812, and it, too, disappeared.

The great star of Fort Pitt had however shed its rays out into the surrounding land. Soon after its establishment a rude log settlement had grown up in its shadow and this began to expand outward into the area we now know as the Triangle. In 1784 the Triangle was surveyed and a plan of lots was laid out for the Penns by Colonel John Wood, but by 1796 there were still only one hundred fifty houses in the town and most of them were still of logs.

LOG STRUCTURES

Logs served for our early churches and schools, but houses of brick and stone began to be constructed. Some of them were built with brick from the demolished installations at the Fort, such as a group of houses on Market Street; among them, on the corner of Market and Third, was the dwelling of Ebenezer Denny, who became the first mayor of Pittsburgh in 1816.

After the turn of the century, the churches in the young city deserted their log shelters for more sophisticated buildings, and public buildings as well as houses began to appear that reflected to a degree the Georgian architectural style of the eastern seaboard. Among these was the first Allegheny County Court House (1799), which was a two story red brick structure of great simplicity with a hipped roof and a sharply pointed turret in the center.

The era of the log church, the log school, and the log house lasted even longer in the ravines, in the hills and valleys that lay in the countryside beyond the new city and its rivers. Most of these structures were modest constructions of one or two floors (they figure rather abundantly in this book) but we are told that there were rather more elaborate examples. One has heard of Croghan's Castle, a large construction of logs near the present site of Lawrenceville built by the trader George Croghan. It may have been a sort of early frontier version of the later mansions raised by Pittsburgh industrialists, but we do not know much about it because, as Charles M. Stotz tells us in *The Early Architecture of Western Pennsylvania,* no real description of it survives. Perhaps if a fort can be a star, even a fancy house of logs can be a castle. It seems particularly appropriate to Pittsburgh that our earliest castle seems to have been not of Spain or of clouds but solidly constructed of logs.

Certainly no castles had been the early log cabins of the first settlers, but the log houses have been more durable. Perhaps the Neal log house (1787-95), still extant in Schenley Park, is a good example of this once numerous group, but unless something is done to preserve this early survival of our eighteenth century past, it will not last much longer. Stotz has written extensively of the materials and construction of the log dwelling, and it would be redundant to discuss it further here.

EARLY STONE AND BRICK BUILDINGS

Along the roads that began to form, throughout Western Pennsylvania, pursuant to the rays of the great star at the Point, as the countryside became more settled, houses of stone and brick began to appear as well. Through some strange magic of the earth, stone from out-croppings in the hills, bursting naked from the verdurous slopes, seemed to form itself into the habitations of men. As we behold today the elemental power of the stone walls of taverns or farmhouses, we sense a kind of atavistic procession from the hill and the field to the sinewy hands, the scarred and hairy arms of our forefathers who built them. Here in these gaunt, eternal walls wherever we may behold them, the essential bone and muscle of the land is forever contemporary with the flesh. Having said this, we again refer the reader to Stotz, who has spoken much about these houses and the materials of which they were made.

Stone houses such as the Frew place (before 1800) in Crafton or the James Miller house (c. 1808) in South Park still testify to the solidity of the hills, but the house built of bricks became increasingly common after 1800. They were either five bay with the main hall and the central door in the middle of the facade, or three bay with the hall and door at one side; so they continued to be until the end of the century whatever the later mutations of "style". The central doorway, for instance, might have begun with a Georgian fanlight, continued through the mid-century as a Greek Revival "side light and transom" entry, and ended as an Italianate-Classical portal. *"Plus ça change, plus c'est la même chose."*

The houses in the young city itself, graduating by degrees from the once ubiquitous log ranks, tended, in the upper echelons at least, to be provincial or vernacular versions of the domestic Georgian eastern style. That these houses did exist and help to form the image of the city in its earliest days is important, but they disappeared long ago leaving behind them only names and shadows. Of later Pittsburgh houses we know something more, but these early ones, perhaps because we do not know too much about them, have a kind of magical quality, evocative of dreams, and perhaps their ghosts sometimes on a summer day shimmer in the waters of the rivers.

It was the inexorable waters of those rivers that tightly hemmed in the Triangle and its buildings. Always in this area there was only a limited amount of space and the ground has been built upon and built upon again. The late eighteenth century and the Greek Revival cities have almost totally disappeared, and now the Victorian and even the Edwardian Triangles are vanishing as well.

EXPANSION

The North Side, the erstwhile city of Allegheny which had been surveyed in the 1780's by Daniel Leet and laid out as a gridiron surrounded by commons, became, as the nineteenth century progressed, an expansive and thriving residential and industrial city. Here because of the relative flatness of the land, closely built blocks of row housing constructed in the Classical urban pattern were, almost uniquely in Western Pennsylvania, not uncommon.

As Pittsburgh itself expanded, the city began to move up the long ascending planes of the lower Hill. (Much of this area has in turn vanished with the urban redevelopment of the 1950's). The rapidly developing heavy industry of the City tended to congregate in the river valleys, where transportation was easy. The County itself became increasingly settled as more land was brought under cultivation and towns and villages were formed.

As prosperity attended the ever-widening commercial and industrial activities about the Point, smoke arose constantly to give the City its infernal reputation from which it was delivered only within the last two decades. Smoky it is no longer but something of its early vigor and power have departed along with the vapors from its forges.

Vigor and power were never absent from Pittsburgh, however. To a degree the City has never lost the adventurous spirit and the rugged character of its frontier days, and the tone of the place has always remained active, restless, masculine. Again something of the elemental simplicity and rude strength of the area's vernacular construction has always informed the County's building history. As a rule our local architecture is inclined to be sober, simple, forthright, and well-muscled. There is little here that is feminine or pretty.

THE "STYLES"

Even while the vernacular continued its course in the rural areas, keeping always its bold youthful freshness, over and above it appeared the architecture of the styles. The nineteenth century, which was to see so many innovations in architectural form and materials, was also a period of numerous stylistic revivals and a concommitant eclecticism. Sometimes an architect would adhere to one style in a design but often he would use several in one composition. In the latter case, making a stylistic analysis of a building is often a highly venturesome procedure. Form is, though, the important factor in architecture, and "style" plays merely a secondary role.

The vernacular sufficed for the traditional well-known building types, but the expanding technology of the nineteenth century required new forms that were constantly being evolved—factories and mills, railroad stations, department stores, great hotels, large libraries and art galleries, exposition halls. The evolution of forms here is various and fascinating, but those types expressive of emergent uses were nearly always clothed in the "styles", thus conferring on Victorian technology the authority of history.

THE GREEK REVIVAL

But most of these new forms were still in the future when we consider the Pittsburgh and the Allegheny County of the Greek Revival. The late Georgian Classical manner lingered on well into the nineteenth century and we may see it keeping company with the new Greek forms as in the Isaac Lightner (1833) and the Nicholas Way (1838) houses. This intensive interest in the architecture of Classical Greece began in Europe during the eighteenth century, but it had not become really established in America until the 1820's; by the 1830's it was the dominant style and the Grecian orders abounded throughout the land. The movement was at once the last phase of the Classical revival which had begun with the Italian Renaissance as well as one of the important nineteenth century stylistic trends.

A herald of the Greek Revival appeared in Pittsburgh from 1813 to 1815 in the person of Benjamin Henry Latrobe (1764-1820), who was the first really professional architect to practice in America. Latrobe was an engineer as well, and the primary reason for his Pittsburgh sojourn was that of developing steam navigation on the rivers. While he was here he did make drawings dated 1814 for the Allegheny Arsenal in Lawrenceville. The severe Classicality of these designs, which were not strictly adhered to in construction, perhaps set the tone for much subsequent Classical work in the Pittsburgh area.

Pittsburgh particularly was a city where the new Greek manner flourished, and this stark and somber Classicism figured forth very appropriately the youthful prosperity and rising importance of the metropolis at the river gateway.

Of the Grecian orders, Pittsburgh, in consonance with its general masculinity of tone, preferred the Doric and the Ionic. John Chislett (1800-1869), the city's first important architect, who had been born in England and trained at Bath, used both orders in the important public buildings that he designed after he opened his office in Pittsburgh in 1833. Ionic colonnades adorned the first Bank of Pittsburgh building (1834) and Doric pillars presided at the doorway of Burke's Building (1836), Pittsburgh's premier office building. Chislett's masterpiece was undoubtedly the second Allegheny County Court House (1842) on Grant's Hill. Its splendid portico of two rows of Doric columns eminently symbolized the spirit of the City. Of these monumental structures only the smallest—Burke's Building—has survived, and it should be preserved. This is largely the known tally of Chislett's Greek works.

Also vanished are the Shoenberger House (c. 1847) on lower Penn Avenue; the Samuel Church house (1833) on the North Side; the Wilkins house "Homewood" (1835) in the East End; and the first Third Presbyterian Church (1833-34) downtown. The magnificent ballroom of the Croghan-Schenley house "Picnic" (c. 1835) has been preserved at the University of Pittsburgh, but most of the subdued glories of the City's Greek Revival have disappeared, leaving only a few glimmerings and shadows of what once had been, as witness the brick row houses (c. 1835) at Chestnut and Canal Street in the North Side or the Smithfield Methodist Church (1848) in downtown Pittsburgh.

10

In the matter of surviving monuments, aside from the Lightner and Way houses, the County is little better off, but a quantity of vernacular work with some Greek Revival characteristics is still extant.

The revival of medieval styles in the eighteenth century gathered momentum during the nineteenth until they rivaled and eventually replaced the Greek style. The Classical stream continued, but it was diverted again to a new interest in the Renaissance, especially that of Italy and France. Of the two revived medieval styles, the Romanesque sometimes kept company with the Renaissance as witness the recently demolished North Side Market House of 1863 and St. Michael's Roman Catholic Church (1857-61) on the South Side. Elements of the Romanesque appear also in a rudimentary or vestigial way in the vernacular architecture of the County— notably in many of the small country churches described in this book.

THE GOTHIC REVIVAL

It was the Gothic Revival, however, that captured most completely the imagination of the century. There was always something mundane, something earth-bound about the Romanesque, but the aspiring structural system of the Gothic seemed for a time at least to be much more in tune with nineteenth century expansiveness. In Western Pennsylvania, the Gothic was used almost completely for church and to a much more limited degree, house architecture. Pointed spires and pointed windows were by no means strangers to the local landscape.

The Gothic first appeared in any memorable guise in this area in 1824 when the second Trinity Episcopal Church was erected on Sixth Avenue after the design of its rector John Henry Hopkins. Hopkins, who published an *Essay on Gothic Architecture* (1836), was a figure of considerable importance in the history of the American Gothic Revival. As an architect, however, he was an amateur in the eighteenth century sense, and there was something rather more literary-picturesque than architectural in the design of Trinity. It did, however, place the Gothic image engagingly before early nineteenth century Pittsburghers.

The second important Gothic church to be erected in the vicinity was St. Peter's Episcopal Church (1851-52) after the designs of the Philadelphia architect John Notman (1810-1865). Constructed entirely of stone, it is a handsome example (unique in Western Pennsylvania) of the archaeological phase of the Revival, which had been so notably advanced by the Cambridge-Camden group in the 1840's in England. Although St. Peter's again illustrates the simple, sober tone of Pittsburgh architecture, it had little influence on local work.

The second St. Paul's Roman Catholic Cathedral at Grant and Fifth (1853-1870) also carried on the Gothic image of its earlier counterpart of 1828-34, but its broad Gothicized body, sharp Germanic spires, and thin octagonal dome made it look rather like stage scenery. More substantial as architecture was the third Trinity Episcopal Church (now Cathedral) designed by Gordon W. Lloyd of Detroit and erected 1871-72. The Gothic had also long since pentrated to the rural areas as witness the small Episcopal chapel of St. Luke's, Woodville (1852), a Gothicized vernacular stone meeting-house.

In the domestic field, the Gothic can also be seen in a modified Tudor form in Chislett's design for the Butler Street gate house (1848) of Allegheny Cemetery and the amazing Gothic-Second Empire stone manor house of John F. Singer (1865-69) in Wilkinsburg—the latter being a highly ornamented, larger than life version of many now vanished suburban houses. Also in this category we may include the frame "steamboat Gothic" cottages ornées of one of America's first planned suburbs, Evergreen Hamlet (1851-52) on the outskirts of Pittsburgh.

THE RAILROAD

And by the middle of the century the era of the suburb had definitely arrived in

11

Allegheny County. The advent of the railroads now made it possible for those engaged in business or commerce in the City to live at some distance from their work. The opening of the Pennsylvania Railroad in 1852-54 ensured that the wide expanse of the East Liberty valley would become chiefly residential in character. Around 1900 it had become a secondary focus of population in the metropolitan area; still residential and diversified with some light industry, it has always remained quasi-suburban in character.

Some of these old railroad suburbs like Edgewood or Oakmont have considerable charm while the old village of Sewickley on the Ohio River became a millionaire suburb. Not only the living but the dead were beginning to desert the city and the planned Romantic suburban cemetery became the mortuary counterpart of the planned Romantic suburb. Pittsburgh, again, possesses one of the earliest of these sylvan graveyards—Allegheny Cemetery, laid out by John Chislett in 1844.

OTHER STYLISTIC REVIVALS

As the century advanced, the new architectural interest in the Italian Renaissance and the French manner of the Second Empire became more insistent. The mansard roof, a full-blown and sometimes coarse use of the more ornamental orders, elaborate portals, and highly decorated window cornices are characteristic of this manner. Perhaps the most salient example in the area was the second Pittsburgh City Hall (1868-1872) designed by J. W. Kerr. Complete with its Louvre-like square domed tower, it was an ornament to Smithfield Street until its demolition in 1953.

Around the middle of the century cast-iron began to be used extensively in building, not only for interior supports but also ornamental exterior details and sometimes whole facades. Many elaborate cast-iron commercial fronts still exist in downtown Pittsburgh although their demolition occurs frequently.

The earlier vernacular Romanesque paled before those magnificent adaptations of the medieval past—the Allegheny County Court House and Jail (1884-88) by the great genius of nineteenth century American architecture Henry Hobson Richardson (1838-1886). Perhaps it was the star of manifest destiny that caused the destruction by fire of the old Doric Court House in 1882 and the selection of Richardson to design the new County Buildings.

Pittsburgh by the 1880's had become one of the great industrial centers of the world, and Richardson must undoubtedly have been impressed by the rough vigor and the masculine vitality of the place. And he was a man to match the City. He felt that the Court House and Jail were the high points of his architectural career, and there is no doubt that they are among his best works.

Both of the structures are Victorian buildings, Romanesque only to a degree, but they are as well, highly eclectic in both mass and detail. In the superb granite masonry of the Jail walls, which has a timeless solidity and grandeur, and the stark fenestration of the courtyard of the Court House we are confronted with a monumental simplicity that places these structures among the great achievements of American architecture.

Also a national treasure is Richardson's small Emmanuel Episcopal Church (1885-86) on the North Side. A massively roofed, simple building, it is not only one of the architect's best late works but also superbly evocative of the tough Pittsburgh spirit. Rather more elaborate and archaeological in treatment is the Richardsonian Shadyside Presbyterian Church (1889-90) by Richardson's successors Shepley, Rutan and Coolidge. This handsome Romanesque lantern church is one of the landmarks in the development of the Protestant auditorium church in America.

Until the end of the nineteenth century the Richardsonian Romanesque manner was enormously popular in this area; in fact Pittsburgh became for a few years almost a Romanesque city as it had once been almost a Greek Revival city. The style was used for public buildings of all kinds, for churches, banks, shops, and houses small and great. There is scarcely a town in Allegheny County that does not retain, as well, some vestiges of the once all-pervasive Romanesque manner.

In the late 1880's and 1890's a new revival of interest in the architecture of the early Italian Renaissance became markedly evident, and Pittsburghers who were still contemplating the Romanesque solidities of the Richardsonian manner now began to find engaging the more delicate graces of the Quattrocento—the Tuscan vaults, the garlands, the arabesques, and the slim columns.

ADVENT OF THE STEEL FRAME

The largest, as it is also one of the earliest local monuments of this new movement is the great Carnegie Institute building, whose very Italianate version of 1891-95 (Longfellow, Alden and Harlow) was much augmented in 1903-07 by a larger more Beaux-Arts addition (Alden and Harlow). This later portion makes use of the steel frame.

The steel-frame building appeared in Pittsburgh in the early 1890's (a little late, perhaps, for one of the steel centers of the world), but it was this structural type that in the next couple of decades was to change entirely the aspect of the city core. The first steel high-rise in Pittsburgh was the Carnegie Building of 1892-93; the steel framework was left uncovered for a time so that the curious might examine it, but finally its Quattrocento skin (designed by Longfellow, Alden and Harlow) was pulled over it. Despite the fact that the structure was important historically it was demolished in 1950.

The Park Building of 1896 is perhaps the best known and the most highly ornamented of the late nineteenth century steel-frame structures. George B. Post of New York, who had designed the Roman-porticoed second building of the Bank of Pittsburgh (1894-96), which stood on Fourth Avenue until 1943, made of his high-rise structure a grammar of ornamental motifs that is still interesting today.

With the advent of the new century, however, Pittsburgh returned to its usual architectural sobriety once more, while at the same time the steel frame began to climb farther skyward. It was the twenty-four story Frick Building of 1901 (D. H. Burnham & Company), which led the procession and introduced the great skyscraper slab to the city. Right in the face of the Court House tower it proclaimed the pre-eminence of the new lofty city core. Here was the signal victory of steel over the smaller towers and the spreading horizontalities of the medieval and Renaissance cityscape of which the Pittsburgh dominated by the Court House was the last representative and the summation.

More and more the downtown area of Pittsburgh was left to commerce and the new steel-frame giants. Everyone who could afford it left to take up residence either in the suburbs or in more salubrious quarters of the city, and they took their churches with them. Those churches that remained in the downtown area tended to become institutional in character.

Representative of this latter group was the First Presbyterian Church on Sixth Avenue, which built its fourth building designed by T. P. Chandler, Jr., in 1903-05. Its rich, highly-textured curvilinear Gothic fabric, sumptuous but tasteful, is closely akin to the great new millionaire palaces that had begun to appear in the late nineteenth and early twentieth centuries in the North Side, the East End, and elegant suburbs like Sewickley.

HOUSES

Those palaces of the North Side tended to be built as "town houses"; that is they occupied sites in a closely built urban context. Representative of this type are the Byers-Lyon and the Snyder houses (built in 1898 and 1911 respectively) still extant on Ridge Avenue. With the decay of the North Side after 1920, however, these mansions were deserted by their wealthy owners for their suburban estates in Sewickley.

Perhaps the greatest concentration of millionaire houses occurred in the East End just before and after the turn of the century. The Greek Revival and Second

13

Empire houses of earlier suburban East Liberty began to be replaced in the late 1880's by Richardsonian Romanesque chateaux (which in their turn have by now almost completely disappeared).

After 1900 a veritable explosion of building activity took place in the East End. Most of the large estates with their sometimes extensive grounds were located along Penn and Fifth Avenues. These new multi-millionaire manor houses—Italian, Tudor, or Georgian—although large and constructed of rich materials, rarely tended to be lavishly ornate (at least on the exterior). For outward appearance's sake the general sobriety of the local architectural tone prevailed.

Most of these great houses have also disappeared and of those that remain, the Frick (remodeled in 1893), the Phipps-Braun (1901-03), and the Benedum (1911-12) houses give some idea of what these establishments were like in their heyday. Some of these huge houses had a life of little more than fifty or sixty years, and certainly none of them, with the possible exception of the Frick house, seemed to generate any ancestral piety. As the difficulty of staffing them and the cost of maintaining them mounted, most of their owners either sold or demolished them.

Meanwhile except for domestic and ecclesiastical work in the near and far suburbs, the County had steadily ceased by degrees to have much architectural significance as vernacular work faded and vanished away. With the loss of the ancient traditional ways of building something has gone from our land that can never be regained.

CHURCHES

There has always been, until very recent times at least, a marked connection between domestic and ecclesiastical architecture. This was certainly true in the East End, and it is here that we may see the last efflorescence of the Gothic Revival in the work of Ralph Adams Cram (1863-1942) and Bertram G. Goodhue (1869-1924), who were not only the heirs of the archaeologists of the nineteenth century, but they were also in possession of talents of the first order that enabled them to work freely and creatively in a style that they found sympathetic. Although for a time they were associated in the firm of Cram, Goodhue and Ferguson, the Pittsburgh work of this stage of their careers can be readily assigned to one or the other partner.

Calvary Episcopal Church (1906-07), which belongs to Cram, is a very handsome example of revived early English Gothic. Goodhue's First Baptist Church (1909-12) in Oakland, which owes something to both late French and English Gothic, is undoubtedly the most elegant example of the revived style in Pittsburgh.

Cram also designed two other East End churches, both of them showing the influence of the Spanish Gothic—the Holy Rosary Roman Catholic (1929-30) and the East Liberty Presbyterian (1931-35). These were built when the area was beginning to fade as a residential district. Their great suave stone towers preside now over an ambiguous collection of decayed houses and shops from which the prosperous middle classes have, for the most part, fled to the farther suburbs.

HENRY HORNBOSTEL

The early twentieth century in Pittsburgh was pre-eminently a period of architectural personalities, and one of these men of some originality and talent was Henry Hornbostel (1867-1961), much of whose best work can be found in one particular section of the city, Oakland, an erstwhile suburb, that had become in the 1890's the "civic" and cultural center of Pittsburgh. Hornbostel contributed some notable buildings to that development. The design of the original campus of the Carnegie Institute of Technology (1904-1923) is almost entirely due to him and the Soldiers' and Sailors' Memorial Hall (1907-11) is one of his most noteworthy monumental compositions. Hornbostel was particularly adept at interpreting the manner of the Ecole des Beaux-Arts in a bold and original way.

14

BENNO JANSSEN

Another outstanding architect of early twentieth century Pittsburgh was Benno Janssen (1874-1964), who also worked much in Oakland during the phase of its monumental development. A very fashionable architect, he was also a designer of great taste who was equally adept in handling the Italianate-Classical theme as well as the Romantic country house style developed in England by Sir Edwin Lutyens. In one category we have two Oakland buildings, the Pittsburgh Athletic Association Clubhouse (Janssen and Abbott, 1909-11) and the Mellon Institute for Industrial Research (1931-37) and in the other the E. J. Kaufmann house (1924-25) and the Long Vue Country Club (1922-26). All these commissions, except the first, were executed by Janssen in partnership with W. Y. Cocken. Well proportioned, suave, and elegant, these several buildings contribute a special fine glow to the local sunset of the "styles."

FREDERICK G. SCHEIBLER, JR.

However, the most original architect that Pittsburgh ever produced was Frederick G. Scheibler, Jr. (1872-1958), who may be considered also Pennsylvania's only proto-Modern designer. He received his training under the old dispensation as an apprentice, not in an academic institution or technical school; he never went to Europe and he knew nothing of the Ecole des Beaux-Arts. His extensive knowledge of the advanced contemporary European architecture of the 1900's he gained from foreign periodicals and books. He was not only a provincial but a parochial architect, and most of his work was confined to the East Liberty valley.

Scheibler was an individualist, a dedicated artist who developed his own design theories and refused to be moved by any other standards than those of his art. His work is similar in some degree to that of Frank Lloyd Wright and also to that of the European modernists of the first decade of this century. There are, of course, visible in his work many reminiscences of the middle European vernacular, witness his Old Heidelberg Apartments of 1905-08, but the subdued Modern note is omnipresent.

The influence of F. L. Wright is particularly noticeable in the Highland Towers Apartments (1913), which is just as striking in design and concept as the Old Heidelberg, if rather different in form and texture. Scheibler's work of the 1920's became increasingly Romantic and his earlier Modern tendencies less evident; he became blind in his later years and did little designing after 1925. His contribution to the architectural image of the City is, however, unmistakable and extremely important.

MODERNITY

Scheibler's experiments with small garden-communities of houses was very agreeably carried on in a large modern garden suburb of forty-five acres: Chatham Village (1932-36). Clarence Stein and Henry Wright were the site planners and Boyd and Ingham were the architects.

Chatham Village has had deservedly an extensive fame among planners, but what might have been a valuable lesson, locally, to future "developers" of land in the Pittsburgh area has been largely ignored. Today the great suburbs of the motor age sprawl endlessly and haphazardly over the once green hills of the County. Here the star of Progress sheds a baleful light on the scarred and misused land near the meeting of the rivers.

In 1900 D. H. Burnham and Company designed a splendid steel and terra cotta domed rotunda to stand before the Pennsylvania Station in the Triangle. Disguised as a cabstand, this handsome building was intended, symbolically, as the gateway to the new century; now it is decayed and threatened with demolition.

Looking out through its wide arches the seeker after architectural truth may behold the great towers of the Triangle. Burnham's huge steel-framed slab for H. C.

Frick was followed by an even larger one for the Henry Oliver Estate erected in 1908-10. For many years the Oliver Building dominated the constantly augmented ranks of smaller high-rises, but it, in turn, was overtopped by new giants in the 1920's—the Grant Building (1927-30) designed by Henry Hornbostel and Eric Fisher Wood; the Koppers Building (1929) by Graham, Anderson, Probst and White; and the Gulf Building (1930-32) by Trowbridge and Livingston.

One of the great visual landmarks of the Triangle, this last tower, whose peaked roof remembers in its pyramidal form the Mausoleum of Halicarnassus, one of the seven wonders of the ancient world, also serves as a weather beacon.

This great tower, half-modern, half-reminiscent of the past, serves as the terminal point of our essay. Since the end of the Second World War there has been much building in the Modern style done in Pittsburgh, but that is not part of our story here.

Perhaps the bright beacon gleaming from the Gulf Building, as it sheds its light on newer and ever larger towers of steel and glass, may reveal emergent marvels. Perhaps the beacon is a star. We hope it augurs well for the future of the land at the Point.

A NOTE

"Significant architecture" is a term difficult to define. The value of a building can vary with the context of the environment in which it is located, it can vary with taste and time, and it can vary with the observer. In this volume we have tried to select buildings that met criteria established by our historian and by a group of people knowledgeable concerning architecture and our local area. Whatever significance our selections may have will be derived, therefore, from age, aesthetics, unique structural or design qualities, and historical associations.

We have tried to be reasonably complete, although even as we write this final note new candidate structures are being suggested to us for inclusion. Any additions must necessarily be left to future editions or the present work itself would never end. We hope that this register will bring to public attention not only the buildings listed in it but others now unknown, and that periodically a supplement can be issued.

In many of the anonymous buildings outside the city limits time and budget did not permit the thorough research we should have preferred; again this labor must be carried out by future architectural historians and students.

We have attempted to set down all the facts that we could gather within the limitations that we faced in order that the reader might at least be acquainted with each building. Our endeavor is to compile an initial list that provides an overview of the County's notable buildings. In this way we will have the future work of preservation planning and historical research delineated.

James D. Van Trump
Arthur P. Ziegler, Jr.

For Touring

This register is divided into City of Pittsburgh and municipalities in Allegheny County. The listings in each area are arranged insofar as they permit in a sequence that enables a person to drive from one to another. However, distances and locations at times precluded our establishing an easy route. At the back of this book is a series of maps that cover the entire County and show street names and local route numbers. You are invited to use them as your guide; we also suggest the purchase of the Road Map of Allegheny County that is published and sold by the Allegheny County Planning Commission.

THE REGISTER

I. PRESERVATION AREAS
II. INDIVIDUAL BUILDINGS

I. PRESERVATION AREAS

LARGE SCALE URBAN REDEVELOPMENT is the major tool used today to revitalize our cities. This process, however, need not always entail demolition as it generally has in Pittsburgh, but can take the form of rehabilitating and restoring architecture that, while it has fallen into decay, retains qualities of design that make it irreplacable. Often the residential urban environment of the eighteenth and nineteenth centuries is more pleasant than that of the contemporary high rise city apartment complex because of its smaller scale, its homogeneity of tone, its carved detailing, and its simple brick and frame materials.

In many cities such areas have been completely refurbished; Society Hill in Philadelphia and Beacon Hill in Boston are two of the most successful examples.

In our City and County we have only a few buildings of the eighteenth and early nineteenth centuries, but we do have clusters of later nineteenth century and Edwardian structures, and we here delineate some districts that we feel form cohesive and unique architectural areas that should be preserved, and when necessary, rehabilitatcd.

Oakland Square, Oakland

This area is definitely an echo—faint and provincial though it is—of some of the Georgian and early Victorian squares of London. Save for the Commons of the North Side, there is nothing else quite like it in the city. It was developed about 1885; Dawson Street bounds it on the west, and on the east, which side is unbuilt, the hillside falls away into Junction Hollow. The wide view up Panther Hollow is quite fine, although the view is not quite "on axis", and it adds another and extremely Pittsburgh dimension to the "square" concept.

Although the small houses lining the square are not of very high quality (some of them do retain a spindly 1880-ish charm) the Square itself is one of the finest urban open spaces in the city, particularly in connection with Parkview Avenue opening to the south. If the area were rehabilitated, it could be one of the most pleasant residential areas of Pittsburgh.

Shadyside

On its largest boundaries, Shadyside the district is bounded roughly by Centre, Negley, and Fifth Avenues and Neville Street and is situated between Oakland, now the cultural center of the city, and East Liberty. By the mid-nineteenth century both Oakland and East Liberty were still suburban villages of no great extent and the Shadyside district, then part of Peebles Township, was largely forest and farmland traversed by somnolent country lanes.

Gradually the rising community began to shake itself free of the vernal anonymity of the ancient wilderness and houses appeared here and there. A district school was established in 1838 near what is now Aiken and Fifth Avenues. However, it was not until the Pennsylvania Railroad was opened to through traffic in 1852 that the East Liberty valley in general and Shadyside in particular became a favored suburban quarter.

The area we have designated for preservation is bounded by Fifth Avenue, Aiken Avenue, Devonshire Street, Centre Avenue, and the Pennsylvania Railroad.

The area was once the Ekin or Aiken farm. The original owner David Ekin, married Rachel Castleman, and their daughter, who married Thomas Aiken, inherited the farm. Thomas Aiken and his son David divided the farm between them. In 1854-55 Thomas Aiken erected a house for himself at what is now Ellsworth Avenue and St. James Street. Both the house and the nearby station on the Pennsylvania Railroad were called Shadyside, and in consequence the name came to be applied to the whole district. After Thomas Aiken's death in 1873, much of his farm was divided into residential lots. The Shadyside Presbyterian Church (q.v.), which Thomas Aiken was instrumental in founding in 1866 was for many years the true center of the district, as was very often the case in nineteenth century American suburbs.

The area has always retained a very open suburban aspect, and parts of it retain that character even today, notably in the streets immediately surrounding the Shadyside Presbyterian Church. These quiet thoroughfares lined with old trees and elegant villas lying on broad green lawns constitute an almost miraculous survival of late Victorian and Edwardian Shadyside. Still to be found throughout the district are early mid-Victorian houses—usually those of the smaller sort—picturesque cottages, and the frame dwellings of small farmers or artisans. Most of the larger houses of this period are gone, but some of the late Victorian and Edwardian mansions survive. Large apartment houses are beginning to intrude on the boundaries of the district but it is to be hoped that these intrusions can be inhibited from encroaching too relentlessly on the green calm of this old suburban quarter.

Since the 1920's the district has been much frequented by professional people, artists, and those members of the upper financial classes (who are to be found in all American towns and cities) who like to live in "restored" old houses. In Pittsburgh, Shadyside has been the focus of their activities; restoration and rehabilitation still continue to be a marked and very pleasant architectural feature of the quarter. The shopping area of the community—that part of Walnut Street called "The Village", has mercifully been spared, for the most part, the black-top horrors of the usual suburban shopping center. It's very real charm, as well as its slightly pseudo "Main Street" quality have unfortunately attracted a raffish Bohemian "beatnik" element that tends at times to give the street a brassy, arty-commercial tone. If means can be

found to check these deleterious influences, perhaps the Village can once again become the true center of the community.

Certainly every effort should be made to preserve this compact, homogenous urban-suburban quarter with its surviving overtones of nineteenth century suburbia.

Thomas & McPherson Boulevards from Fifth Avenue to Dallas Avenue in Point Breeze

This area, laid out c. 1885, is an interesting example, in a miniature way, of an attempt to emulate some of the grand city planning of the Baron Haussmann in the Paris of the Emperor Napoleon III. The pallor and insubstantiality of this local shadow of the Champs-Elysées need hardly be exaggerated, but the attempt to combine Haussmann with American suburban amenity was not unpraiseworthy. Although the district has decayed somewhat, it still has a kind of leafy ordered "presence" and it could well be preserved as an example of its kind.

Lawrenceville

William B. Foster, father of Stephen C. Foster, bought in 1814 a tract of land comprising one hundred and twenty-three acres on the Allegheny River about two and a half miles from Pittsburgh. In April of that year he sold thirty acres to the Federal Government, which established there the Allegheny Arsenal (q.v.). The rest he laid out as a community, named in honor of the naval hero of the War of 1812, Captain James Lawrence of the frigate *Chesapeake,* whose dying words "Don't give up the ship!" later formed part of the seal of the borough of Lawrenceville.

In its early days most of the community life centered around the Arsenal, which stood between Penn Avenue and the Allegheny River, and 39th and 40th Streets, and many of the male residents were employed in government work. In 1834 Lawrenceville was incorporated into a borough. Industry, aside from the Arsenal, had begun to enter the area and the population was increasing. Churches as well were beginning to be established.

Until the later nineteenth century, some prominent Pittsburgh businessmen maintained summer homes at Lawrenceville.

Since Lawrenceville was developing into part of the metropolitan area, it became part of the City of Pittsburgh in 1868. After the Civil War the Arsenal gradually ceased to be of any importance but many new industries had located in the region between Butler Street and the Allegheny River. In 1907 the upper portion of the Arsenal grounds became a city park but even in 1844 the park-like Allegheny Cemetery had been established on a large hillside tract between Penn Avenue and

Butler Street. Later St. Mary's Roman Catholic Cemetery was laid out on a neighboring plot of land.

Two hospitals were founded in the area—St. Francis in 1866 and St. Margaret's in the 1890's; they are still functioning on their original sites.

The last decades of the nineteenth century found Lawrenceville not only a flourishing industrial quarter but a prosperous middle class residential area as well. The early half-rural aspect of Foster's "community" had long since vanished and the long ascending hillside streets between Butler Street and Penn Avenue had been gradually built up with later Victorian houses of two and three stories, sometimes in rows, sometimes double and semi-detached, sometimes single and standing in their own yards. Stylistically these houses were for the most part in the Second Empire-Italianate manner or less frequently the Richardsonian Romanesque. It is this area between Penn and Butler and extending from 40th to 46th Street that we wish particularly to designate as a preservation district.

After the middle of the nineteenth century there was a marked influx of Germans into the area, similar to that which occurred in parts of the North Side and the South Side and some of these red brick hill streets have a curiously Germanic quality —solid, gemütlich, and, occasionally, rather crudely ornate.

Butler Street, the main business and commercial thoroughfare, divided the area in half. There was considerable housing mixed in with the industrial installations below Butler, some of it quite solid, but in Victorian times when most people preferred to live close to their work, the hillside streets were the most desirable as they were removed to some degree from the bustle and smoke of the river valley.

There is little Edwardian architecture in Lawrenceville because the area had been largely built up by 1900 and most later building took place farther out in the East End, very notably and effulgently in such districts as the not too distant Baum Grove. Also toward the end of the century and later, immigrants from central and eastern Europe, including many Slavic groups, began to come into Lawrenceville and many of their descendants now live there.

There is another smaller area on the up-river side of Allegheny Cemetery, a district bounded by Stanton Avenue, 54th, Butler, and Carnegie Streets, which is filled with neat two story workers' housing that is worthy of note and which could well be retained and rehabilitated to advantage.

Throughout Lawrenceville there are a number of survivals from the pre-1850 town, notably some Greek Revival houses, including those dwellings noted separately in the Register as of the Arsenal type. There are also several Romantic, picturesque "cottages" in the "Gothic" manner.

It is, however, for its character as a solid Victorian neighborhood of the period between 1860-1900 that we wish to designate Lawrenceville as a preservation district. Every effort should be made to retain its essential character as an evidence of the past life of the city. Although some unfortunate remodelling has occurred, many of the houses in the area have been well maintained and kept in repair so it should not be too difficult to keep these streets at their present level of maintenance—provided the character of the neighborhood does not change too radically.

The Mexican War Streets, North Side

Developed after the Mexican War (April 1846-September 1847) this tract of land north of the Commons was originally owned by William Robinson. All of the streets are shown as well built up in the Hopkins Atlas of 1882. The tract is bounded on the south by North Avenue, west by Buena Vista Street, north by Taylor Street, and east by Arch Street.

The boundary areas are in the weakest condition today and the center, particularly Resaca Place, is very good. Along with the Beech Street block between Allegheny Avenue and Galveston Avenue, Resaca Place is perhaps the most pleasing of the small thoroughfares built up on the Classical urban pattern in Allegheny.

All of the streets have a rather consistent scale of small two story constructions and although a few outrageous intrusions (and demolitions) have occurred, they do not unduly trouble the general line. The houses vary in form and style from very

Map of the Mexican War Street preservation district showing in grey the density of the houses to be preserved. The Allegheny Commons and Lake Elizabeth are directly opposite the district on the lower side of North Avenue, and the North Side campus of the Community College of Allegheny County and Allegheny Center, a shopping-residential-office complex, are within a few blocks.

simple Greek Revival types to mid and late Victorian examples (some with mansards) and even the early twentieth century is represented. A fine Romanesque house now in deplorable condition stands at the corner of Buena Vista and Eloise Streets. It is built of stone and has a circular third floor porch. A rather less interesting stone row house is further up this side of the street, and at 1241 Resaca stands a three story brick house with a Romanesque stone facade and carved stone faces at the porch entrance. The latter houses may all have been influenced by the Allegheny County Court House and Jail (q.v.) and the North Side Carnegie Library (q.v.). Another thunderous stone building—a sturdy but severe hulk—anchors the corner of Monterey and Taylor.

Abutting the alleys that parallel the streets are various small brick houses in random states of decay, and each has a parent brick house on the main street.

The interiors of these houses vary considerably. The decoration was always rather simple, although several have rather handsome fireplaces. Most of them, however, cannot compare in decorative treatment inside or out with the houses of Liverpool Street (q.v.), excluding those along North Avenue, which generally are three story and rather grand even if they maintain the somewhat grim Pittsburgh tone. The houses at the corners tend to be exceptional in style and design, although several along the blocks have fine woodwork in the porches and good wrought iron fences. The Wickersham Music School at 414 West North Avenue is an amusing Victorian structure, and the Unitarian Church next door supplies a pleasant variation.

The area is nicely contained by Taylor Street, the houses of which form a wall to the north, and the park to the south. The opening of Allegheny Center and Community College coupled with the generally good condition of these houses of manageable size will very likely spark the area as a major restoration effort in nineteenth century housing.

Manchester, North Side

This district which comprises most of the residential part of the city neighborhood known as Manchester is, for our purposes, bounded by West North and Columbus Avenues and Chateau and Bidwell Streets. The site consists of part of the lower North Side's rolling alluvial plain that is relatively flat in contour and that permitted the establishment of a gridiron layout for the streets.

Manchester, so-called from its earliest days, was laid out in 1832, erected in 1843 into a borough that in 1867 became part of the City of Allegheny by reason of common commercial and industrial interests. When Allegheny amalgamated with Pittsburgh in 1908 the area became the twenty-first ward of the latter city.

We have designated the residential area of Manchester as a preservation district because of its numerous mid and late Victorian houses. There were no millionaire townhouses, although on North and Pennsylvania Avenues there are still extant some large private dwellings of upper-middle class or even lower-upper class status in their prime. Most of the district housing is middle-class, of two or three stories and much of it is brick, although there is some frame construction.

There is considerable row housing in the area as well as a fair number of those party wall double houses which at one time were a residential staple of the North Side. A good example of the latter type of construction is the 1300 block of Liverpool Street (q.v.) where the closely-built, block-long row of double dwellings on the northern side of the street, gives the impression of a single row. The most interesting single example of these doubles, a handsome Ruskinian Gothic structure at 1233-1235 Sheffield Street has recently been demolished, but almost as good is the still extant building in the Italianate-Second Empire style at 1400 Pennsylvania Avenue at the corner of Manhattan.

Also in the 1400 block of Pennsylvania are two single houses standing in their own grounds. One of these, number 1414, is a red brick Italianate-Second Empire house (c. 1870) with its own stylistic version of the earlier Italian villa tower. Number 1410 is a house of about the same period with interesting Gothic detailing. At 1224 West North is a large Norman Shaw-W. M. Hunt-Richardsonian chateau with fantastically variegated gables standing on a high terrace. Next to it (number 1220) is another extensive dwelling, Picturesque-Richardsonian in form with some Colonial Revival detailing. At 1431 Liverpool Street is the rectangular rather severe bulk of the former Max Rosenbaum house which is now derelict and in extremely bad condition. At 1430 Columbus Avenue there is a three story brick and stone house

27

of about 1880 whose bold, intricate massing lends piquancy to another otherwise not particularly distinguished street.

Among the smaller single houses of the area is a two story and mansard, red brick at 1112 Liverpool Street which has an elaborate cast iron porch applied to its standard Italianate-Second Empire facade. There are not many of these ornamental filigree porches left in the Pittsburgh area, and although the house itself is in very bad condition, the porch should be saved.

There is still interesting row housing in the area, some with verandahs in front and some whose walls rise directly from the sidewalk. Among the latter is a row of houses in the 1200 block of Sheffield with coarse Ruskinian Gothic detailing. There is some Richardsonian stone-faced row housing in the 1200 block of West North and in the 1300 block of Liverpool, but most dwellings of this type tend to fall stylistically into the Italianate-Second Empire category with debased Classical portals and elaborate window cornices.

There seems to be little Edwardian housing in the district which would seem to indicate that even by 1900 the area had passed its prime as a favored place of residence. The district generally seems to be in a much more advanced state of decay than the Lincoln-Beech area and it would seem apparent that if the area is not to become totally derelict, some strong preservation and rehabilitation measures will have to be undertaken without delay.

Lincoln-Beech, North Side

This district comprises the area bounded by Lincoln, Beech, and Allegheny Avenues and Brighton Road.

As the City of Allegheny expanded outward from its original gridiron core, the area beyond the western common (later West Park) became a desirable residential district about the middle of the nineteenth century. Streets were laid out and they began to be built up with upper middle class and upper class housing of various types—single family houses standing in their own grounds, row housing, large double houses, and small or large single family houses built wall to wall in the Classical urban pattern. Although much of this construction has been demolished, a great deal still remains, even if in poor condition. The area is also a graphic illustration of the rotting process that has invaded the older quarters of so many American cities.

Ridge Avenue, the next street south of Lincoln, was always the most fashionable and was especially favored by the iron and steel millionaires of the later nineteenth century. On lower Western Avenue some Greek Revival houses survived until well into the present century, but on that part of Western that bisects our district, the housing is for the most part smaller post-1860 and more closely built. Lower Western Avenue is now a dreary commercial desert, but many of these later houses have survived, possibly because they were smaller. It is possible that some of these could be rehabilitated.

Lincoln Avenue, once second only to Ridge Avenue in residential favor although it is only two blocks long, once had a wide variety of upper class housing of which something still remains. Toward the Park some of the large three story double houses of the 1860's are still extant but they have been badly treated and for the most part have lost their character. Midway in the block is a charming small two bay, two story and attic, single house of the Classical urban type (No. 838). It is stone fronted and stylistically it is one of those fascinating amalgams of the Richardsonian Romanesque and the Classical. The facade is well proportioned, the scale is good, and the detailing is restrained. It would be pleasant if this house could be preserved as a good example of the small upper-class townhouse of the 1890's.

At Galveston (once Grant) Avenue is the decaying domed building of the North Presbyterian Church (q.v.) and cater-corner to it the red brick Classical building of the old Allegheny Preparatory School. It is these quasi-public buildings that helped to anchor the residential district of the nineteenth century into a pattern of existence that for its time was viable. Houses, church, and school existed side by side in a closely connected unity of necessary function that vanished as those who upheld that unity—which in this case was essentially upperclass—moved elsewhere to form a new pattern that was essentially the same pattern in a suburban context.

28

That the context was changing is abundantly evident in the preserved presence of the house of William Thaw (930) which is a strange compromise between the three bay row house of the 1880's and the more open urban private house that had also been characteristic of Allegheny or the North Side from the very beginning. The image still presented to us that has somehow been miraculously preserved is, again, that of the standard three bay townhouse built close to the sidewalk, repeated twice from its more usual version of a hall door and parlor on one side into another unit with a recessed front porch, and again in a further section with a loggia in front (glassed in but we do not know when this was done)—probably an enclosed version of the standard American front porch beside it. At any rate Mrs. Thaw tired of this compromise and near the turn of the century in pursuit of the fullness of suburban life moved to the suburban East End, where she lived on a hilltop in a much detached Edwardian-Georgian Revival house.

There is little else remaining in this block of Lincoln between Galveston and Allegheny Avenues that is especially noteworthy—indeed one side of the street has been almost completely demolished. Perhaps the one area that would lend itself to rehabilitation with the least difficulty is that block of Beech Avenue between Galveston and Allegheny, inasmuch as these rather closely built two and three story houses would recommend themselves to would-be restorationists of moderate income. For the most part, also, these houses would seem to be better preserved than many of the remaining large houses on Lincoln.

Crouching at one end of the block like a great dragon is the huge serrated bulk of the Calvary M. E. Church (q.v.), whose soaring spires are a landmark in the North Side. Also at the Allegheny Avenue end of Beech is a large red brick double house (948-950) that is grossly ornamented in the most violent manner with colored tiles. It is said that Mary Roberts Rhinehart, the Pittsburgh novelist, lived in one of these houses at the corner in her youth. As we proceed along Beech toward Galveston, the houses become smaller, although none of them is by any means diminutive. On the Church side of the street there is some row housing but it is not in very good condition.

On the other side of the street is a type of city dwelling that again marks a compromise between the Classical urban type of structure built very closely together at the edge of the sidewalk and the detached city house. These dwellings—no matter how limited the area between—have their verandahs on the side instead of in the front. All these houses with their nice scale and good proportions could certainly be restored to advantage. Their variegated red brick facades presided over by the great gawking crocketed spires of the church would certainly make for a preservation area of the liveliest interest.

South Side

This area that occupies the flatlands on the south bank of the Monongahela is indissolubly connected with one of Pittsburgh's prominent early families—the Ormsbys. Although it has undergone many changes since the land was Ormsby acreage, the district between 13th and 33rd Streets and from Bingham and Sydney Streets to the hill still has a marked individuality—perhaps because of its very mutations—that should be respected and preserved.

John Ormsby, the pater familias of the Ormsby clan, came to America from Ireland in 1752 and entered the British Army. He was with General Forbes when Fort Duquesne was taken in 1758. Grants from the government warranted to Ormsby most of the land between the Smithfield Street Bridge and Beck's Run—some two or three thousand acres later to be known as South Pittsburgh, Birmingham, East Birmingham, and lower St. Clair. Ormsby called the area Homestead Farms, an appellation that now seems wildly improbable.

While the elder Ormsby chose to build his estate in the section which today is East Birmingham, he deeded to his daughter Jane, the land from 6th to 17th Streets. Jane eventually married Dr. Nathaniel Bedford who in 1811 laid out a town on this land and named it for the English city.

Birmingham grew rapidly and by 1816 fifty houses had been built, many of them brick. There were also evidences of a varied industry—a glass works, a saw mill run by steam, an extensive pottery, where it was said "beautiful ware" was made. A square of land named for its donor, was given by Dr. Bedford to the settlement with the stipulation that it was to be used only for public purposes. Nearly fifty years later the South Side Market (q.v.) was built there.

By 1826 Birmingham had grown to such an extent that it was made a borough, the first to be created in Allegheny County after Pittsburgh. Glass factories and iron works comprised the major industries; coal mining in the hills also helped keep the population employed. The Ormsbys continued to be the prominent family of the South Side. Four daughters of John Ormsby married into the Page, Phillips, Wharton, and York families, and all of them built handsome houses along the Monongahela. Not only the Christian names of the daughters but some of the family names are preserved in the streets that run parallel to the river for most of the length of the South Side.

After the Civil War it was so apparent that this now well populated and industrially flourishing district was part of the metropolitan area, that it was all incorporated into the City of Pittsburgh in March 1872.

From the time of its founding until the early 1860's the South Side was largely populated by the original English, Irish, and Scotch settlers and by Germans who arrived in steadily increasing numbers after 1830. It was the Germans particularly who left a marked impression on the district as they did in other sections of the city.

Beginning about 1863, however, an influx of the Slavic peoples began that was slowly to change the population patterns of the South Side. We have noted this pattern of change in other sections of the city, notably Lawrenceville (q.v.). The first of these nationalities to arrive were the Poles; then Lithuanians began arriving and

after them Slovaks. The Ukrainians, last of the eastern European peoples to replace the earlier ethnic population elements in the South Side began emigrating to Pittsburgh about the last quarter of the nineteenth century as near as can be known from a rather cursory sampling of the present day population. The district is still populated to a large degree by the descendants of these Slavic groups. As time goes on, however, it is possible that these people may follow the heirs of the earliest settlers to the suburbs.

These Slavs have left little impress of their own vernacular tradition on the domestic architecture of the South Side; for the most part they either took over those houses built by the earlier settlers or if they did build, the construction was done after the American fashion. This would be true for other portions of the city in which the Slavs as relative late-comers settled.

It was quite another matter with their churches. The church was the one building in which these nationality groups could and did express themselves architecturally. In some cases where they took over the brick Victorian churches of the earlier inhabitants of the quarter, they might add an onion dome to a tower or place an iconostasis in the interior. When they did build as in the Ukrainian Church of St. John Baptist at Carson and Seventh Streets (q.v.) the form of the structure proclaimed unequivocally that it was of eastern origin. Its grouped turquoise-colored domes add an unmistakably exotic note to an industrial Pittsburgh valley.

East Carson Street, which runs the complete length of the district, was and still is the main business and commercial street of the South Side. Early in the nineteenth century it was the Washington Pike, the chief route between Pittsburgh and Washington, Pennsylvania, where it connected with the National Road. The street widens as it leaves the older Birmingham district behind. The street yet retains many architectural reminders of its prosperous nineteenth century days and at intervals there are some really imposing Second Empire-Italianate commercial buildings still extant. Although the seediness of these structures and the street generally testify to the fact that the South Side is no longer important industrially as it once was, every effort should be made to preserve as many of these buildings as possible since they serve as anchors for the residential quarters behind them.

Only a few short years ago a good number of the early Greek Revival houses of the area around Bingham Street and Bedford Square were still extant, but now little remains of old Birmingham except the former Bedford School (q.v.) and a couple of ecclesiastical survivals like the Ninth Presbyterian Church (q.v.).

The South Side is now chiefly known for its solid gemütlich red brick houses and churches that line the residential streets named for the Ormsby daughters. These streets have still a marked Germanic quality and in those areas where they are built closely together they show the influence of the Classical urban pattern of row-housing that was still a strong force in nineteenth century city building. In Pittsburgh, however, due to the nature of the topography, this pattern is only notably visible here and in the North Side.

32

These portions of the South Side are still well kept and the inhabitants remain vigorous and out-going in their demeanor in contrast to certain sections of the North Side where a hopeless decay and creeping blight seems to have infected not only the streets but the people who live among them. The atmosphere of the South Side is still hopeful and those concerned with urban preservation should make it their study to keep it so.

Sewickley

Sewickley on the Ohio River is known far beyond the bounds of Pittsburgh and Allegheny County as the most eminent of all well-to-do Pittsburgh suburbs, a character that it began to assume after 1850. Originally the land comprising the present borough was part of the "Depreciation Lands", of which Major Daniel Leet and Nathaniel Breading surveyed those portions in which Sewickley now lies. Allotments were then appropriated to the redemption of the depreciation certificates given to the officers and soldiers of the Pennsylvania line in payment for their services in the Revolution. Lot Number One called "Loretto" now includes the western half of the borough; adjoining on the east was a tract called "Aleppo".

Since Sewickley was on the road from Pittsburgh to Beaver, it was not long before a village with taverns and churches began to form. Until 1840 it had no official title but in that year the name Sewickleyville was chosen by the citizens. The town became a borough in January 1854 under the title of Sewickley. In 1851 another important event took place when the railroad was opened between Pittsburgh and New Brighton, and Sewickley became a station on the line. Since the village was not too distant from Pittsburgh, its character as a residential suburb of the City was assured.

The *History of Allegheny County* published in 1876 says of it—"There are few more beautiful places in the whole country than the borough of Sewickley. It is in one of the most favorable situations on the Ohio and has been settled by wealthy families who have united in making it an elegant suburban place of residence. For this purpose they have strenuously opposed all attempts to introduce manufactories into the place". When it is remembered that most of the choice riverside sites in the County have been preempted by heavy industry, the fact that Sewickley is still free of any large commercial activity seems little short of miraculous.

Toward the end of the nineteenth century, many industrial millionaires who maintained large town houses in the North Side began to establish extensive country estates in the hills behind Sewickley. In 1894 General Jacob Coxey, whose "Army of the Commonweal" passed through the town, referred to it as "the bedroom of Pittsburgh capitalists". It was not until after the turn of the century with the development of the automobile that many of the country houses in the "Heights" became places of year-round residence. After the Second World War changing social conditions led to the breakup of most of these great estates into smaller plots on which are located smaller dwellings. The day of the great Sewickley country house is definitely past.

But our chief concern is with the village of Sewickley itself, which we here designate entirely as a preservation district. The main business district located on Beaver Street is curiously nondescript in its architecture, but at least it has never become too modern or too quaint, nor does its vitality seem to have suffered any serious inroads from competing shopping centers. Broad Street, which leads to the Ohio River Boulevard and which intersects the Beaver Street commercial area, is visually an important element in the townscape. Here some of the public buildings of the borough are located. At Broad and Thorn Streets are the handsome Classical Public Library (q.v.) and cater-corner to it the large aggressively Victorian Gothic mass of the Methodist Church (1884) with its red brick clock tower and slate spire. Farther down the street at Frederick Avenue is St. Stephen's Episcopal Church. Some of the large residences along Broad Street have already gone for parking lots and others have been let as offices. Care must be taken that this commercializing tendency does not go too far as Broad Street represents the monumental core of the town.

During the mid 1920's the Pennsylvania Railroad moved its line to the river bank, unfortunately eliminating the Ohio River beach and making the river itself very difficult of access from the town. Although it was the railroad that brought Sewickley its widest suburban renown, it counts for very little now in the life of the borough and the fine Classical station erected on its new right of way is now disused.

It is interesting in this sequence of transportation that the former railroad line has now become the Ohio River Boulevard, the chief means presently of approaching or leaving the town. The Boulevard is a wide rather dull stretch of concrete, acting as an assembly belt line of traffic that is more divisive and essentially more menacing to life and limb than the railway line ever was. It is now lined through most of its borough length by some excruciatingly bad modern housing, a motel which is not badly designed and the scattered remains of some of the estates that used to line the railway line.

Although the Boulevard now carries most of the through traffic, Beaver Street still handles a considerable volume of motor cars. There is danger that commercialism may also spread out along this highway, menacing some of the large houses that line the street and creating visual hazards for such public buildings as the Sewickley Presbyterian Church (q.v.).

Sewickley, generally, is a kind of museum of suburban residential construction dating from 1800 to the present day, and this, with its concommitant ancient green and heavily verdurous setting, should be preserved at all costs.

Thornburg

By reason of its isolated position on a hillside overlooking the valley of Chartiers Creek, this little borough has been able to maintain a remarkable homogeneity of

34

tone and architecture. It was laid out in 1900 and became a borough in 1909. The streets or roads have all been named for well-known academic institutions—Yale, Dartmouth, Harvard, Hamilton, and Princeton, and the area is heavily wooded with old trees.

The houses are all fairly large and most of them seem to belong to the first two decades of this century, although there are a few from the 1920's and even one or two modern ones. Most of these suburban villas seem to be upper middle class of a very settled and established sort and they are nearly all well maintained, but none of the "yards" or the gardens are excessively manicured.

Although some of the architecture is pedestrian, much of it is rather on the "original" side, and a rewarding study could be made of these houses as good examples of early twentieth century domestic work.

Elizabeth Borough

Elizabeth should be recommended as a preservation area because in spite of all the changes that have taken place in the Monongahela River valley, it has still retained a certain homogeneity of appearance due to the presence of so much of its early nineteenth century and later Victorian architecture. The single railroad track that runs through the town along First Avenue has been planked, a once common practice that one rarely sees now. Along the right of way are stations now looking very deserted and put to other uses. Water Street has a good collection of houses of the early nineteenth century. Lafayette is supposed to have spoken from the porch of 108-10 when he visited Elizabeth in 1825. There are a number of interesting houses on Second Avenue where is also the Methodist Church with its tower and spire which is the visual focus of Elizabeth—the distant "point of interest", as it were, which "signals" the town when it is seen, say, from the hills behind, where the later Italianate-Second

Empire houses are lined up, or even from the new approach of the Route 51 bridge, which swings the highway widely behind the town.

It is, however, Water Street with its early nineteenth century brick houses and taverns that recalls most strongly Elizabeth's early importance as a river town. Stephen Bayard, a successful Pittsburgh business man, laid out the town in 1787 and named it for his wife, the daughter of Colonel Aeneas Mackay; Bayard also established the Elizabeth Boatyards in 1788, which were an important factor in opening up the western territory because many emigrants had boats built here to complete their journey westward by water. In 1800 Bayard began building sea-going vessels. Steamboat building was launched here by the firm of Walker and Stephens in 1826 and for some time the town continued to be an important center of shipbuilding.

The entire length of Water Street, although there have been some unfortunate later excrescences and intrusions, is of sufficient merit architectually speaking to warrant preservation.

Boston, Elizabeth Township

Boston in Elizabeth Township is a quiet, pleasant little town on the Youghiogheny River. It is of no great extent; it has no outstanding industry or special renown and perhaps its great name, seemingly applied in such a haphazard, incongruous fashion to this diminutive village, rather recommends it to our half-humorous regard and even, as Americans, our affections. It so captures our attention because, for all its small superficial modernities, it seems to have been arrested at some earlier point in both our local and our national history. In some strange way we seem to be able to recapture in its physical entity the image of a western Pennsylvania hamlet of an earlier day.

Boston lies in the land between the Monongahela and Youghiogheny Rivers that was from 1758 peculiarly free from Indian depredations, which may have had something to do with the activities of General Forbes in that neighborhood. The only blockhouse in this peninsula was situated near Boston, and the walls of a fort, used as a retreat for the fighters at the Forks, were said to be visible as late as 1930 on the farm of M. M. Wilson.

In 1897 a group of prominent people in the area petitioned the Court of Common Pleas of Allegheny County to make Boston a borough, but their petition was rejected, thus seeming to cast the place farther back into the mists of history.

A brother of the Duncan of Duncan, Cornell and Werhing (see below) is said to have given Boston its name, but no one seems to know why. Whimsey, perhaps, or some sentimental memory? The mists of history give us no answer, but the name survives.

Most of what is now called Boston was property "taken up" by Sam Finley in the right of James McKinney under the name of "Two Friends". This property of 165 acres was surveyed 25 May 1770, patented 1 April 1802, and assigned to Robert Smith. Other owners of large amounts of acreage in the area were John Norton, John Wilson, David Hindman, and Fanty Muse.

Coal was first discovered in the Boston area in 1815, but it was not until 1852 that coal mines began to flourish. Lumber was also abundant in the area. For a time the firm of Duncan, Cornell and Werhing were prominent in the coal business. There was at one time a salt works that stood where the highway bridge now crosses the river.

The town retains a number of interesting old houses that, if of no outstanding architectural merit, do contribute notably to the town's air of existing in the past. 5715 Smithfield Street, a frame house built in 1867, was originally the Kerr home. Opposite on the same street is the frame Werhing house of 1870. The brick dwelling to the right of the bridge as one crosses from Versailles is the John Duncan house of the 1870's. On the site of the Cornell house is the Super Dollar Market.

This last item in the landscape is possibly portentous as it has been in so many other rural or suburban contexts. However, one would be willing to bet on Boston that it will not need really serious preservation attention. Wrapped in the minor mists of history, remote, unhurried, calm, it will probably preserve itself.

Even as a ruin, Roman in its magnificence, the Fourth Avenue Post Office defies the ominous, omnivorous parking garage. A demolition scene taken in August 1966.

II. INDIVIDUAL BUILDINGS

A Word About Format

Each individual entry in this register follows a particular format. First the building is listed by name if known and by type if it lacks a name. In the case of structures that have changed hands, the last name of each owner is generally listed; thus the Stewart-Schlag house was originally owned by a family named Stewart and is now owned by a family named Schlag.

Next the street address is given, followed by the function of the building, (e.g. "house") if that is not clear from the initial entry. If the use of the building has changed, both the original and the present uses are noted.

In the next line the name of the architect, when known, is followed by the date of construction. The next entry defines the style, and following that, in the next line the wall construction, the number of stories, and the building's current condition are noted. For the latter we have selected "very good", "good", "fair", and "poor" as the categories, and all judgments are made from our somewhat cursory examinations of the structures and should not be construed as final or as thorough engineering opinions. More than anything, they suggest what the buildings appear to be.

Any missing information is noted only by its omission in the format.

The abbreviation l.r. refers to the local county route number of a road and c. means approximately. A building with the date c. 1850 was built about 1850. Q.V. refers the reader to a separate entry for the structure so designated.

The format is therefore as follows:
Structure (by name or type)
Street address
Use (if not clear from the name)
Architect   Date
Style
Wall construction, number of stories, condition

The section of the book called "Within the City Limits" lists all entries in a sequence that can be followed as a tour. "Beyond the City Limits", because of governmental boundaries and long distances between structures, lists all entries by municipal sub-division. These cities, boroughs, and townships appear in alphabetical order.

39

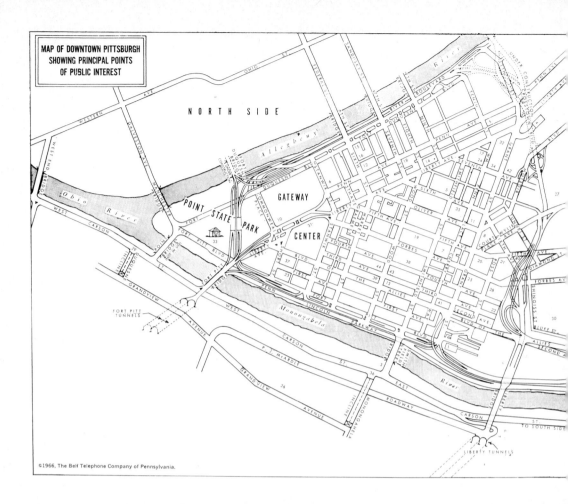

MAP OF DOWNTOWN PITTSBURGH
SHOWING PRINCIPAL POINTS
OF PUBLIC INTEREST

©1966, The Bell Telephone Company of Pennsylvania.

40

II. INDIVIDUAL BUILDINGS

Within the City Limits

Between the Allegheny and Monongahela Rivers

Downtown

FORT PITT BLOCKHOUSE
Point Park
Original use: redoubt   Present use: museum
————— 1764
Brick   1 story and loft   very good

According to C. M. Stotz, the oldest building of any sort of verified date in the district, the Blockhouse was built as an outlying redoubt of Fort Pitt by Colonel Henry Bouquet after he had raised the siege of Fort Pitt in Pontiac's War of 1763. It stood outside the walls of the Fort between the Monongahela and the Ohio bastions. After 1784 the redoubt with additions was converted into a dwelling and Isaac Craig was the first occupant; his son Neville B. Craig was born there. The structure remained a dwelling until 1 April 1894, when it came into the possession of the Daughters of the American Revolution by deed of gift from Mrs. Mary Croghan Schenley, the granddaughter of General James O'Hara. Operated for many years as a museum by an association under the auspices of the DAR, the building will have a prominent place in the new Point Park. As the oldest building in the city, its preservation is mandatory and now seems assured.

OFFICE BUILDING
127-29 Fort Pitt Boulevard
For sale
————— 1872
Brick and cast iron   —————   good

A rather elaborate cast iron front building with Renaissance styling and round-arched windows.

42

SMITHFIELD STREET BRIDGE
Smithfield Street spanning the Monongahela River
Gustave Lindenthal   1883, 1889
Steel trusses on stone piers   ——————   good

This bridge, designed as a two lane bridge, was erected in 1883 as a one lane (twenty feet wide) span. In 1889 another lane with truss above (also twenty feet wide) was added on the upstream side. In 1911 the upstream truss was widened several feet. The designer was Gustave Lindenthal (1850-1935), one of the most famous of bridge engineers, who had set up a private engineering practice in Pittsburgh. He also designed the former Seventh Street Bridge, which was opened in 1885. The Smithfield Street span makes use of the Pauli or double lenticular truss. Now the oldest and one of the most graceful of Pittsburgh's river bridges, this span should be preserved if possible.

PITTSBURGH & LAKE ERIE RAILROAD STATION
Smithfield Street at Carson Street
William George Burns   1898-1901
Classical
Brick and terra cotta over steel frame   7 stories   good

This is the best preserved of the large Pittsburgh railway stations still extant (there are only two of them left) but it is a question of how long it will be allowed to stand because of expensive maintenance, which the P&LE might not want to pay. The station is a combination of the terminal headhouse type with through tracks on one side toward the river.

The building itself, which contains some 80,000 feet of floor space, is, like the Pennsylvania Station (q.v.), of the office building type. Designed in 1898 by William George Burns, it was completed in 1901. Its large single span train shed, 100 **feet**

43

wide and 500 feet long, was extended some 200 feet in 1911, only to be demolished in 1935.

The compact but hollow cube of the station is in keeping with the Pittsburgh tradition of the "no nonsense" type of architecture. Burns has sparsely adorned the muscular brick and stone flesh of the building with very subdued Beaux-Arts detailing. The one lively note on the exterior is a large relief of a moving locomotive, "Number 135" in the square pediment at the centre of the ornamental roof balustrade. It advances proudly, emitting clouds of stylized smoke, serving admirably to announce on the facade the purpose of the building.

On the interior the great waiting room is undoubtedly, after the foyer of the Carnegie Music Hall, the finest Edwardian interior space extant in Pittsburgh. The staircase that descends into the room like a waterfall is especially noteworthy and the ornate detail that adorns this great two-story hall contributes a general air of subdued corruscating richness to the whole great convoluted space. Every effort should be made to preserve this elegant structure and perhaps if it should no longer be needed as a station, some other use could be found for it.

GRANT BUILDING
330 Grant Street
Henry Hornbostel;
   Eric Fisher Wood, Associate architect   1927-30
Beaux-Arts—Modern
Brick and cast stone over steel frame 40 stories very good
This structure together with the Koppers and Gulf Buildings represents the great high-rise of the 1920's, a period of much local building activity in this field not to be matched again until the 1950's and '60's. The lower floors are faced with Swedish granite and the upper walls with buff brick and brown cast stone.

The exterior ornamentation as executed was much simplified from the early designs of Hornbostel. His early sketches are quite Beaux-Arts in character but the actual detailing of the building is rather Modernistic. There is a beacon on the roof. The building lobby was modernized in 1965-66, but not inappropriately.

CITY-COUNTY BUILDING
414 Grant Street
Palmer, Hornbostel & Jones
   and Edward B. Lee, Associate architect 1915-17
Neo-Classical
Stone over steel frame 9 stories very good
An architectural competition was held in which Palmer, Hornbostel & Jones, and Edward B. Lee, associate architect, won the commission. This handsome building

44

is an interesting combination of severe neo-Classical mass with Beaux-Arts detailing. The great arched loggia on the Grant Street front is extremely impressive as is the long interior hall with its gilded metal columns. The Supreme Court room with its ornate detailing is also an extremely effective interior space.

The Guastavino tiled vault drawings for the Grant Street loggia (now at Columbia University in New York) date from 1916; there is also a much simpler Guastavino vault in the Ross Street loggia.

The exterior of this building in its massive, stark simplicity, continues notably the Pittsburgh tradition of masculine architecture.

COUNTY OFFICE BUILDING
542 Forbes Avenue
Stanley L. Roush   1929-30
Romanesque-Classical
Stone over steel frame   6 stories   good
This is a handsome exercise in the Romanesque manner of the 1920's and represents the last flowering of the style before its ultimate eclipse in the 1940's. The lower story is not ill-designed but there is something of Victorian density and profusion both in the use of great polished granite pillars and their elaborately carved capitals where the carved beasts and monsters of the Court House are echoed. The vaulted lobby is elaborately medievalistic. The structure was probably intended to have more stories added to it but they have never been built.

There is no question about the preservation of the structure as it stands, barring drastic remodeling. If the building were enlarged, care would have to be taken that the new additions did no violence to the original construction.

UNION TRUST BUILDING
435 Grant Street
Frederick J. Osterling   1915-16
Gothic
Stone and terracotta over steel frame   11 stories   very good
Built as the Union Arcade in 1915-16 by Henry Clay Frick, who had bought the site from the Roman Catholic Diocese which had located St. Paul's R. C. Cathedral there 1828-1903, it was originally erected as an arcade building of four floors with office suites on the floors above. There are eleven stories in all with three more in the two small towers; the latter also contain the elevator machinery. There is a legend without foundation in fact that one of these towers contains a chapel, placed there in accordance with a stipulation in the deed sale with the Diocese.

The style of the building is that of the late North French and Flemish Gothic

of the fifteenth century. Erected on a steel frame, the lower floors are encased in sandstone with a base of Westerly granite. The elaborate canopied cornice of late Gothic "lacework" is made of terra cotta as are the surfaces of the steeply pitched mansard-type roof, the ornamental balustrades, and the towers. The flat part of the building roof, with its balustraded light wells and turreted towers possesses great visual importance in the cityscape, and in some ways it bears comparison with the famous roof of the sixteenth century Chateau of Chambord.

The interior with its superb central rotunda rising through eleven stories is perhaps the finest interior space in the city, but it was even finer as originally constructed, with its two cross-arms of the Arcade that rose four stories.

In 1923 the building was bought by the Union Trust Company and the first four floors of the Fifth Avenue side were remodeled after the designs of Graham, Anderson, Probst and White of Chicago, the successors to D. H. Burnham. Since then the other arm of the cruciform interior space has been closed up; two minor arms were never open since they had to serve as elevator platforms.

The fine, rich ornamental character of this building is a real asset in our cityscape and every effort must be made to preserve it.

ALLEGHENY COUNTY COURT HOUSE AND JAIL
436 Grant Street
Henry Hobson Richardson   1884-1888
Richardsonian Romanesque
Granite   7 stories   very good
These are the architectural lions of Pittsburgh and buildings that must be preserved at all costs. The Court House consists of a large hollow rectangle 301 feet by 209 feet, having a basement, five stories and attics on each side with an interior court 145 feet by 70 feet. The plan is essentially the same on all five floors of the building; the court rooms and offices are grouped around the outside of the structure connected by interior corridors that face the courtyard.

The style of the Court House is generally Southern French and Spanish Romanesque, but the form of the building harks back to other sources as well. The tower is perhaps the most salient element in the composition, although it has lost some of its effectiveness through the near juxtaposition of the Frick Building. The

46

47

interior court, which is almost free of architectural historicisms, is superbly designed.

Not quite so archaeological in treatment as the Court House, the Jail is, no doubt, in greater aesthetic favor at the present time. It has been expanded and remodeled at various times, notably in 1909 when F. J. Osterling designed a new wing as well as extensions to the earlier wings and enlarged the area of the jail yard. All this new work was carried out in the original style and the structure as it now stands seems like an amplification of Richardson's original scheme. It is generally conceded to be one of the most magnificent buildings erected in America during the nineteenth century.

The Court House seems now to be safe from those who would demolish, but ever since 1925 there have been recurring questions about the Jail. The situation seems not at the moment to be serious but constant vigilance must absolutely be maintained.

FRICK BUILDING

437 Grant Street
D. H. Burnham & Company   1901
Neo-Classical
Stone over steel frame   21 stories   very good

When the twenty-one story H. C. Frick Building was built in 1901, it was the largest skyscraper in the city. It was designed by D. H. Burnham & Company of Chicago, who had earlier designed the Union Trust Company on Fourth Avenue (1898) for Henry Frick. With its steel frame enclosed in a severe neo-Classical envelope, it marks the emergence of the great slab skyscraper in Pittsburgh. Massive and powerful in both form and detail, eminently suited to the spirit of the city and the time, the building leaves little doubt that Frick, one of Pittsburgh's great industrial leaders, intended it as a kind of monument to his financial might. The marmoreal severity of the lobby is relieved by a large stained glass window "Fortune" by John LaFarge, and two bronze lions by Alexander Phimister Proctor (1862-1950), which are stationed at either side of the Grant Street entrance.

PENN SHERATON HOTEL

Grant Street, Oliver and Sixth Avenues
Janssen & Abbott; Janssen & Cocken   1916; 1929
Italianate
Brick and terra cotta over steel frame   20 stories   very good

Designed in 1914, the first section—that on William Penn Way—was built in 1915, opened in 1916. The architects were Janssen & Abbott. Like the Union Trust Building (q.v.) next door, this hotel building was built on land owned by H. C. Frick. Frick had bought the property, which included the site of the Third Presbyterian Church some years before.

The materials are brick and terra cotta over a steel frame; the style is Italianate, a continuation and augmentation of the same manner that the young firm had used a few years earlier in the competition design for the now demolished

49

Y.W.C.A. on Chatham Street. This was the building that really started the firm on its career, although the PAA Clubhouse (q.v.) finished in 1911 remains their *chef d'oeuvre.*

D. H. Burnham had died in 1912; his last Pittsburgh commission from Frick had been that for the Highland Building (1911) in the East End. In his later building ventures in this city, Frick employed Janssen and Abbott for the hotel and Osterling for the Union Trust Building (q.v.). The early skyscraper scheme of the Classical order is much in evidence—base-column-entablature with a stone and terra cotta lower floor and high arched windows, then ranges of brick above. Finally at the seventeenth floor—the ballroom floor—is a kind of *piano nobile* on stilts; again appear the high arched windows surrounded by terra cotta ornament. However, the building is not highly ornamental—the detail is rather delicate and restrained and definitely of the best early twentieth century type. Its simplicity also gives it a definitely Pittsburgh flavor.

In 1928-29 a new section of the same height and in the same style was added —only the treatment was a bit more elaborate—as perhaps suited the ebullience of the 1920's. This new version quite filled the whole block, thus making it the largest "mammoth" metropolitan hotel of the early skyscraper age in Pittsburgh; it has some eight hundred rooms. At the ballroom level in the older section are little bridges faced underneath with Guastavino tiles. The public rooms of the older section—the lobby with its elaborate coffered ceilings, the formal Italian Dining Room (now replaced by a pseudo-Colonial tavern called the Harp & Crown in the new wing), the Ballroom—were all rather Italian in decoration, mixed with French touches.

The Urban Room next to the Ballroom on the seventeenth floor was designed by the theatrical designer Joseph Urban; now a little worn and dim, it was when it was opened in 1929, a particularly good example of the "Modern" of the 1920's.

FIRST LUTHERAN CHURCH
615 Grant Street
Andrew Peebles   1886-88
Gothic
Stone   1 story   very good
This is a pleasant edition of the "Decorated" Gothic parish church very loosely and assymetrically disposed both in elevation and plan. The church was organized in 1837 and erected its first building in 1839-40; the congregation bought a lot at Penn Avenue and Ninth Street in 1874 and asked James H. Windrim of Philadelphia to prepare plans, but financial difficulties forced postponement of building activities. In 1885 ground was bought at Grant Street and Strawberry Alley and in May of that year Andrew Peebles of Pittsburgh, was asked to prepare plans. They were adopted with some modifications and the cornerstone was laid in November. Constructed of sandstone, the church is in the form of a Greek cross; the tower and spire are 170 feet in height. The church was consecrated on 4 November, 1888.

The mosaic reredos and wall decorations were installed in the chancel after 1892, when the marble altar was also put in place. All work in the chancel was completed in 1897. The north transept windows were designed by Frederick Wilson of the Tiffany Studios as a memorial to the Black family (1898). Unfortunately the church is being dwarfed by the new high-rise buildings being erected on all sides.

NEW POST OFFICE & FEDERAL COURTS BUILDING
Grant Street at Seventh Avenue
Trowbridge & Livingston;
      Joseph A. Wetmore, Acting Supervisory Architect   1930-32
Classical
Stone over steel frame   11 floors and 4 basements   very good
This, one of the last Classical buildings to be erected in the city before the advent of the Modern style, is, like the Mellon Institute for Industrial Research, designed in a rather stark, stripped version of the Classical manner.

UNION OR PENNSYLVANIA RAILROAD STATION & ROTUNDA

1100 Liberty Avenue
D. H. Burnham & Company   1898-1903
Beaux-Arts neo-Baroque
Brick and terra cotta over steel frame   12 stories   good

The Pennsylvania Station was commissioned in 1898 from the office of D. H. Burnham of Chicago, one of the chief purveyors of the new monumental Classicism. Burnham's first important commission in Pittsburgh, it was the prelude to many other jobs in the city, most of them office buildings. The first studies of the building were published in the *Inland Architect* (March 1899) showing the structure as a relatively small four story office building with a rather dull entrance pavilion. In the final plans dated 8 June 1900, the head house became the present twelve-story office tower and the rotunda is fully developed into its present form.

The detailing of both the headhouse and the cab stand is noteworthy; the standard Beaux-Arts stylistic devices were used with restraint and taste (Burnham's

office was particularly good at this sort of thing) and the brown brick and terra cotta envelope of the building has a smooth, even texture, a decorative suavity, that is especially commendable. Both the headhouse and the cab stand were finished in 1902, but the now demolished trainshed (a splendid creation of the Pennsylvania Railroad's engineers) was not finished until 1903.

It is the domed rotunda, above all, with its magnificent four-centered arches and its elegant turrets that is especially distinguished. Very nearly related to the Exposition architecture of the time, it has at once a bright festal gaiety, and in the interior a mysterious cave-like air; it is a pavilion of enchantment and light and a grotto of contrived, curvilinear shadows, endlessly fascinating. One of the finest things in Pittsburgh from an architectural standpoint, it is certainly one of the most fantastic and delightful railroad structures ever erected. Every effort should be made to preserve it.

FORT PITT HOTEL
Penn Avenue at 10th Street
Alden & Harlow; Janssen & Abbott   1905; 1909
Italianate
Steel frame and brick   8 and 11 stories   fair

Once one of the city's most elegant hotels, the Fort Pitt was built in two sections; the eight story part at 10th and Penn was constructed in 1905 after designs by Alden and Harlow. The building material is rough brick with recessed mortar joints and there are a number of ornamental wrought iron "window balconies." Also in evidence are metal cornices and a low-pitched roof of tiles, very common to Italianate designs of this period.

The eleven story tower addition to this hotel constructed in 1909 and designed by Janssen and Abbott is of the elongated palace type and like the earlier section of the hotel was constructed in the same type of material.

The building contains some handsome public rooms, notably the Jacobean banqueting room, but these have suffered with the passage of time. The Norse Room, a cafe in the basement, is a "tour-de-force" showing the early twentieth century interest in ornamental fired-clay products. The decoration is entirely of Rookwood tiles in a quasi-Celtic-Norman style featuring large wall panels illustrating Longfellow's poem "The Skeleton in Armor"—a most peculiar theme for a cafe. The room was designed by John Dee Wareham and executed by the Rookwood Potteries of Cincinnati. It was finished in 1909 and is said to have cost $85,000.

With the decline in passenger traffic on the Pennsylvania Railroad, the Fort Pitt gradually fell from grace among travelers. It still functions in a limited way but part of it is now closed and the rest limps along in a much reduced category. It is hoped that the structure might be revived as an apartment or retirement hotel, but with the development of the new Penn Park, the future looks ominous for its survival.

PENNSYLVANIA RAILROAD BRIDGE
Eleventh Street
Pennsylvania Railroad Engineers   1901-04
Steel trusses on stone and concrete piers   ———————   very good

This double-decked through truss bridge was erected to replace an earlier one built in the middle of the nineteenth century. Designed by the Pennsylvania Railorad's own engineers, it was constructed by the American Bridge Company in 1901-04. It was raised in 1918. This is perhaps the most rugged and powerful of Pittsburgh's river bridges and its Herculean girders are a great visual asset to the downtown riverscape.

SIXTH, SEVENTH & NINTH STREET BRIDGES
Stanley L. Roush   Sixth 1927-28; Seventh 1925-26; Ninth 1925-26
Steel on stone piers   ————————   very good

These are three identical structures of the self-anchored suspension type so called because the pull of the top chords is resisted by steel girders in the superstructure itself.

The Sixth Street Bridge received the 1928 award given by the American Institute of Steel Construction for the most beautiful bridge constructed in the United States or Canada during that year. Its north abutment contains the original masonry that has supported four bridges at this site—the original covered wooden bridge of 1819, Roebling's multiple-span wire cable suspension bridge of 1859, the two-span, bow-string truss designed by the noted engineer Theodore Cooper and completed in 1892, and the present structure.

FULTON BUILDING
107 Sixth Street
Office building
Grosvenor Atterbury   1906
Proto-Modern-Renaissance
Brick and granite over steel frame   12½ stories   good

Designed by Grosvenor Atterbury, a New York architect who did considerable work for Henry Phipps, one of the partners of Andrew Carnegie, this skyscraper was intended to be a companion piece to the Bessemer Building (erected 1904 and recently demolished) on the opposite side of Sixth Street. A steel frame building with an envelope of brick and granite, it has (continuing a tradition found in several early commercial buildings) a skylighted interior court that serves as a lobby. This great court with its monumental staircase and galleries is unusually spacious for such a building and gave rise to a legend that the structure had originally been constructed as a hotel, which was not the case, although there was a restaurant in the basement when the building was first opened. Above the skylight an open court rises to the roof and this space opens out toward the river by means of a great archway. The top story with its low pitched tile roof and arcaded galleries was treated by the architect in emulation of certain Spanish sixteenth century palaces. It is a great pity that the Bessemer Building was demolished because the two structures together formed a monumental entrance, a kind of triumphal arch at the river entrance to Sixth Street. However, the surviving structure is of sufficient architectural interest that it should be preserved.

53

BUHL BUILDING
204 Fifth Avenue
Office building
Janssen & Abbot   1913
Italianate
Terra cotta over steel frame   6 stories   very good

First called the Bash Building, this structure was under construction by mid-1913. Henry Buhl, Jr., bought it in October 1913 while it was still being constructed. A very "open" Edwardian building of six stories with large areas of glass, its curtain wall is composed of blue and white figured terra cotta. The architects chose this material in imitation of Italian Renaissance Sgraffito, a form of decorative plaster work by which portions of the top coat of one color are scratched off in order to expose an undercoat of another color, thus producing the desired pattern. The building now adds a very graceful and colorful note to the rather tawdry stretches of lower Fifth Avenue and it should be preserved.

KEENAN BUILDING
643 Liberty Avenue
Office building
Thomas Hannah   1907
Classical
Brick and terra cotta over steel frame   18 stories   fair

A high-rise building constructed by Thomas J. Keenan, Jr. (1859-1927), its brick and terra cotta envelope is extremely elaborate, but its most notable feature is a concrete shell dome covered with tiles which was once surmounted by a gilded eagle. There are also ten bas-relief portraits in terra cotta about twenty feet above the sidewalk; these include historical Pennsylvania portraits as well as turn of the century Pittsburgh figures. The building may well have been constructed in emulation of the domed Spreckels-Call Building of San Francisco, which was rebuilt after being burned out in the San Francisco earthquake of 1906. For its form alone it would be pleasant if the building could be preserved.

It is not now fully occupied and the chief danger to it is the abundance of new and modernized office space becoming available in the city.

OFFICE BUILDING
805-807 Liberty Avenue
——————— C. 1865-75
Renaissance
Brick and cast iron   4 stories   good

A building notable for its cast iron front.

SMITHFIELD METHODIST CHURCH
408 Seventh Avenue
——————— 1848
Greek Revival
Brick   2 stories   very good

The first Methodist group in Pittsburgh was formed in 1788. Their first church was built on First Avenue in 1810, the second erected on the present site in 1818, and the present structure followed in 1848. A signature stone in the front gable gives the date. It has been remodeled to some extent from time to time but it still retains its general form and appearance.

In form it is the standard nineteenth century brick hall church on a high basement. We encounter here also the simple Greek Revival gabled temple form, another commonplace of the 1830's and 1840's. There is no portico, however, and the temple image is supported by ranges of brick pilasters alone.

This is the Methodist downtown institutional church, and it has been well

maintained; it is also, along with Burke's Building on Fourth Avenue (q.v.) one of the two surviving Greek Revival buildings in downtown Pittsburgh. When it is considered that the city was at one time especially rich in examples of this style, it will be understood how rapidly the older architecture in this area has been disappearing. Since the church comprises an important link with the architectural past of the city, every effort should be made to preserve it.

CHAMBER OF COMMERCE BUILDING
411 Seventh Avenue
Offices
Edward B. Lee & James A. Piper   1916-17
Modern-Classical
Brick and terra cotta over steel frame   16 stories   very good
The chief interest of this building is its brick and terra cotta envelope. The design of the terra cotta ornament displays perhaps the first attempt in Pittsburgh to "modernize" the Classical ornamental grammer.

BELL TELEPHONE COMPANY BUILDINGS
416 Seventh Avenue
Frederick J. Osterling; Alden & Harlow; John T. Windrim
    1890; 1904-05; 1908-14; 1930
Original building brick and stone. Later additions brick and stone over
    steel frame   various stories   very good
The first building of the Telephone Company was that erected in 1890-1892 in the Richardsonian Romanesque style after the design of Frederick Osterling. The rugged arched walls still remain but the turreted roof has been removed and the interior has been remodeled. In 1904-05 an eleven story addition designed by the firm of Alden & Harlow was built at the rear. Between 1908 and 1914 the stone-faced highrise along Seventh Avenue, designed by John T. Windrim of Philadelphia, was constructed. A further addition to this structure in 1929-30 features a sidewalk arcade vaulted with Guastavino tiles along Strawberry Way.

This complex of buildings is especially interesting because it so graphically illustrates changing forms and construction methods in downtown buildings.

GULF BUILDING
435 Seventh Avenue
Offices
Trowbridge & Livingston;
    E. P. Mellon, associate architect   1930-32
Modern-Classical
Stone over steel frame   44 stories   very good

This is one of the great monumental structures of the Triangle and an important element in the visual impact of downtown Pittsburgh as seen by the visiting eye, whether from distant points in the hills, from some of the entry points of the city, from the air, or even from the streets of the downtown area.

This is also the last great Pittsburgh skyscraper to wear Classical dress as it also wears upon its crown an adaptation of one of the seven ancient wonders of the world, the Mausoleum of Halicarnassus.

This architectural motif of the stepped pyramid topping an arcade of columns has fascinated architects since the beginning of the Renaissance. Many architects during that period had made reconstructions of it from literary sources, but it was not until archaeological excavations were made at the site of the Mausoleum in 1856 that some real information was made available to the eclectic architects of the nineteenth century. From that time the conjectural form of the Mausoleum was used many times in many versions in actual buildings.

One of the latest and most original of these versions was that advanced by Trowbridge and Livingston in their Banker's Trust Company Building for J. P. Morgan & Company in 1914 in lower Manhattan. This recapitulation of the Mausoleum is quite Classical, but when, toward the end of the Eclectic period, the same firm was asked to do another version of the same theme, they produced for the Gulf Building an arcade and pyramid stripped to its basic form, the stepped roof of which now serves as a weather beacon.

Left to right: Chamber of Commerce Building, Gulf Building, Bell Telephone Buildings, Koppers Building.

KOPPERS BUILDING

436 Seventh Avenue
Offices
Graham, Anderson, Probst & White;
    E. P. Mellon, advisory Architect   1929
Modern-Medieval
Granite and Indiana limestone over steel frame   35 stories   very good

This handsome structure, along with the Gulf Building, its neighbor across the street, represents a modernized version of earlier Eclectic skyscraper forms as well as a preview of emergent trends in high-rise construction. This is essentially the last edition, so to speak, of the elongated chateau that had been a commonplace of the high-rise world, almost since the inception of the steel-frame building.

This tall, suave, ribbed building with its discreet touches of "moderne" ornament and its green peaked roof is a real ornament to the city; it contrasts very well with the stone Halicarnassian tower of the Gulf Building. Even more expressive of the expansive élan of the 1920's is the marble-lined lobby, an exceptionally good example of the modernistic decor popularized by the Paris Exposition of Decorative Arts of 1925. The building is a rich and unusually splendid document of its period, and as such should be preserved.

HARVARD-YALE-PRINCETON CLUB

William Penn Way near Seventh Avenue
Original use: housing; present use: Club
Edward B. Lee for the remodelling.   1894;
    remodelled 1930-31
Georgian
Brick   3 stories   very good

This small court of houses is one of the last vestiges of residential downtown Pittsburgh and it is an uncommonly agreeable small urban space located in an area where such spaces have almost totally disappeared. It is a matter for alarm nowadays that our urban planners seem to be able to work only in the grand manner; very often the sense of human scale seems to have fled away from their vision. To come upon such a little enclosure of the past among the increasingly platitudinous acres of downtown Pittsburgh is a very agreeable visual surprise.

The narrow flagged court with its preserved architectural fragments gives a pleasant sense of enclosure, a necessary note of quiet, from the raucous clamor of the downtown streets. The rear vista of the rose window and spire of the Smithfield Congregational Church (q.v.) is one of the most delightful picturesque vignettes in Pittsburgh. Since we have lost almost everything else of this sort in Pittsburgh, may we not keep this lone survivor? We hope it may be so.

DUQUESNE CLUB
325 Sixth Avenue
Longfellow, Alden & Harlow, 1889, 1902;
    Janssen & Cocken, 1930-31
Richardsonian Romanesque
Brownstone front section; brick over steel-frame addition;
    5 stories in old; 13 in 1931 section   very good

The Duquesne Club was founded in 1873 and incorporated in 1881. In 1879 the organization moved to the present site. In the mid-1880's an architectural competition to provide plans for a new clubhouse was held. Among participants were Shepley, Rutan & Coolidge of Boston, Heins & LaFarge of New York, and Longfellow, Alden & Harlow of Pittsburgh and Boston. The latter firm won the competition and in 1888-89 the first part of the building was erected. This brownstone structure with its bay windows and Richardsonian Romanesque detailing, set the tone for later additions.

In 1902 another brownstone section was added on Sixth Avenue in the same style and at that time the clubhouse was rearranged. In 1930-31 a twelve story addition, designed by the Pittsburgh firm of Janssen & Cocken, was built to the rear of the older structure in the fashionable medievalistic brick style of the 1920's, which agreed rather well with the original Romanesque detailing of the facade. Also in the new building is a garden court (once open but now covered) in the suave Romanesque manner of the Twenties.

In this case the architecture reflects very eminently the history and standing of the club. From the standpoint of social history this is one of Pittsburgh's important buildings. Every effort should be made to preserve its special character, both inside and out. The building was severely damaged by fire in 1966 but has been restored.

TRINITY CATHEDRAL (EPISCOPAL)
Sixth Avenue
Gordon W. Lloyd   1871-72
Gothic
Stone   1 story   very good

The Trinity congregation had been formed in 1787 but it did not become a parish until 1805. Land (the site of the present church) was given to the group in 1787 by the Penns; however, the congregation did not proceed to build on it at once but erected an octagonal building at Wood, Sixth, and Liberty. In 1824, however, they removed to the present site, erecting thereon a brick and stucco church in the Gothic style after the design of the parish's rector John Henry Hopkins, who later became Bishop of Vermont. This structure served the congregation until 1869 when it was demolished. The present church, which became the Cathedral of the Diocese in 1928, was dedicated in 1872.

Constructed entirely of stone with a timber barrel roof, the building is a good example of the High Victorian interpretation of the English 14th century Decorated style. At the entrance to the chancel is a handsome pulpit designed by Bertram G. Goodhue (1922). The tower, the handsomest element in the general composition, is quite well designed. The graveyard beside the church contains the graves of early Pittsburghers and is thereby of some historical importance. The church interior has recently been discreetly renovated. There is no question about its preservation.

FIRST PRESBYTERIAN CHURCH
Sixth Avenue
Theophilus Parsons Chandler, Jr.   1903-05
Gothic
Stone   2 stories   very good

The First Presbyterian Church of Pittsburgh was incorporated by an act of legislature in September 1787. In the same year the Penns gave the congregation land and a log structure was begun. This shelter served until a new brick church was completed in 1802. Another stone church was built facing Wood Street in 1853; the graveyard occupied the land where the present building now stands. The present church was begun in 1903 and dedicated in 1905. Designed by the well known

Philadelphia architect, Theophilus P. Chandler, who had also designed the present building of the Third Presbyterian Church (q.v.), the First Presbyterian with its twin towers is a highly sophisticated example of Edwardian Gothic, crisp, richly textured, and curvilinear, seemingly related to the contemporary Art-Nouveau style. Set back from the sidewalk and on an elevated court above the street which it shares with Trinity Cathedral, the church with its neighbor provides the reason for a refreshing open space among the surrounding skyscrapers.

300 SIXTH AVENUE BUILDING
(formerly McCreery Department Store Building)
300 Sixth Avenue
Original use: department store; present use: offices
D. H. Burnham & Company   1903-04
Classical
Terra cotta over steel frame   13 stories   very good

This building was erected by the Oliver interests on land leased from the First Presbyterian Church for the purpose of housing the local department store of a New York company that opened its Pittsburgh premises in 1904. The construction was quite light and open with ample glass areas in the cream-colored Classical terra cotta walls. In 1937 the store was closed and it was liquidated in 1938. The Oliver Tyrone Corporation has since transformed it into an office building, thus proving that it is possible to adapt older buildings of special use to modern functions.

Large stores of this kind tend to become local landmarks and if their buildings have any architectural merit, as this one does, efforts should be made to preserve them, even if new uses have to be found for them. Oliver-Tyrone is to be congratulated on its efforts in this instance.

In 1966 a fourteenth story was added to house the Pittsburgh Press Club.

GRANITE BUILDING
Sixth Avenue at Wood Street
Original use: offices and bank; present use: offices and shops
Bickel & Brennan   1889-90
Richardsonian Romanesque
Granite   8 stories   good

A surviving example of the once large number of Pittsburgh bank buildings executed in the Richardsonian Romanesque manner, this building has nonetheless lost its bank. Here the banking premises have long since been remodeled into shops, but enough of its wide Romanesque musculature of wall remains to give us an intense, clear picture of the bank building clothed in medieval habiliments.

The ornate outer texture of this building also confers considerable visual interest on the cityscape. Now that so many of these buildings are being demolished, it would be salutary to preserve this structure.

BUILDINGS ON WOOD STREET
Wood Street
Various uses
——————— 1860-1900
Various styles, materials, heights, and conditions

There are a number of worthwhile small buildings on this street, some of which have now been altogether spoiled or at least badly treated at street level.

515-517 is a three story cast iron front with very rich late-Renaissance, almost Rococo detailing, and 418-422, also cast iron but four stories high, has, faintly, the same stylistic quality. 411, built in 1876, has polished granite pillars at the upper windows while 417 is a three story Ruskinian Gothic structure probably built around

61

1875-80. A white terra cotta Beaux-Arts building stands at 518 and an Italian Renaissance structure, rather Classical in tone at 524.

There are others of note; below the Allies Boulevard toward the river is a handsome structure that is partially covered with ivy, a unique sight in a city area.

We call attention to this and other streets (First Avenue, Fort Pitt Boulevard, and Market Street are good examples) that have older buildings of random styles, each reflecting architectural taste at the time of its building and indicative of a scale sympathetic to the pedestrian.

The damage to most of these buildings at street level indicates how desperately control of graphics and remodelling is needed. Their solid qualities are lost behind artificial tiles, anodized screens, banners, garish paint, and other mutilations.

SHERWYN HOTEL
Third Avenue & Wood Street
Original use: club; present use: Point Park College dormitory
Modern-Medieval
Janssen & Cocken   1928-29
Brick and stone over steel frame   21 stories   good
This is a particularly ebullient architectural document of the 1920's although it has lost something of its original quality and its tone. Intended as an out-sized high-rise fashionable clubhouse for the Keystone Athletic Club and clothed in the most elegant medievalistic habiliments of the very late Eclectic period, it did not long survive the financial crash of 1929 as a clubhouse. After 1934 the Club lingered on for awhile in restricted quarters but since the mid-1930's the building has functioned with varying fortunes as a hotel, and it is now a college dormitory.

It is interesting that its long brick flanks still rise above the downtown streets, its sidewalk arches of bland stone recall the Trecento graces of Florence and Siena and, high up, its strange Celtic gargoyles point outward to a nameless future.

The building still seems to be in fair condition and it is very probable that it might be more useful in the future to use it rather than demolish it.

THIRD NATIONAL BANK BUILDING
Wood Street at Oliver Avenue
Original use: bank; present use: shops
D. H. Burnham & Company   1903
Edwardian Quattrocento
Brick and terra cotta   2 stories   good
This small building is representative of the minuscule minor structures in the Quattrocento style so popular at the turn of the century, of which the Morgan Library in New York City is perhaps the most salient example.

OFFICE BUILDING
101-103 Wood Street
———————— c. 1860-70 (?)
Renaissance
Brick and cast iron   4 stories   good
A four story cast iron front building, it has considerable distinction of style.

HART-WEST PENN BUILDING
14 Wood Street
Offices
Charles Bickel   1906-7
Classical
Terra cotta on steel frame   12 stories and penthouse   very good
This building displays a very elaborate curtain wall of white terra cotta with an extensive and rather free rendering of many of the standard Beaux-Arts ornamental motifs. The shell appears often—in the spandrels between the floors with palm

62

fronds and ribands, and with garlands on the copper cheneaux above the almost excessively consoled classical cornice of terra cotta. At the twelfth floor between the triplets of windows are large lion heads and beneath them huge panel-like cartouches between flaming torches. Depending from the cartouches are garlands.

Like an Amazon's bride cake, the violent richness of this building notably enlivens the quarter in which it stands.

THIRD AVENUE BUILDINGS
Third Avenue below Smithfield
Various dates, architects, styles, heights and conditions
This, like First Avenue, Wood Street (q.v.), and Fort Pitt Boulevard, still is at least partially lined with various examples of 19th century building.

At 518 stands a two-story and attic red brick townhouse with cast iron cornices above the windows, but it is in poor condition. 510 is a small two story and attic townhouse with a dormer, while 330-32 is a four story white terra cotta structure with ornamental figures. (It probably dates from about 1910.) 209-213 is a three story cast iron front structure of about 1870 with still extant Victorian shop fronts, but it also is not in good condition.

The Romanesque Magee Building (q.v.) also is situated between this street and Fourth Avenue and at the corner of Smithfield stands the Fort Pitt Federal Building (q.v.).

FORT PITT FEDERAL BUILDING
301 Smithfield Street
Bank and offices
Frederick J. Osterling   1890
Richardsonian Romanesque
Stone   5 stories   very good
Stylistically related to the nearby Magee Building (q.v.) this five-story structure

63

displays the same heavy stone Richardsonian Romanesque envelope. There is visible, as well, a quantity of ornate, sometimes whimsical carving, the most salient example of which is the dragon on the corner of the building. Once occupied by the Marine National Bank, the first floor premises have been remodeled in the modern style for the present occupant.

DOLLAR SAVINGS BANK
Fourth Avenue at Smithfield Street
Isaac H. Hobbs & Sons 1868-71, with 2 wings added in 1906
Classical
Brownstone   1 story   very good

Established in 1855 as Pittsburgh's first institution devoted to mutual banking—a bank operated solely for the benefit of its depositors—the present structure was begun in 1868 after the designs of Isaac H. Hobbs and Sons of Philadelphia. The central section was completed in 1871, and the two wings added in 1906.

The use of the colossal Roman Composite order gives a kind of heavy authority to a rather eccentric composition whose debased Classical details recall the solemn caprices of Baalbek or Palmyra. The two lions at either side of the main portal, who seem to be guarding not only the bank's treasure but public morality as well, are completely delightful examples of large-scale Victorian sentimental sculpture.

Having been set back from the street, the building, in spite of its massiveness, does not overwhelm the pedestrian and a handsome wrought iron fence helps maintain an appropriate sidewalk scale.

Although the building was constructed of brownstone that has spalled to some degree, the ravages of time have been skillfully repaired.

MAGEE BUILDING
334-36 Fourth Avenue
Offices
Frederick J. Osterling   1892
Richardsonian Romanesque
Stone and brick   8 stories   fair

This early pre-steel-frame high-rise, erected for the Pittsburgh *Times,* represents a curious compromise between the old American loft building and the developing skyscraper. Built on a long narrow lot between Third and Fourth Avenues, the facades on these two streets are of stone executed in a heavy Richardsonian Romanesque manner; the side walls are of brick on the longitudinal axis, and the structure is bisected by a long corridor. In the center of the passage the elevator shafts rise and the stairs ascend around them. At one time the shafts were enclosed in open work metal grills that opened the space all the way to the top of the building. The two stone facades have recently been cleaned.

UNION NATIONAL BANK BUILDING
306 Fourth Avenue
MacClure & Spahr   1906
Neo-Classical
Stone over steel frame   22 stories   very good

Tradition has it that Benno Janssen, who was in the MacClure & Spahr office at the time, had a considerable hand in the design of this building. Simply designed, this structure employs the same severe neo-Classical manner to be found in the Frick Building and the First Union Trust Building. Unfortunately much of the interior marble ornamentation was stripped out in 1966.

MACHESNEY BUILDING (now Benedum-Trees Building)
221-225 Fourth Avenue
Offices
Thomas H. Scott   1905
Classical
Granite, enameled brick and terra cotta over steel frame
     19 stories   very good

At the time the building was constructed, Fourth Avenue was still the chief financial artery of Pittsburgh and an attempt was made to indicate architecturally by the use of large granite Corinthian columns and much Classical terra cotta ornament on the floors above, something of the "weight" and importance of the street. In the way of ornament, very few elements of the Beaux-Arts grammar have been neglected—cartouches, brackets, consoles—all are richly present. Although the building was constructed on rather a narrow lot, the steel frame and the elevator enabled it to move skyward. The building is a handsome and well maintained example of the Edwardian skyscraper.

65

BURKE'S (or Meyer) BUILDING
211 Fourth Avenue
Office building
John Chislett   1836
Greek Revival
Brick with stone facade   3 stories   poor

One of the first office buildings in Pittsburgh, it is now the earliest extant. According to Charles M. Stotz, it contained banking quarters at one time. It was built in 1836 by the Burkes on a site purchased from the Irwin family. It escaped the Great Fire of 1845, but advancing years have not treated it kindly. The main portal with its Doric columns, portions of which have spalled, has been painted and the original window sashes have been removed; the masonry facade also seems to have separated from the brick sidewalls. A small portion of the original interior finish seems to have survived, but inside and out the structure appears dingy and unkempt. Although restoration would be extremely expensive, a very strong effort should be made to preserve this building since it is unique in the city.

PARK BUILDING
355 Fifth Avenue
Office building
George B. Post   1896
Renaissance
Brick and terra cotta over steel frame   15 stories   very good

Designed by the New York architect who had been responsible for the design of the second bank of Pittsburgh building (1896), the Park Building was one of the early steel frame high-rise buildings in the city; in fact it is probably now the earliest extant skyscraper in the downtown area. It was constructed by D. E. and W. F. Park, Pittsburgh steel men. Its brick and terra cotta envelope was very exuberantly designed. Near the top of the structure, above a Corinthian colonnade, a frieze of terra cotta telamones upholds the cornice. Some of the terra cotta detailing has already failed and unfortunately the brass entranceway has recently been replaced with a less auspicious aluminum. Although it is not of the first architectural importance, it would be very pleasant if so ornate a specimen of early skyscraperdom could be preserved.

MELLON NATIONAL BANK & TRUST COMPANY
Smithfield Street, Oliver and Fifth Avenues
Trowbridge & Livingston in association
    with E. P. Mellon   1923-24
Classical
Stone over steel frame   4 stories   very good

This great granite structure, the main office of the Mellon National Bank & Trust Company, is four stories high with a basement and a sub-basement beneath. The colossal order of the main facade is very simply, even severely treated, and the temple porch has here been reduced to a lofty entrance recess flanked by two Doric pillars. Enormous bronze doors open into the great central banking room, which is 62 feet high and amply lighted by large windows and a skylight. Basilican in form, this hall is lined on all four sides by marble Ionic columns.

67

Since the demolition of the Bank of Pittsburgh on Fourth Avenue, this has become the sole remaining example in the city of the great Classical bank building, the "temple of finance".

HENRY W. OLIVER BUILDING
535 Smithfield Street
Office building
D. H. Burnham & Company   1908-10
Classical
Stone and terra cotta over steel frame   25 stories   very good

The largest of the early slab skyscrapers in Pittsburgh is this structure named for Henry W. Oliver, the noted industrialist, who died in 1904; it was built as a memorial to him. An expanded version of the Frick Building, it was designed by the same architect in the same coldly Classical style, but the outer severity of this immense slab is softened by some Renaissance ameliorations of detail. The austerity of the recessed entrance on Smithfield Street with its great Doric pillars is matched on the interior by the marmoreal simplicity of the lobby. Well maintained and situated as it is on Mellon Park, it will probably continue to be well tenanted.

SMITHFIELD CONGREGATIONAL CHURCH
620 Smithfield Street
Henry Hornbostel   1925-26
Gothic
Stone over steel frame   3 stories   very good

This building represents one of Pittsburgh's historic congregations. In 1787, the heirs of William Penn granted to the German Lutheran and Reformed congregations a plot of land at what is now Sixth Avenue and Smithfield Street, and the church was built in 1791 or '92. In 1812 the Lutheran and Reformed congregations united and adopted the name German Evangelical Protestant Church; church buildings replaced one another in 1815, 1833, and 1875-77. In 1925 the organization united with the Congregational fellowship and in 1961, with the merger of the Congregational and Evangelical Reformed churches, it became part of the United Church of Christ.

In 1924 part of the congregation's land was leased for commercial purposes and in 1925 the present church was designed by Henry Hornbostel. It was dedicated in December 1926. The design is interesting as that of a compact urban church that pays homage to the Gothic image of what a church building should be, and it is entirely modern in that all of its subsidiary functions are adequately housed. Although Hornbostel had never much used the Gothic style, this is an arresting essay in medievalistic design. The auditorium is rather elaborate with its fan vaulting and pendants. There is much stained glass, including a rose window from the 1875 church.

The most important architectural feature of the church is the open-work spire of cast aluminum, which marks the first large scale use of this material in architecture.

The building is in excellent condition and the interior of the structure is at present being remodeled to meet present-day needs.

DUQUESNE UNIVERSITY ADMINISTRATION BUILDING
801 Bluff Street
——————— 1883-84
Victorian Medievalistic
Brick and stone   5 stories   very good
The University was founded in 1878 as the Pittsburgh Catholic College of the Holy Ghost. The present five story Administration Building was built 1883-84 and dedicated in 1885. The bands of stone that vary the sober pattern of the brickwork give the structures a curious striped appearance that, architecturally speaking, was quite fashionable after the mid-century, although it had practically disappeared after 1900. At one time there was a kind of open cupola in the center of the roof. Situated high on its bluff, the structure, although it is no architectural master-piece, is a well-known landmark and should be preserved. A complete search of records, history, and archives of the school failed to turn up the name of the architect.

ST. MARY'S HALL
Bluff & Colbert Streets
Original use: St. John's Hospital;
    present use: college building
——————— c. 1850
Italianate
Brick   3 stories   good
This is a large three bay Italianate brick building with elaborate cornices over the windows and doors. It was used as a hospital during the Civil War and was then known as St. John's Hospital. About 1882 it was moved across the street to make way for the Administration Building (q.v.) of the University.

MERCY HOSPITAL
Pride Street & Forbes Avenue & Allies Blvd.
——————— 1848, 1882, 1903
Brick and steel frame   various number of floors   good
Mercy Hospital was first opened on 1 January 1847 by a group of Roman Catholic nuns, the Sisters of Mercy. Land was bought on Boyd's Hill above the Triangle

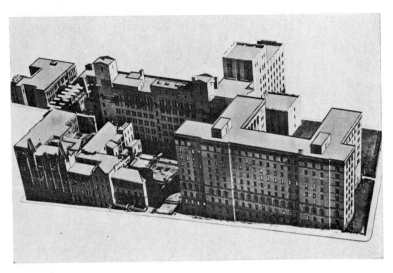

and an architect named Haden Smith was asked to prepare plans for a hospital that was opened in May 1848. Part of this building still exists in the very large complex that the hospital now comprises. New wings were added (notably in 1882) and around the turn of the century Edward Stotz designed several buildings that culminated in 1918 in the South Wing, a high-rise structure, and the Nurses' Home of 1925-26. The Modern style made its appearance in 1938 with the the south-east wing (Kaiser, Neal, and Reid, architects).

Mercy remains the essential local example of the large urban hospital that has remained near the old metropolitan core and as such it is important. Undoubtedly since the buildings are all in operation, most of the complex will continue.

METHODIST RESIDENCE FOR YOUNG WOMEN
2000 Fifth Avenue
——————— Before 1894; addition c. 1910
Romanesque-Classical
Brick and stone   4 stories   good
This building is an interesting combination of the small "loft-type" hotel and the classical type of urban townhouse on a narrow corner lot.

ST. AGNES ROMAN CATHOLIC CHURCH
Fifth Avenue & Robinson Street
John Comes   1917
Romanesque
Buff brick and limestone   1 story   very good
During the first three decades of this century, Comes was perhaps Pittsburgh's most active and prominent ecclesiastical architect. He was a Roman Catholic and his commissions stemmed largely from that religious body. This church, in buff brick and limestone, is a higly competent twentieth century exercise in the Italian-Romanesque basilican manner with some Byzantine details. Felix Lieftuchter decorated the interior and the windows are by Sotter. There is no question as to its preservation.

HOUSES
2701-03 Fifth Avenue, 1-7 Robinson Street
——————— c. 1875-80
Victorian
Brick   2 stories plus attic   fair to good
This is a row of separate three bay Victorian houses facing out on the great Soho curve on Fifth Avenue. They are still solid citizens.

70

EPIPHANY ROMAN CATHOLIC CHURCH

Epiphany Street
John T. Comes   1903
Romanesque
Brick and terra cotta   1 story   very good

This building in red brick and red terra cotta is a good example of Comes' early manner. The form is basilican, the style Romanesque, of that type which existed through much of the nineteenth century and well into the twentieth, independent of the Richardsonian version of the style. This is one of the few buildings to survive the general clearing of the Lower Hill for the new group of structures that is gradually forming there. Erected not far from the downtown area, it was at one time a church especially frequented by printers and newspapermen working on the early shift. Masses were said at early morning hours when they could attend.

The murals on the interior of the apse by Taber Sears are illustrated in Edwin Blashfield's *Mural Painting in America* (1912), p. 242.

This church also served as the cathedral of the Roman Catholic diocese during the time that St. Paul's Cathedral was building in Oakland.

The building has been well maintained and since it was the sole survivor among structures on the Lower Hill, its future preservation is probably assured.

PASSAVANT HOSPITAL

Reed & Roberts Streets
J. W. Kerr; Edward Stotz for later additions;
    1851, 1898 and 1917
Tudor and Classical
Brick   3 stories   fair

The first section of what has been called the first Protestant hospital in America was built in 1851 after the designs of the Pittsburgh architect Joseph W. Kerr (1815-1886). The hospital had been founded in 1849 as the Pittsburgh Infirmary by the philanthropic local Lutheran minister, Rev. W. A. Passavant (1821-1894).

This first square structure 60 x 24 feet was designed in the Tudor style and still stands at the right of the range as one faces the hospital from Reed Street. Variations of the Tudor style theme were used by Stotz in his additions, which also reflect more advanced methods of hospital construction.

Due to the rapidly changing character of the neighborhood in the present day and because of the Lower Hill redevelopment, the Passavant Hospital (so named soon after the death of its founder) has moved to a new building in the North Hills. Here we have another salient example of the tendency of such institutional buildings to follow the population trend to the suburbs.

The building still used and well maintained is in a fairly good state of preservation. Since the original section of the building is probably the oldest surviving hospital structure in the city, all efforts should be made to preserve it.

HOUSE
520-522 Herron Avenue
———————— c. 1850
Vernacular
Brick   2 story   poor
This is a three bay double house of red brick with gable curtains on sides.

HOUSE
Wick Street
———————— c. 1800-1830
Vernacular
Stone   2 stories and attic   fair
A large stone house in two sections, this is an exceptionally good building of its type in the area, but because of its remote location is difficult to view.

ST. BRIGID'S ROMAN CATHOLIC CHURCH
91 Crawford Street
Henry Moser   1895
Victorian "Decorated" Gothic
Brick and stone   1 story   good
This late commission of Henry Moser's is a Pittsburgh version of the standard Victorian "Decorated" parish church; as architecture it has no particular distinction but visually it is very important in the cityscape above the Civic Auditorium. In this connection it is very unfortunate that the spire has been removed from the tower and only a stump remains. Spires now are difficult to maintain.

The parish was originally that of the Holy Trinity, but when the neighboring church of St. Brigid was demolished in the 1950's, Holy Trinity became St. Brigid's. The earlier St. Brigid's was a large church of the Classical persuasion erected in the 1850's.

HOUSE
1853 Arcena Street
———————— c. 1850-60
Greek Revival
Brick   2 stories   poor
A three bay very late Greek Revival house, square, with large multi-paned windows that have shutters in the lower story. It has a Victorian verandah.

IMMACULATE HEART OF MARY ROMAN CATHOLIC CHURCH
3000 Brereton Avenue near Bigelow Boulevard
William P. Ginther   1904-06
Late Italian Renaissance
Brick and stone   1 story   good
The great copper-covered late Renaissance dome and its two smaller subsidiary domes form a kind of visual focus and turning point about half way out Bigelow Boulevard from downtown. This great Edwardian church of buff brick and stone was built, like many churches of its type in the Pittsburgh area, as the rallying point of one of the many nationality groups that settled on the local hills and in the valleys; this parish was predominantly Polish, but it is no longer so homogeneous nor are its members so numerous.

The style of the building is generally late Italian Renaissance and Baroque, and it resembles, on the exterior, early Baroque Roman churches in an Edwardian version. The interior, which tends toward over-elaboration, owes something to Christopher Wren's church of St. Stephen Walbrook in London.

Visually the church is one of the valuable elements in the Pittsburgh landscape and every effort should be made to preserve it.

Bloomfield

BLOOMFIELD BRIDGE
Liberty Avenue & Bigelow Boulevard
─────────── 1913-14
Steel   very good
This is a deck-cantilever span over a broad valley. Because of the lattice work of steel on its underside, the bridge is most effectively viewed from the valley bottom.

The Strip

ST. JOHN THE BAPTIST ROMAN CATHOLIC CHURCH
Liberty Avenue at 36th Street
John Comes for Beezer Bros.   1902-03
Italian Romanesque
Brick, stone and terra cotta   1 story   good
The first church of the parish was located at Liberty Avenue and 32nd Street and it was built in 1878. The cornerstone of the present church was laid in June 1902 and it was completed in 1903. Although Beezer Brothers are the architects of record, the design was really Comes'; it was one of his early ecclesiastical commissions in Pittsburgh and displays his facility in handling the Romanesque style.

The rather stilted basilican form of the church and its tall campanile once looked very effective rising above the gaunt working-class quarter which lies along the descending ridge traversed by Liberty Avenue. Unfortunately the tower has now been much truncated and the church thereby is much diminished as a visual element in the cityscape.

SIXTEENTH STREET BRIDGE
Sixteenth Street
Warren & Wetmore, designers   1923
Steel and stone   very good
This is a late and very good example of the large expansive through-truss bridge encased in Baroque architectural adornment. It comprises three arch-truss spans of the braced rib type with tie in the plane of the floor. The spans are 229, 437, and 229 feet long respectively. At either end of the superstructure are two tall stone piers topped with groups of bronze winged horses holding armillary spheres. The bridge with its sculptured adornments is one of the most elegant things of its kind in Pittsburgh and it should be preserved.

ST. STANISLAUS ROMAN CATHOLIC CHURCH
21st Street (off Smallman Street)
1891-92
Brick and stone 1 story good

This organization, the first of Pittsburgh's Polish R. C. parishes, was founded in 1875, and its first church building was located in a former Presbyterian church at Penn Avenue and 15th Street. In 1891 a lot was bought at 21st and Smallman Streets and the same year the church was begun; it was dedicated in 1892.

The broad Romanesque face of the church, of brick vigorously striped with stone, provides a welcome visual relief in a district that is now almost completely commercial. In a sturdy and forthright way it testifies to values other than those of business and it should be preserved for its upright presence in the market place.

Lawrenceville

LAWRENCEVILLE PRESERVATION AREA
(See under Preservation Areas)

UNITED STATES ALLEGHENY ARSENAL
Penn Avenue, 39th, 40th Streets and the Allegheny River
Original use: Arsenal; present use: various
Benjamin Henry Latrobe and others 1814 and later
Classical
Brick various stories poor

It is difficult to imagine now what Lawrenceville was like in its earlier days when it was dominated by the Arsenal, which was erected on thirty acres of ground bought in 1814 from William B. Foster, father of Stephen C. Foster, the composer. Later six more acres were purchased. At one time the Arsenal grounds extended from Penn Avenue to the Allegheny River and from 39th to 40th Streets.

Under the regime of Colonel A. R. Wooley, the first commandant, the first buildings were erected after the designs of Benjamin Henry Latrobe, who lived in Pittsburgh from 1812 to 1814. Six of Latrobe's studies for the Arsenal buildings are

now in the Library of Congress. (They are dated October 1814.) Much of the Latrobe work including the Commandant's house has been demolished within the last few years, but even when the buildings were still standing, comparison of

Arsenal type house, 513 Carnegie Street

the drawings with the executed work showed a number of departures from Latrobe's designs.

Talbot Hamlin, in his recent biography of Latrobe states that the architect recommended to Colonel Wooley the services of a young bridge engineer Thomas Pope, who was resident in Pittsburgh in 1814. Apparently Pope had something to do with the erection of the first buildings but by 1815 he was no longer employed at the Arsenal.

The officers' house, which balanced that of the Commandant in the northern part of the Arsenal area, which faced Butler Street, is still standing and it gives some idea of what the demolished structure was like. It is a severely Classical stone building with two stories and five bays on the main facade. It has been so badly treated, however, (it is now the Arsenal Terminal Warehouse) that it is only a shadow of the former substance. Possibly, though, it is not beyond restoration.

These two houses served as models for a number of houses in Lawrenceville; these later houses we have labeled as the Arsenal type and each of them has a separate entry below.

The Powder Magazine in Arsenal Park was built 1814-20. The L-shaped structure is half buried in the ground. Beneath its timber roof is a masonry barrel vault. As Talbot Hamlin says in the Latrobe biography — "The great gable coping stones (keyed up at the outside edge) of the powder magazine and its simple arched entrance have a character of exciting power."

The structure was partially remodeled in the 1930's as part of the Arsenal Park and it now serves as a combined "comfort station" and shelter house for the park personnel.

In the northern part of the old Arsenal complex a long two story brick building with arcades on the first floor still survives (now the Pittsburgh Industrial Engineering Company). This is called a storehouse on old maps, but again the structure has been much changed to enable it to be used for present day commercial purposes. Near the river is a portion of a two story Greek Revival structure of brick and stone with pilasters and a Classical stone cornice. There is also a two story stone building with a hipped roof. Aside from a couple of indifferent brick structures of uncertain date, and some bits of the wall that enclosed the area, these fragments are all that is left of the Arsenal.

In its early days the Arsenal was one of the most extensive in the country. Ammunition, infantry and horse equipment, caissons and gun carriages were manufactured there and the buildings included an armory, barracks, a smithy, a carriage shop, a machine shop, a paint shop, stables, and a powder magazine. The place was very active in the Civil War but after 1868 no more manufacturing took place there and the Arsenal became merely a military post for the storing and distribution of arms.

Gradually, however, it lost all importance and in 1907 the southern part above Butler Street was given to the City of Pittsburgh for a park; in 1926 the remainder was sold at public auction. The real heart of the Arsenal between Butler Street and the river is now a dreary industrial and commercial wilderness.

This entry is merely a contemporary record of remaining fragments. It would seem that the Arsenal is probably beyond restoration even if some omnipotent Maecenas or official agency would attempt it, but the area does need more study as one of Pittsburgh's important early architectural monuments.

WASHINGTON CROSSING BRIDGE
40th Street over the Allegheny River
Janssen & Cocken;
    Charles S. Davis, associate engineer   1923-24
Classical
Steel and concrete   ——————   very good

This steel-arched bridge represents, along with the through-truss Sixteenth Street Bridge (q.v.), that combination of architecture and engineering as rather separate activities (a *mariage de convenance* between art and science in which both parties, however, retain distinct and marked identities) which attended during the nineteenth and early twentieth centuries the development of modern technology. In this case the steel arches, as in the case of the truss frames at Sixteenth Street, are firmly

held, one might almost say clamped in the embrace of architecture of the old dispensation. Today the two have coalesced as could already be seen in the 6th, 7th, and 9th Street bridges (q.v.) in the late 1920's. The effect here is, however, still Classical—and it is appropriate that Washington should be commemorated in this place by a Roman bridge—or that which at least is Roman in intent. As for Washington, there is nothing that here eminently recalls him; between the modern industrial desolation of the one bank and the busy highwaymanship of the other, there is little that remembers him specifically, only the flat course of the river and the low, recessive hills recall that remote time when he beheld them.

HOUSE
257 40th Street
————————— c. 1830-50
Vernacular Greek Revival
Brick   2 stories   good
This house of the Arsenal type is a three bay structure with a flattened hipped roof. There is a side light and transom central doorway.

HOUSE
513 Carnegie Street
————————— c. 1840-50
Vernacular Greek Revival
Brick   2 stories and attic   good
A house of the Arsenal type, it is five bays wide, with multi-paned windows that have ornamental stone lintels featuring blocks at the ends. There is a simple Classical cornice.

EMERSON HOUSE
5300 McCandless Avenue
————————— c. 1845
Vernacular Greek Revival
Brick   2 stories   fair
Another house of the Arsenal type, this one is also five bays wide. As is usual in houses of this group, the style is rather severe provincial Greek Revival. The windows are multi-paned and there is a side light and transom doorway. It is said that the house was built for Mary Schenley's physician—a story which, transferred from the latitude of legend, might possibly refer to a physician attending on the Croghan family.

HOUSE

186 Home Street
————————— c. 1840-50
Vernacular Greek Revival
Brick   2 stories   poor

This is a five bay house of the Arsenal type. It is a severe rectangular structure having a heavy attic with a corbeled brick cornice. One of the outstanding features of the house is the wall toward Home Street, which is blank with a stark paneled treatment. There is also a simple Classical cornice below a low hipped roof.

PATRICK J. KANE HOUSE

4745 Modoc Alley
————————— c. 1830-40
Vernacular Greek Revival
Brick   2 stories   fair

This is another five bay brick structure with small side wings. It is two rooms deep with chimneys at the side. This house in its extreme simplicity of treatment and in the general disposition of its mass would seem to have been influenced by the Commandant's house at the Arsenal. It should be preserved if possible.

BUTLER STREET GATEHOUSE, ALLEGHENY CEMETERY

4734 Butler Street
Gatehouse and entranceway
John Chislett; Barr and Moser   1848; 1868-70
Gothic Revival
Stone   2 stories   very good

Allegheny Cemetery, one of the early examples of the Romantic, park-like cemeteries of the nineteenth century, was chartered in 1844. John Chislett, who was Pittsburgh's most prominent early architect, was appointed first superintendent and it was he who was responsible for the lay-out of the grounds. The gateway on Butler Street designed by him bears the date 1848. This gatehouse was enlarged in 1868-70 by the addition of a building containing a chapel and offices, after the designs of Henry Moser of the local firm of Barr and Moser.

The general effect of the gateway is charming; the rather tasteful massing and the chaste detailing constitute a delightful architectural composition. The picturesque effect of the earlier structure is considerably augmented by the new work, although the quality of the latter suffers a little by comparison. The elongation of the forms and the coarseness of detail are characteristic of the 1860's and 70's, although the arcade of five bays, rather resembling a segment of a cloister that flanks the side of the chapel and connects with the gate screen, is an exception to

the prevailing, heavy-handed detailing; this open passage with its groined vaults is designed and executed with a crisp archaeological competence.

This delightful little architectural vignette of gate, chapel, and tower, is, on the whole, extremely attractive and it may be taken as the very type of Romantic picturesque architecture. Having been recently cleaned, the buildings' chances for survival are good.

SEVENTH UNITED PRESBYTERIAN CHURCH
44th Street and Cessna Way
—————— 1873
Victorian Second Empire
Brick   1 story   good
Founded as the First United Presbyterian Church of Lawrenceville in 1860, it became in 1872 the Seventh United Presbyterian Church of Pittsburgh after Lawrenceville became part of the city in 1868. The present church building is a brick hall church on a very high basement. The date 1873 is inscribed on a signature stone in the gable; the building was dedicated in 1874.

ST. MARGARET'S HOSPITAL
265 - 46th Street
Ernest Flagg and others   1891-1910
Baroque and Modern
Brick   various stories   very good
The will of John H. Shoenberger (d. 1889) provided for the erection of a Protestant Episcopal Church Hospital that was to bear his first wife's name—Margaret. The site of the hospital had been part of Shoenberger's country estate in Lawrenceville. In December 1891 the charter was granted and Ernest Flagg, who had designed St. Luke's Hospital in New York, was selected as architect. His design, rather Baroque in conception, featured a central building with wings disposed about a courtyard; at the rear of the central section is a handsome chapel. The

80

cornerstone was laid in 1896 and the hospital was occupied in May 1898, but it was not formally opened until October 1910.

Flagg's original design has almost disappeared under subsequent additions and remodelings, but the Chapel still remains as perhaps the finest Baroque small space in a city where the Baroque is notably absent. The Chapel should be preserved at all costs, but at this moment a remodeling project may spoil it.

ST. MARY'S ROMAN CATHOLIC CHURCH COMPLEX
300 - 46th Street
Church, school, convent
James S. Devlin, John Comes
Vernacular Gothic and Greek Revivals
Brick   various stories   very good

This interesting group of buildings forms an isolated religious enclave on the hillside below the lower gate of St. Mary's Cemetery. The rather plain Victorian Gothic church of brick trimmed with sandstone was built in 1874 after the design of James S. Devlin. In 1906 twenty stained glass windows by Mayer of Munich, were installed. At one side of the church near the sanctuary is the Chapel of St. Anne, designed by John Comes, which was dedicated in 1921.

Next to the church is a two story brick structure with pilasters and corbeling, rather late Greek Revival in style. Known as the Academy Building, it was probably

erected some time around 1850. It has a curious ornamental cast iron porch, like a two story portico.

The two story brick convent next door, built in 1867, has an exceptionally good ornamental cast iron porch.

ST. AUGUSTINE'S ROMAN CATHOLIC CHURCH
220 - 37th Street
Rutan & Russell (John T. Comes)   1899-1901
Romanesque
Brick and terra cotta   1 story   very good

Comes was probably chiefly responsible for this design and it is certainly related to work that he did later when he became the chief ecclesiastical Roman Catholic architect in the Pittsburgh area. Comes was at this time working in the office of Rutan & Russell. Certainly St. Augustine's bears little relation to the rest of the work emanating from the Rutan & Russell office at this time.

The building with its two towers and octagonal dome, recalls not only Italian Romanesque sources but also the Romanesque churches of the Rhineland (the parish in the past was largely made up of Germans). Not only is it an interesting structure of its type but it ought to be preserved as an important visual asset in its neighborhood.

82

ST. FRANCIS GENERAL HOSPITAL BUILDINGS
45th Street near Penn Avenue
Sidney F. Heckert and others   1871; 1891; 1907-10; 1932; 1964
Various styles
Various materials and heights   very good

St. Francis Hospital was founded by the Franciscan sisters, who came from Buffalo at the request of a Pittsburgh citizens' committee to provide home care for the needy and victims of smallpox until May 1866 when a frame dwelling at the present site of St. Francis was fitted up as a hospital accommodating thirty patients. In 1871 when the first large building was erected, the frame structure was used to isolate smallpox patients, but a few years later it was employed to house neuro-psychiatric cases. By 1891 the hospital had a 150 bed brick building for psychiatric patients. The long north wing on 45th Street, designed by Sidney F. Heckert, was begun in 1907 and finished in 1910. This building, in the Renaissance style, has a mansard roof, foundations of concrete and Indiana limestone, and upper floors of brick.

The high-rise nurses's home (designed by Schmidt, Garden, and Erickson of Chicago, who have specialized in hospital construction) was opened in 1932. This again was the medievalistic, Romantic tall building of the 1920's with its sloping chateau roof. In 1964 this structure changed its function and became the Community Mental Health Center, the same year in which the remodeling of the building began.

Shadyside

SHADYSIDE PRESERVATION AREA
(*See under Preservation Areas*)

SACRED HEART ROMAN CATHOLIC CHURCH
Walnut Street at Shady Avenue
Carlton Strong; Kaiser, Neal & Reid   1924-53
Gothic
Stone   1 story   very good

Designed originally by Carlton Strong (1869-1931), Sacred Heart was finished by the firm of Kaiser, Neal and Reid. The style, like that of the First Baptist Church, is late English Gothic rather freely treated and enlivened by some French touches;

a dramatic feature of the interior is a painted beamed roof. The construction of the church proceeded over a period of years, but the Gothic style was still adhered to long after the Revival had come to an end. The church has a large and flourishing congregation and is in an excellent state of preservation.

CALVARY EPISCOPAL CHURCH

Shady Avenue at Walnut Street
Ralph Adams Cram (Cram, Goodhue & Ferguson)   1906-07
Gothic
Stone   1 story   very good

The old Calvary Church (its second building), erected 1860-1885 and located at Penn Avenue and Station Street, had by the turn of the century grown too small for this congregation and in 1906-07 the present structure was built. One of the architectural monuments of East Liberty as well as a suave relic of Edwardian religious expansiveness, it is a chaste, handsome exercise in the early English Gothic. The arcading of the west front and the tall narrow lancets of the transepts are very effective, but the best features of the building are the superb tower and spire, which are centrally placed over the crossing. (Cram himself was very proud of the tower,

and he felt that the handling of the transition between the square lower structure and the octagon of the steeple was quite original).

The rather austere interior, especially the nave, displays a nice regard for scale and proportion; in the chancel is some very rich woodwork inspired by Devonshire and Essex work of the fifteenth century.

The church is well maintained and since the congregation is large, active, and well-to-do, there is no question of its adequate preservation and maintenance. East Liberty has changed vastly in the years since it was built, but Calvary Church has managed to hold its own.

Although the architect of record is nominally the firm of Cram, Goodhue and Ferguson, the building was designed by Cram, who headed the Boston office of the associated partners.

CALVARY CHURCH RECTORY
400 Shady Lane
Original use: house
——————— 1860-70
Gothic-Second Empire
Brick   2 stories and attic   very good

Formerly the Carnahan residence, this large brick version of the Gothic-Second Empire manor house became the rectory of Calvary Church some few years back. With its verandahs, porte-cochere, barge boards, and oriel window it conveys very forcibly the impression of what a large East Liberty mansion of the mid-nineteenth century was like.

It is in good condition and a "big" house of this period was fortunate in being so sympathetically preserved. Most other Pittsburgh examples of this type have vanished and every effort should be made to retain it not only for its own merits but for the part that it plays visually in the cityscape.

BURGWIN HOUSE
5219 Fifth Avenue
_____ 1830-1870
Western Pennsylvania Vernacular
Brick   1½ stories   good

This three bay house is reputed to date back to 1830, but despite the side light and transom front door, much of the interior detailing of the house would suggest a later period, c. 1860-1870. The structure has the curious air of an urban house of the period detached from a closely built urban setting and isolated in a quasi-suburban context; there are no windows in the side or "party" walls. The house is placed on a long narrow lot, and behind it is a very pleasant secluded garden.

GWINNER-HARTER HOUSE
5061 Fifth Avenue
_____ 1870-1880
Victorian Second Empire
Brick   2 stories and mansard   very good

This well preserved house represents the image of the large East End suburban mansion midway between the Greek Revival temple-house and the Richardsonian Romanesque chateau or the Norman Shaw manor house; it is especially notable because it is such a well maintained example of a type that has almost disappeared. It was bought by the Gwinner family in 1911, remodeled by F. J. Osterling, and remodeled again in 1923. Painted grey and displaying a Classical porch of Edwardian inspiration, it still boldly asserts its Second Empire beginnings.

86

SPINELLI HOUSE
5302 Westminster Place
—————— c. 1870
Picturesque cottage
Board and batten   2 stories   very good
This handsome white-painted Shadyside version of the asymmetrical Romantic suburban cottage orné with its wide lattice windows would by its smoothness of style seem to date a little later in the nineteenth century than the two nearby cottages at 918-920, St. James Street (q.v.).

ABBOTT AND MARSHALL HOUSES
918 and 920 St. James Street
—————— c. 1860
Picturesque Cottage
Board and batten   2 stories   very good
Asymmetrical and Romantic in silhouette, these are very charming examples of the mid-nineteenth century suburban cottage.

APARTMENT BUILDING
5425-31 Walnut Street
Frederick G. Scheibler, Jr.   1908
Early Modern
Stone and brick   3 stories   good
This is an interesting apartment house in Scheibler's early manner. The strong, stark treatment of the monolithic stone work of the shop fronts is contrasted with the simply handled white brick and the casement fenestration of the upper floors. Some of the original iron work that adorned the facades has disappeared. Although

the interior of the flats have not been examined by us and there have been some changes on the lower floor, the building would seem to be in relatively good condition. It should be preserved.

SCHOOL HOUSE LANE HOUSES
School House Lane, Fifth and Aiken Avenues
——————— c. 1860-1880

Vernacular

Frame   2 stories   very good

Although the School House Lane houses are not particularly old nor architecturally important, they are good examples of single vernacular Victorian houses that have been remodeled into pleasant urban dwellings. The buildings, according to one account, were moved into this secluded court from another site in the late 1920's and rehabilitated. Originally these were the houses of people who worked in the area during the last half of the nineteenth century.

MORELAND-HOFFSTOT HOUSE
5057 Fifth Avenue

Paul Irwin   1914

French Renaissance

Terra cotta and stucco   2 stories   very good

This building illustrates the Edwardian passion for ornamental terra cotta, as well as for French architecture of the seventeenth and eighteenth centuries. The basic form of the house is that of the Grande Trianon at Versailles (1687-88), which had been notably and more skillfully used by the New York firm of McKim, Mead and White in "Rosecliff" (1901-02) at Newport, Rhode Island.

Pittsburgh's Trianon is a provincial model of the Newport house. Possibly these American Trianons are reflections of the Palais Rose constructed in Paris by

Comte Boni de Castellane with a portion of the Gould millions. At Pittsburgh evidently the Moreland funds did not extend to the back premises, which are extremely dull in utilitarian plaster. This is a prime Edwardian example of the Victorian "Queen Anne front and Mary Ann behind." It can also be seen that the white terra cotta envelope of the front and side elevations is a rather solemn version of rococo insouciance.

Nevertheless, the house with its elaborate and well preserved decoration is a well cared for period piece and adds considerably to the Shadyside stretch of Fifth Avenue. It would be a great loss to the area were it to disappear, as so many of the Fifth Avenue mansions already have.

SHADYSIDE PRESBYTERIAN CHURCH
Amberson Avenue at Westminster Place
Shepley, Rutan and Coolidge;
    Wilson Eyre & McIlvaine   1889-90; 1892; 1937-38
Romanesque
Stone   1 story   very good

This congregation was formed in 1860, growing out of a Sunday School established in the neighborhood. An earlier building designed by James W. Windrim of Philadelphia and erected in 1874-75 was demolished to make way for this church, which was erected in 1889-90. The Chapel on Westminster Place was completed in 1892. In 1937-38 the interior of the church was completely remodeled by the firm of Wilson Eyre and McIlvaine of Philadelphia. In 1952-53 a new parish hall was constructed in a modernized Romanesque style by the Pittsburgh firm of Hoffman and Crumpton.

The church building itself, aside from its subsidiary buildings, is one of the important architectural monuments of Pittsburgh, not only for its intrinsic merit as an architectural composition, but also because it was designed by H. H. Richardson's successors, the Boston firm of Shepley, Rutan and Coolidge, not long after the

89

great man's death in 1886. The building is an interesting Richardsonian document because it was very probably influenced in its lantern form by a first project for Emmanuel Church (q.v.) that was never used. Stylistically much more archaeological in treatment than Emmanuel, it is a highly significant monument in the development of the Prostestant auditorium church in America.

The lantern theme was first used by Richardson in his Trinity Church Boston (1876) but at Shadyside, designed by his successors, the great central dome *is* the church. This huge centrally planned structure thus gives significant architectural form to one of the main Protestant tenets, the preaching of the Word. Architecturally, Shadyside has been influential not only in Pittsburgh, but throughout America as well. It is an interesting comment on rapidly changing urban conditions that Shadyside has managed to preserve about it a little enclave of residential elegance. The congregation is large and well-to-do and there should be no question of its preservation.

SHADYSIDE RAILROAD STATION
Amberson Avenue and the Pennsylvania Railroad
Wilson Brothers & Co.   1887
Vernacular
Brick   2 stories   poor

This is a good example, along with the slightly earlier Homewood station, (1883) a little further out the Pennsylvania line from Pittsburgh, of the vernacular brick and shingle stations of the 1880's. The scale and form of both these structures is essentially domestic, most appropriate to the small suburban station. The picturesque massing of gables and chimneys is charming; here the verandahs have become passenger shelters. Abandoned now, its future is highly problematical, but it should be preserved as one of the last survivors of the railroad commuter era.

RODEF SHALOM TEMPLE
Fifth Avenue between Devonshire and Morewood
Palmer and Hornbostel   1906-07
Beaux-Arts Neo-Baroque
Brick   1 story   very good

The congregation was chartered in 1856 and at the turn of the century it occupied a building on Eighth Street near Penn Avenue that was taken over by the Second Presbyterian Church when the Temple moved to Oakland. In 1906 an architectural competition for the present structure was won by Palmer and Hornbostel. Construction began in May 1906, and the building was finished by 1907. In 1938 the school fronting on Devonshire Street was built, and in 1956 the Social Hall on Morewood was finished.

90

The Temple proper is a large square domed structure of brick and terra cotta; the interior of the dome is vaulted with Guastavino tiles and the exterior with green roofing tiles. The large looming mass of the structure, which displays Hornbostel's vigorous massing to good advantage, is a Shadyside landmark.

FIRST CHURCH OF CHRIST SCIENTIST OF PITTSBURGH
635 Clyde Street
S. S. Beman   1904
Classical
Stone and brick   1 story   very good
This small stone and brick building with its Classical portico adds a graceful note to a street on the edge of Oakland. The cornerstone was laid in 1904, and the first service was conducted in the completed building in 1905.

Oakland

EPISCOPAL CHURCH OF THE ASCENSION
Neville Street and Ellsworth Avenue
William Halsey Wood   1896-98
English Gothic
Stone   1 story   very good
This is a rather original, rugged, but not quite successful example of the late nineteenth century Gothic Revival designed by an architect who, if he had not died at a comparatively early age, might have made more of a mark on American architecture. Wood was an advocate of the ideals of the High Church party in the Episcopal Church, as well as the architectural tenets of that group, but here his neo-medievalism is much tempered by the necessity of providing for a large Protestant congrega-

tion. Wood, who began his career as a disciple of H. H. Richardson. designed the first of the Carnegie Library buildings, that at Braddock (q.v.) as well as competition designs for the Allegheny and Pittsburgh Carnegie Libraries.

Wood later turned to the Gothic and designed many churches, of which the Ascension is the sole Pittsburgh example. The tower, which Montgomery Schuyler called "one of the best things in Pittsburgh" was modeled after the late Gothic tower (1506) of Wrexham Church in Wales. The church has a large and flourishing congregation so there should be no question about its preservation.

ST. PAUL'S ROMAN CATHOLIC CATHEDRAL
Fifth Avenue at Craig Street
Egan and Prindeville   1903-06
Gothic
Stone   1 story   very good

The first St. Paul's Church (which later became the first Roman Catholic Cathedral) located at Grant Street and Fifth Avenue (the site of the present Union Trust Building) was begun about 1828 and completed in 1834 after designs by John Behan. This was in the same kind of literary picturesque Gothic represented by the slightly earlier Trinity Episcopal Church (q.v.). This early structure of St. Paul's was destroyed by fire in 1851.

The second St. Paul's was erected 1853 on the site of the earlier structure. It has been attributed to both Thomas Walsh of New York and Charles Bartberger of Pittsburgh. Of stone and brick, it had two thin spikey towers on the main Grant Street facade. The plan was cruciform with five aisles and there was a Gothic "cupola" over the crossing. It was abandoned in 1903 and demolished in 1904 to make way for the Union Trust Building. The Church of the Epiphany (q.v.) in

92

the lower Hill district became the temporary Cathedral until the new St. Paul's in Oakland was completed.

The new structure bears some relation to the old—in plan at least—since it also has five aisles and is designed to seat a large congregation. The style, as well, is Gothic, but of a much more suave and archaeological kind than the older version on Grant Street. The mass of the building is impressive and the two towers with their spires are especially imposing, but there is in the general design of the building a curious mechanical quality that detracts from its effectiveness. Generally the Cathedral, however, bears itself very well in the eclectic architectural symphony of Oakland.

MELLON INSTITUTE FOR INDUSTRIAL RESEARCH
4400 Fifth Avenue
Janssen and Cocken   1931-37
Classical
Stone over steel frame   9 stories   very good
This is an extremely interesting document in the transition from the great Classical architectural tradition to the Modern style—a phenomenon observable generally in the architectural history of the 1930's—especially in the so-called "Fascist" architecture of Mussolini and Hitler. During the 1930's, at the time the Institute was built, functionalists objected violently to the idea of housing laboratories for industrial research in a hybrid Greco-Roman temple. Essentially, their objections are still valid, but visually the Institute is a very handsome addition to the Oakland complex of cultural buildings. Stylistically, we have here the classical forms and formula stripped down to its barest essentials. The structure is surrounded, except at the corners, by rows of huge monolithic columns of the Ionic order but without fluting (36 in all). The interior is equally severe, with some ornament of a "modernized" Classical sort; there is also a handsome library of the English seventeenth century sort with carved woodwork in the manner of Grinling Gibbon.

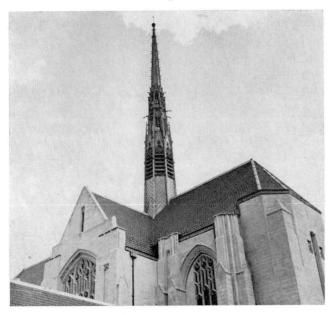

FIRST BAPTIST CHURCH
Bellefield Avenue at Bayard Street
Bertram G. Goodhue of Cram, Goodhue and Ferguson   1909-12
Gothic
Limestone   1 story   very good
This congregation founded in 1812, built in 1867-76 a handsome church in the

93

pre-Richardsonian Romanesque style at Fourth and Ross Streets designed by David Gendell of Philadelphia. This building with its facade ornamented by a large wheel window and two squat towers was demolished about 1909 to make way for the City-County Building. The present Oakland Church may lay claim to being the best piece of Gothic Revival work in Pittsburgh from the standpoint of design and function. The church, constructed of limestone, is cruciform in plan with side aisles and transepts almost suppressed. The style of the church is late English Gothic "Perpendicular", not without some French touches.

The interior is vaulted with Guastavino tiles, although the ribs are stone. The glass—all contemporary with the erection of the church—is grisaille with touches of color. The carving of the interior woodwork is rich and subdued and of that suave sharp archaeological character which Henry-Russell Hitchcock has labeled "Second Gothic Revival."

The matter of the baptismal tank—central to the tenets of the Baptist denomination—has been well managed and under ordinary circumstances the installation looks like a curtained recess. The choir and organ loft are placed above both this tank and the preaching platform.

The church is institutional in character and still has a large congregation despite urban dispersal to the suburbs.

SCHENLEY HIGH SCHOOL
Centre Avenue at Bigelow Boulevard
Edward Stotz   1915-16
Classical
Stone over steel frame   3 stories   very good
The stark, stripped Classical exterior of this building and its unadorned interior efficiently illustrate that type of school building that bridged the gap between the Romantic Electic period and the Modern manner. The triangular plan also makes it unique among Pittsburgh schools.

RETAINING WALL
Parkman Avenue above Bigelow Boulevard
—————   c. 1900
Stone   —————   good
These great masonry walls are to be found throughout the Pittsburgh area. They were used extensively wherever retaining walls were necessary before the advent of reinforced concrete. These heavy, rugged surfaces, so nearly allied to the hills that they retain, are among the finest things in Pittsburgh visually. They are so simple and powerful that they have invariably worn well. Other excellent examples are the walls at the first great curve of Perrysville Avenue as it ascends the hill; the great retaining wall in North Dallas Avenue not far from the Pennsylvania Railroad tracks, and the wall along Bigelow Boulevard where it meets the Crosstown Boulevard. Unfortunately the best part of the latter was removed when the Crosstown road was constructed. The wall under discussion here is particularly effective both because of its great height and its sweeping curve. In springtime, long streamers of yellow forsythia cascade down over it making it, in season, a delight to the eye. This wall was constructed when the streets of the residential area of F. F. Nicola's Schenley Farms tract were laid out (c. 1905).

TWENTIETH CENTURY CLUB
Bigelow Boulevard at Parkman Avenue
Janssen and Cocken   1929-30
Italianate Classical
Limestone over steel frame   5 stories   very good
The Twentieth Century Club, formed in 1894, had its first headquarters at 408 Penn Avenue in the old James Laughlin house on Duquesne Way. It remained there from 1898 to 1910, when it moved to Nicola's Schenley Farms and erected

a brick structure on the present site. In 1929 this building was remodeled and enlarged after the design of the firm of Janssen and Cocken.

The result is practically a new building, of limestone with a low-pitched tile roof, designed in the Italianate palazzo manner that Janssen had used earlier at the nearby Pittsburgh Athletic Association Clubhouse (q.v.). The building features a colossal order and is nicely scaled to its narrow corner lot.

PITTSBURGH ATHLETIC ASSOCIATION
Bigelow Boulevard at Fifth Avenue
Janssen and Abbott   1909-11
Venetian Renaissance
Stone and terra cotta over steel frame   5 stories   very good
The Pittsburgh Athletic Association was formed in 1908 by a group of young businessmen. In 1909 they bought land in Nicola's new Schenley Farms tract. They commissioned the firm of Janssen and Abbott, which had only recently been formed,

to design the present clubhouse. It was opened in April, 1911. A fine, smart, sophisticated version of the Italianate manner, then very much in vogue, the Pittsburgh Athletic Association is a quite grand exercise in the Venetian High Renaissance. Indeed, Venice very notably presides over this elegant building; the form is effulgently "palatial" and it was intended to be. The order used on the facade is reminiscent of the Grimani Palace (1549) in Venice as the frieze with its cupids and garlands recalls that of Sansovino's Library of St. Mark (1536). Montgomery Schuyler, the architectural critic, writing in 1911 called the Pittsburgh Athletic Association Clubhouse the architectural lion of its day in Pittsburgh, and it is still possibly the finest Classical building in this city. The interior has been much changed (this is only to be expected in clubs and hotels), but rooms like the main lobby have managed to keep their chief architectural features. The marble and terra cotta swimming pool with its Guastavino tiles is a fine Edwardian period piece. Since the club is at present flourishing, there is no question as to the preservation of this building.

SOLDIERS AND SAILORS MEMORIAL HALL
Fifth at Bigelow Boulevard
Palmer and Hornbostel   1907-11
Beaux-Arts neo-Baroque
Stone and steel   2 stories   good
In "Shall Oakland be the City's Trade Center", an article in the Pittsburgh *Leader*,

25 October 1904, C. H. Chance gave it as his opinion that the Memorial Hall of the Grand Army, permission for the erection of which was recently given by the County Courts, would be placed on the old Charles J. Clark property then owned by Murry Verner. The site of the hall was finally located in that part of F. F. Nicola's Schenley Farms area that was to be devoted to cultural and civic uses. The final working drawings for the structure are dated 18 October 1907; Palmer and Hornbostel had earlier been given the commission as the result of a competition. It opened in 1911. Stylistically the huge stone building is a reworking of the form of the Mausoleum of Halicarnassus (one of the seven wonders of the ancient world), a theme that was much used by the eclectic architects of the nineteenth and early twentieth centuries, but the basic borrowed mass serves as the core for an elaborate Beaux-Arts composition which features a large public auditorium. The building adds a considerable note of grandeur to the Oakland district, and it should be preserved.

SCHENLEY HOTEL
Bigelow Boulevard at Fifth and Forbes Avenues
Present use: University of Pittsburgh Student Union
Rutan and Russell   1898
Classical
Brick and stone over steel frame   10 stories   good
Opened in 1898, this building, which was Pittsburgh's first large steel-framed skyscraper hotel, was also one of the early monumental buildings erected in Oakland, which in the 1890's was beginning to develop as Pittsburgh's cultural center.

The Schenley was the Pittsburgh equivalent of the quasi-institutional "class" hotel; like the Plaza or the Bellevue Stratford, it was a hostelry of the elongated "Palatial" type, although it lacked the New York and Philadelphia ebullience of roof and cornice. It was also that American phenomenon, the "residential" hotel, and for many years it was an upper class social center, but it became in 1956 part of the University of Pittsburgh. With some changes, it has become the "Student Union" of that institution. The grand air of its former days could, unfortunately, not be preserved, but it is probable that its shell will be maintained.

PRESBYTERIAN-UNIVERSITY HOSPITAL
Fifth Avenue, Lothrop, Terrace, and DeSoto Streets
Various architects, dates, and styles
Stone over steel frame   various stories   very good
This large complex of hospital buildings was conceived in the 1920's as the result of a need for a teaching hospital in connection with the University of Pittsburgh Medical School. The nucleus of the group was the Presbyterian Hospital, which had been founded in 1895 in the North Side. Its third and final building in that lo-

cation is now the Divine Providence Hospital (q.v.).

In the early 1920's the University bought the H. K. Porter estate and added to it other parcels in the Fifth Avenue, Lothrop, DeSoto, Terrace Streets block. The first unit erected was the Children's Hospital (designed by York and Sawyer in association with E. P. Mellon), and it was opened in 1927. Alfred D. Reid Associates designed the addition of 1958-59.

The large towered building in the center of the complex, designed by E. P. Mellon and completed in 1938 consists of the Presbyterian-University Hospital in the center, flanked by the Eye and Ear Hospital in one wing. This great winged building with its tile-topped tower is probably the last Pittsburgh hospital of the irregular, Romantic high-rise type. Deeter and Ritchey designed the new front wing addition, erected 1963-65.

Scaife Hall, which houses the University School of Medicine, was designed by the firm of Schmidt, Garden and Erickson of Chicago and erected in 1955-56; it was connected by a wing with the central tower of Presbyterian.

Although the inclusion of such large building complexes may not really be germane to a preservation list, the hospital is an extremely important building type, and it is advisable to record the mutations of the structure, with a possible eye to preservation of some aspects of any given building or complex of structures.

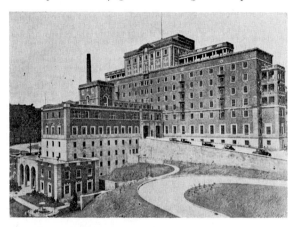

MONTEFIORE HOSPITAL
3459 Fifth Avenue
Schmidt, Garden and Erickson and others   1927-1966
Georgian
Brick and stone over steel frame   various stories   very good
As early as 1898, discussions were underway concerning the foundation of Montefiore. In June 1908 the Montefiore Hospital and Training School for Nurses was opened at 3000 Centre Avenue in the old Jacob Ewart house, a Greek Revival structure with a Doric portico. Gradually this building was enlarged. In the 1920's it was decided to move the hospital, and a site on Fifth Avenue between Chesterfield Road and Darragh Street was acquired. In 1927 the present large brick and stone hospital in the Georgian style was begun; it was finished and opened in July 1929. In 1950 two floors were added to this building and in September 1953, the new Nurses' Residence on Fifth Avenue was opened. In 1964 more building operations were inaugurated (architects: James H. Ritchie and Associates with E. M. Benswanger).

ST. PETERS EPISCOPAL CHURCH
Forbes Avenue at Craft Avenue
John Notman   1851-52
Gothic
Stone   1 story   very good
Designed by the Philadelphia architect John Notman (1810-1865), this structure

98

is an excellent example of the early archaeological phase of the Gothic Revival. It formerly stood at Grant Street and Forbes Avenue (on part of the present site of the Frick Building). When H. C. Frick bought the property, he presented the building itself to the congregation, and that group elected to have it moved stone by stone to its present site. Vrydaugh and Wolfe of Pittsburgh were the architects of the reinstallation. Designed shortly after Notman's famous Philadelphia church St. Mark's (1845-51), St. Peter's resembles its prototype to a marked degree although there are certain minor differences in plan, mass, and detail. St. Peter's

also exemplifies most clearly that simplicity, sobriety, and coolness of tone so characteristic of Pittsburgh architecture, whereas St. Mark's displays the elegance, richness, and traditional character of the more settled eastern seaboard.

Unfortunately, the neighborhood to which it was moved was already in a transitional state at the time of the removal, and since then it has continued to change—not for the better residentially—with the result that the congregation is now sparse. The building has, however, taken on an almost institutional character as a kind of chapel and social center for the Juvenile Court Home next door. The church has been well maintained and generally seems to be in good state of preservation. Architecturally, this is one of Pittsburgh's really important buildings, and all efforts should be made to preserve it.

IROQUOIS APARTMENT HOUSE
3600 Forbes Avenue
Frederick J. Osterling   1901-03
Classical
Brick, stone and steel   6 stories   good
This was the first example in Pittsburgh of the large, more or less "palatial" apartment house rather on the high-rise order, although the chief dimension of these facades is still lateral. Flat houses of this order were already well-established in New

York, beginning with Hardenburgh's Dakota Apartments of the 1880's, and they reflected a marked change in American living habits, especially of the upper classes after the mid-nineteenth century. In 1898 the Schenley Hotel (q.v.) had already established in Oakland the image of the large high rise urban hotel that could also be "residential". Wealthy Pittsburgh manufacturers and industrialists often lived there during the winter.

The broad width of the Iroquois was treated by Osterling with some restraint as regards ornament. Except for a heavy cornice there is a minimum of classical detailing on the Forbes Avenue facades. There are four projecting wings facing Forbes; on the ground floor are shops, and the entrances to the apartments were at one time between the wings, except that of the center which was a shop.

Until about 1950, these long entry corridors were quite elaborate with much mosaic, dark oak woodwork, bronze maidens holding electric lights, and wrought iron elevator cages. In the early 50's these entries were removed and shops substituted. Much earlier the large apartments had already been split up into smaller ones, but since the building had ceased to be fashionable, it was partially remodeled for office space in the 1950's. Entrances were then placed at the back. The interior has been radically changed, but there are not many changes on the exterior, save those already noted.

COLTART HOUSE
3441 Forbes Avenue
YMCA
——————— 1843
Greek Revival
Brick   2 stories   poor

This is the last remaining example of a group of Greek Revival houses that stood in Oakland. The Childs-Magee house that once stood on Halket Street and the Moorhead house on Fifth Avenue just across the street from the Coltart Mansion were also good examples of the local Greek Revival style.

Although the detailing of the house is Greek Revival, the plan, with its small subsidiary wings, was influenced by eighteenth century Virginia mansion houses. In southwestern Pennsylvania there was considerable architectural influence from Virginia during the early nineteenth century. Despite the fact that the house is now surrounded by commercial properties, attempts could be made to restore it.

FERGUSON HOUSE
435 Atwood Street
Offices

——————— c. 1850, remodelled 1915-16
Greek Revival
Brick   2 stories   good
This is a small three-bay, perhaps late Greek Revival brick house with a much
later Classical porch, probably dating from the remodeling of 1915. It now seems
to be used for offices.

OAKLAND SQUARE
(See under Preservation Areas)

HOUSE
319 Oakland Avenue
——————— c. 1860
Second Empire Medieval Manor House
Brick   2 stories and attic   good
This is a large Medievalistic-Second Empire manor house complete with bay windows and barge boards. Due to its proximity to Forbes Field, its once large "grounds"
are now used as a parking lot.

CATHEDRAL OF LEARNING
Forbes Avenue at Bigelow Boulevard
Charles Z. Klauder   1926-37
Gothic
Limestone over steel frame   40 stories   very good
This huge building, possibly the last great monument of the Gothic Revival in
America, is, when one has accepted its basic premise, well designed, at least from

a compositional and visual standpoint. A joint product of the educational idealism of its then Chancellor John G. Bowman and the general élan of the 1920's, it is as much a product, a summation, and a symbol of that expansive era as is the tower of Carnegie Tech's Machinery Hall (q.v.) of the Edwardian period. Conceived in the early 1920's, the commission was put into the hands of Charles Z. Klauder, of Philadelphia, who had, in his day, achieved a considerable reputation as a designer of academic structures.

It was to be a "Cathedral" of learning and also a great skyscraper; fifty-two floors were planned, and even the school children of the city were asked to contribute their pennies and dimes to the "cloud-capped" tower of culture. There were voices, however, that cried out against the structure as impractical. Finally the height was fixed at forty stories, a sufficiency as it turned out. Perhaps the Depression, beginning in 1929, also helped to abridge its height as it certainly lengthened its period of construction. By the time of the Second War the exterior was complete, but only recently have parts of the interior been finished. The great Commons Room on the ground floor, a vaulted Gothic *tour de force*, was finished by 1939; in its Romantic, theatrical way, it is quite effective. On the ground floor also is the ring of Nationality Rooms, representing peoples who settled in Pittsburgh.

Functionally, the dissenting voices of the 1920's were correct, however. Whatever the "Cathedral" has been as a symbol, as a functioning building it has left a little more than something to be desired. Most of the classrooms had to be placed on the first five floors where they could be easily reached. Even so, congestion in the halls and elevators when classes change is formidable.

The building nevertheless is the "center piece" of Oakland, a highly important visual element in the landscape, that must be preserved.

CARNEGIE INSTITUTE
4400 Forbes Avenue
Museum, art gallery, music hall, and library
Longfellow, Alden and Harlow; Alden and Harlow 1891-95 and 1903-07
Italianate; Beaux-Arts neo-Baroque
Stone (over steel frame in later addition)
    variable stories   very good

This huge structure, which covers more than five acres of ground, and which in many ways constitutes the cultural heart of Oakland, was constructed in two installments, although it was always intended to serve four main functions, since it comprised a music hall, art gallery, natural history museum, and a library under one roof. Andrew Carnegie gave the sum of one million dollars to erect the building that was begun in 1892 and dedicated in 1895. Longfellow, Alden and Harlow were the architects of this first version of the building, which originally included two Venetian towers on either side of the Music Hall. The style of the building was for the most part that of the early Italian Renaissance. Large as the new structure was, however, it became apparent at the turn of the century that it was too small, not only for all the functions that it contained but also for the growing number of people it had to serve.

Accordingly Carnegie gave the sum of $5,000,000 to remodel and enlarge the building, and Alden and Harlow made the plans. Excavation was begun in 1903, and the great building was dedicated in April 1907.

In the second building with its great square dome, the Italianate detailing has been retained to some degree, but the general conception of the ensemble is the neo-Baroque of the École des Beaux Arts. The foyer of the music hall is exceptionally grand, and certain of the interior rooms are quite fine including the sculpture court. The building is generally one of the great Pittsburgh landmarks and worthy of preservation.

BOARD OF EDUCATION BUILDING
Forbes Avenue and Bellefield Street
Boyd and Ingham   1926-27
Italian Renaissance
Stone   4 stories   very good

This is a very pleasant, very chaste version of the Italian Renaissance town palace,

103

a type that was soon to disappear after 1940. The tall round-arched windows of the Board Room facing Forbes Avenue echo the Albertian arches of the Carnegie Institute building across the street. Built of limestone, the building has a handsome interior court. The building has been well maintained and there is at present no question about its preservation.

CARNEGIE INSTITUTE OF TECHNOLOGY
Forbes Avenue at Morewood to Frew & Margaret Morrison
    Streets
Palmer and Hornbostel, Henry Hornbostel   1904-23
Beaux-Arts neo-Baroque
Brick, stone and terra cotta over steel frame   various stories
    very good

In 1900 Andrew Carnegie offered to give a million dollars towards a technical school if the city of Pittsburgh would provide the land. In 1903 the City bought the Flinn-Magee tract next to Schenley Park's Flagstaff Hill. In 1904 an architectural competition was held that was won by Palmer and Hornbostel of New York.

    Henry Hornbostel (1867-1961) came to Pittsburgh as supervising architect and also became Tech's first professor of architecture in 1905. It was he who designed most of the Tech buildings up through the Gymnasium of 1923. The buildings along with the Rotunda of the Pennsylvania Station (q.v.) are perhaps the most effective examples in Pittsburgh of the Beaux-Arts neo-Baroque style. Stylistically the structures are a mixture of Italian Quattrocento forms and details with Baroque massing and lay-out; French seventeenth century planning principles are much in evidence. Porter (once Industries) Hall (1905), Margaret Morrison Carnegie College (1906-07), Engineering Hall (1908-09) are the earlier buildings in this well-designed campus layout. Machinery (now Hammerschlag) Hall (1912-13), Administration (now Baker) Hall (1914) and the College of Fine Arts (1912-16) are more elaborate and represent Hornbostel's mature effort at Tech.

Machinery Hall is probably his masterpiece, and it closes the vista at one end of the great mall about which the main campus is arranged.

Some modernization has taken place among the Hornbostel buildings on the campus but they have not been changed to any marked degree. They represent eminently Beaux-Arts principles applied to the design of college campuses, and due both to its homogenity and its quality, the Carnegie campus is one of the best of its time and type in this country. It is unfortunate that as much cannot be said for the more recent buildings.

PHIPPS-BRAUN HOUSE
Warwick Terrace
J. Edward Keirn   1901-03
Italianate
Brick and terra cotta over steel frame   3 stories and attic
        very good

One of the few remaining great Edwardian houses of East Liberty, the Braun house, although it is by no means the largest of this once numerous group, is thoroughly representative. Constructed of brown brick and terra cotta, it is architecturally very much a "school" piece representing provincial Italianate taste in America at the turn of the century. Based essentially on the form of the Georgian center hall house, the structure is yet asymmetrical in both plan and elevation.

The house has been very well preserved in something like its original condition and appearance, and the interior is especially notable for the sympathetic maintenance given it by the present owner. Some of the original fittings such as the wall hangings and rugs made for the house when it was built are still in place.

The Phipps-Braun house should by all means be preserved as the best surviving Pittsburgh example of what is by now practically a dead species. It is an almost perfect document of the way of life of Pittsburgh's great moguls of the turn of the century.

PHIPPS CONSERVATORY
Schenley Park
Lord and Burnham   1893
Iron and glass   1 story   very good

In 1891 Henry Phipps offered to build a conservatory in Schenley Park if the City would give him permission. The City accepted the gift, and in December 1893 the building was opened to the public. The nine display houses were augmented three years later by another three houses given also by Mr. Phipps. The firm of Lord and Burnham of Irvington-on-the-Hudson designed and erected the original buildings. In 1900 the City erected nine growing houses at a lower level behind the main building.

These airy structures of glass and iron made to house collections of tropical plants were among the important constructions of the nineteenth century, and this one has a special significance for Pittsburgh as the home of the semi-annual flower shows. As a great domed winter garden, the building, with its Richardsonian Romanesque stone entrance pavilion, is also a fine Victorian period piece. It must be preserved in its present form, but regrettably the pavilion is now being demolished.

NEAL LOG HOUSE
Serpentine Drive, Schenley Park
Derelict
_____   1787-95
Log   1 story and loft   poor

Built by Robert Neal on ground purchased by him in 1787, this is the oldest of the log houses in Stotz's *Early Architecture of Western Pennsylvania*. Here is the log house in its simplest form, a single room with only a loft above reached by a ladder and with no cellar underneath. The large chimney of field stone laid up in clay mortar serves two fireplaces. The structure has a roof of later date.

The building is one of the last vestiges of eighteenth century architecture in the city, and standing on its knoll in the park, it adds a charming picturesque note to the landscape. Stotz calls it one of the most interesting log houses in twenty-two western Pennsylvania counties.

It has been allowed to deteriorate to the point where it must either be completely restored or removed. The Pittsburgh History & Landmarks Foundation hopes to initiate a campaign to carry out the former course.

Swisshelm Park

Jackson-Horrocks House
1071 Windermere Drive, Swisshelm Park
─────────────── c. 1846
Vernacular
Brick and stone   1½ stories   very good
Reported to be a house once owned by the Swisshelm family, this unpretentious, three bay building is pleasantly sited on a ridge near the Penn-Lincoln Parkway Valley. It stands on a high basement.

Squirrel Hill

WIGHTMAN HOUSE
1227 Wightman Street
─────────────── c. 1870
Provincial Second Empire—Italianate
Brick   2 stories and attic   very good
This three bay, grey painted brick house, which once stood in its own grounds, now looms at the edge of a high stone embankment with a fancy ironwork balustrade. Its front verandah has obviously been removed, and there are ornamental cast-iron Italianate cornices above the windows. A house of no great architectural distinction, it still is representative of the prosperous farmhouse of the Squirrel Hill region. It now contains two apartments.

THE CHURCH OF THE REDEEMER
5700 Forbes Avenue
E. Donald Robb of Frohman, Robb and Little   1936-37
    a re-working of an earlier stucco building of 1913
English Gothic
Stone   1 story   very good
The parish of the Redeemer was founded after the turn of the century on Wightman Street, but in 1903, the Forbes Avenue site was acquired and a church erected there in the same year. The records of the church state that Henry Hornbostel made designs for a new church, but they were never carried out. In 1936 the remodeling (to the designs of E. Donald Robb) was begun. The building was turned around, set on new foundations, encased in Gothic stone work, and a stone tower was added. The parish house was begun in 1922 and in 1940 the second floor was added. The stone rectory designed by Lamont Button, which faces on Darlington Road, was erected in 1938.

    Extremely simple in design, the church has a fineness of scale and proportion and an amiable forthrightness of aspect that make it one of the best things of its kind in Pittsburgh. The appointments of the church are well designed and executed with a proper regard for material and workmanship; typical are the handsome stained glass windows all designed by the late Howard Wilbert, a parishioner of the church.

Together with the parish building and the rectory with its gardens, the church constitutes a delightful, but not "quaint", simulacrum of the small English village church. Thus it has become a necessary religious note in a neighborhood that is becoming increasingly commercial as well as an ornament to its denomination in the city. The congregation is flourishing and there is at the moment no question as to its preservation.

HAMILTON COTTAGES
5635-5663 Beacon Street
Frederick G. Scheibler, Jr.   1910-14
Early Modern
Brick   2 stories   good

The cottages comprise five rows containing nineteen two-story brick veneer houses built for the Hamilton Realty Corporation of Wilkinsburg. This is one of the most interesting of Scheibler's sites for small housing units in what must have been at the time they were built, a suburban area. The houses themselves are a pleasant variation of Scheibler's two-story row house theme, as exemplified by the contemporary Vilsack Row, although they are not intrinsically (as buildings) of the same quality.

The superior interest of the Hamilton Cottages project lies in the relation of the houses to the site. The central court appears again as at Meado'cots (1912), (q.v.) but here the general disposition of the elements is more open. The complex is still in good condition (unlike Meado'cots the surrounding neighborhood is still good), and the group should be preserved.

JUDGE FORWARD HOUSE
2361 Tilbury Street
————————   1840
Vernacular Greek Revival
Frame   1 story   fair

Built in 1840, this one story hipped-roof structure was the country house of the Hon. Walter Forward, at one time President Judge of Allegheny County and also Secretary of the Treasury under President Tyler.

It is approximately square in shape with a one and a half story wing in the rear; the exterior has been inselbricked, but the house is presumably of frame construction. The windows are multi-paned and there are large square chimney stacks symmetrically placed on the roof. The house would be quite charming if it were properly restored.

TAYLOR ALLDERDICE HIGH SCHOOL
Forward at Shady Avenue
R. M. Trimble   1927
Classical
Stone on steel frame   4 stories   very good
This is a late example of the high school building as "temple" of learning, perhaps the last local specimen of the type. The building, with its Ionic portico, is a pleasant embellishment to its neighborhood, and is worthy of preservation.

East Liberty

ARTS AND CRAFTS CENTER
Shady and Fifth Avenues
Original use: house
Charles Barton Keen   1911-12
Classical
Stucco   2 stories and attic   good
The main headquarters of the Arts and Crafts group occupies this former house of Charles D. Marshall. Keen was commissioned by the Marshall's in April 1911, to prepare designs for the house.

A handsome exercise on the Edwardian Classical theme, done very broadly in white stucco, it is vaguely Georgian, with some suave Italianate touches. One of the last built of the great East Liberty millionaire mansions, it is also one of the few survivors of a once numerous group. It was given to the newly founded Arts and Crafts Center by the Marshall family in 1945.

109

BERRY HALL, CHATHAM COLLEGE
Woodland Road
Original use: house   Present use: college dormitory
John Bissell   1893
Georgian Revival
Brick   3 stories   very good

An interesting example of the Georgian Revival of the late 19th century as reflected in the local scene, this house rather echoes the work of the New England architect, Charles Bulfinch (1763-1844) in Pittsburgh, where there is little specific influence from his work. Designed by an amateur, John Bissell, it mirrors rather infelicitously the four-square, three story domestic image popular in the late eighteenth century in New England.

ANDREW W. MELLON HALL, CHATHAM COLLEGE
Woodland Road
Original use: house   Present use: college dormitory
——————   1897 and 1917
Tudor
Brick and stone   3 stories   good

Built originally for the Laughlin (J & L Steel) family in 1897, the house was bought by Andrew Mellon in 1917 for himself and his two children. At that time the house was considerably renovated and enlarged. Done in the style of an English Tudor manor house, freely interpreted, it was for many years the great mansion of the Woodland Road area (a quasi-suburban preserve of millionaire estates). Andrew Mellon also added tennis courts, bowling alleys, and a sixty-foot underground swimming pool, which last was vaulted with Guastavino tiles. The interior of the house also contains much elaborate carving in the Tudor style.

In 1921, when he became Secretary of the Treasury, he turned the house over to his son Paul and Paul's wife who lived there until 1940 when it was given to Chatham College for use as a student center. It should be preserved as one of the few remaining examples of the great millionaire houses of its period in the East End of Pittsburgh.

110

FRANK-ANDERSON-MORELL HOUSE
East Woodland Road
Walter Gropius and Marcel Breuer   1939
Modern
Stone, brick and concrete on steel frame   3 stories   very good

A period piece, much admired in its day, this house, although it has not the great popular appeal of the Frank Lloyd Wright house Fallingwater, has a certain historical importance as heralding the full advent of the International Style in Pittsburgh. It is, as well, one of the first American design documents of two important Bauhaus architects. This house should be preserved because of its importance in architectural history in this country.

GREYSTONE (now Benedum Hall)
East Woodland Road
Original use: house   Present use: college dormitory
W. H. Vantine   1911-12
Edwardian Classical
Stone   2 story and attic   good

The site on a hillside above Fifth Avenue was formerly the estate of Thomas M. Howe, who had built a house on the brow of the hill just prior to the Civil War. His name is commemorated in Howe Spring, where South Highland Avenue intersects Fifth; this was a favorite drinking fountain during the latter part of the nineteenth century, but it is now closed. In 1911, M. L. Benedum bought the seven acre site from the Howe Estate and demolished the old house, which had also been called Greystone from the material of its construction.

Part of the old house's foundations were used in the construction of the new, much larger dwelling. Curiously enough the exact texture of the finely cut masonry of the demolished mansion was imitated in the new house. The later builders, however, deserted the medievalistic style of the Howe place for an exceedingly expansive Edwardian version of the Classical theme. This is probably one of the last, if not the least, of the East Liberty millionaire houses and it has a broad, bland, rich elegance of manner that is architecturally and socially very reassuring. The view of the serried architectural monuments of East Liberty rising above the trees of the Italianate terracing above Fifth Avenue is extremely impressive.

The interior of the house, again, is extremely solid, handsome, and spacious, with wide formal rooms decorated in the English seventeenth and eighteenth century styles. The marble solarium, which still retains some of its original white wicker furniture, is a real period piece. In the dining room is some splendid carved wood paneling.

In 1960 the Claude Worthington Benedum Foundation gave the house to Chatham College and it is now used as a dormitory. It should be preserved as one of the last extant structures of its kind.

HOWE-CHILDS-GATEWAY HOUSE
6000 Fifth Avenue at Woodland Road
Original use: house; present use: college dormitory and guest house
————————— c. 1860
Mid-century Picturesque Cottage
Frame with stone basement   3 stories   good
This asymmetrical frame house in the Picturesque Cottage Style was probably built by Thomas Howe just prior to the Civil War when he built his stone mansion on the hill just above. The latter site is now occupied by Benedum Hall. After 1890 this smaller house was occupied for many years by members of the J. H. Childs family, who were related to the Howes by marriage. M. L. Benedum leased the structure to Chatham College and it is now a dormitory and guest house for that institution. It was once known as Willow Cottage.

112

HAMNETT HOUSE
579 Briarcliff Road
Frederick G. Scheibler, Jr.   1910
Western Pennsylvania Vernacular
Stone   2 stories and attic   very good
This house, very impressive in its way, is rather different from most of Scheibler's early constructions in that it seems to follow in its general form northern English or Scotch or even Western Pennsylvania Vernacular, rather than the "progressive" German or Austrian trends so usually evident in his work of this period. It is also constructed of stone and built on a stony hillock and in this it seems to foreshadow Scheibler's later Romantic manner of the 1920's.

BARNES-AMBROSE HOUSE
592 Briarcliff Road
Frederick G. Scheibler, Jr.   1916
Vernacular and Romantic
Frame   2 stories   very good
A small frame house built on the edge of a great ravine, this house shows Scheibler's vernacular simplicity of approach to the small suburban house, which saves it from being artfully "quaint". It has been kept in excellent condition by the present tenants, one of whom is the daughter of the man for whom the house was built.

OLD HEIDELBERG APARTMENTS
Braddock Avenue at Waverly Street
Frederick G. Scheibler, Jr.   1905, addition 1908
Early Modern
Brick   various stories   very good
This complex consists of a three-story central building, built in 1905, and two wings of two-story cottages on either side. There is also a small two-story and attic house next to it that faces on Braddock Avenue.

His work in essence reflects very strongly some facets of the more advanced architectural trends of the late nineteenth and early twentieth centuries as exemplified in the work of Voysey and Mackintosh in Great Britain, and Loos, Wagner, and Hoffman on the continent. Scheibler never traveled and his associations with European work were formed via his library which contained many of the more progressive-

ly oriented periodicals and books of the first two decades of this century. Scheibler's practice was undoubtedly influenced also by those minor "modernist" architects of Germany and Austria published in the German magazine *Moderne Bauformen.*

In Scheibler's proto-modern style, there is visible an exploration of vernacular sources as opposed to an acceptance of the grand tradition of the styles, and this preoccupation led to a simplification of form, a search for new structural concepts and a contemporary architectural vocabulary in which traditional ornament and even native or folk stylistic reminiscences tend to disappear.

The main building, constructed of brick covered with two coats of Portland cement and roofed with red tile, is symmetrical both in plan and disposition of mass, but the freely devised naturalistic ornament (like the mushroom relief of the facade) and the great variety of opening and fenestration (always a favorite Scheibler device) create a feeling of asymmetrical movement in the general composition. The porches, which display a highly original treatment of a standard architectural motif of the period, have exposed I-beams, an uncommon practice of the time which the architect also used in his later work. Perhaps the general composition of the central building with its attendant cottages is perhaps overly romantic, but it is still quite attractive to the modern eye as well as functional in a high degree.

The buildings attracted considerable attention at the time of their erection and they were published both here and abroad.

The structures are in a fairly good state of preservation and the neighborhood surrounding them has not deteriorated to any marked degree. This complex is one of the key monuments in the development of modern architecture in Pennsylvania, and every effort should be made to preserve it.

APARTMENT HOUSE
201 East End Avenue
Frederick G. Scheibler, Jr.   c. 1905-10
Early Modern
Stucco over brick   3 stories   good

A three story brick apartment house with stucco and wooden porches, this building has six units and is similar in style to the Linwood Apartments at McPherson Boulevard and Linden Avenue in the Point Breeze area (q.v.).

This is essentially the great gabled form; the northern roof-tree, the "house" that a child draws, used so effectively at the Linwood and also on a much larger scale at the Old Heidelberg. There is, as well, a central projecting wing at the back with its recessed porch and stairway, found also in the architect's other apartments. The building is a good example of the early Scheibler apartment house and should be preserved.

CLAYTON
7200 Penn Avenue
House
Frederick John Osterling (remodeling)   c. 1870; remodeled 1893
Richardsonian-Hunt Chateau Style
Brick   3 stories   very good
This is a remodeling, undertaken in 1893 (after a design by Frederick J. Osterling) of an earlier house (c. 1870) that had been bought by H. C. Frick in 1882. Stylistically as it now stands, the house seems to be a vaguely Richardsonian Romanesque version of the R. M. Hunt chateau type. On the interior there is a mixture of styles and luxurious *gemütlichkeit* extremely characteristic of the period. The porte-cochere, still survives as part of the original building and, from its style at least, the small dining room toward Homewood Avenue would seem to belong to this same construction. The house has been extremely well maintained and it should be preserved as a good example of the East End mansion.

PARKSTONE DWELLINGS
6937-43 Penn Avenue
Apartment house
Frederick G. Scheibler, Jr.   1922
Early Modern-Romantic
Schist stone and stucco   2 stories   very good
This, one of the later developments of Scheibler's personal manner, is a four unit apartment house, or it may be a double duplex. Many facets of his earlier manner are still apparent—the moulded forms, leaded colored glass, the medieval massing—but his romanticism seems here to have taken on a heavier, richer quality than

115

in his earlier work; the forms are twisted and prolonged in search of dramatic effect, the texture is generally rather extravagant.

The building has been well maintained for the most part; the neighborhood is still good and the Dwellings should be preserved as the best example of Scheibler's late manner.

THOMAS AND McPHERSON BOULEVARDS PRESERVATION AREA
(*See under Preservation Areas*)

LINWOOD APARTMENTS
6801 McPherson Boulevard
Frederick G. Scheibler, Jr.   c. 1907
Early Modern
Stucco   3 stories   fair

This is a particularly good example of Scheibler's early apartment house construction, which, although merely a variation on the Edwardian multiple dwelling theme, is notable for its freshness of approach and its felicity of treatment.

Although the neighborhood in which it stands has become considerably tarnished, it is to be hoped that this apartment house can be preserved.

Homewood

HOLY ROSARY ROMAN CATHOLIC CHURCH
Lang Avenue at Kelly Street
Ralph Adams Cram (Cram & Ferguson)   1929-30
Gothic
Stone   1 story   very good

This suave limestone church whose sophisticated French and Spanish Gothic masses rise above the dull latitudes of a flat Edwardian quarter (which now in its decay is something rather more than dull) is startling to a degree. It is possibly a monument to clerical ambition and "culture", if not to parochial piety.

116

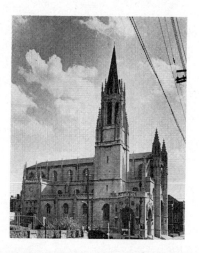

At any rate the hierarchy established in Homewood the latest grand image of the Gothic Revival, the last flowering of the revived style before its eclipse. It is a document also of that free-flowing eclecticism that made the 1920's so abundantly the last extraordinary decade—if anything so totally extra could be so-called—of the nineteenth century.

The interior of the church is reminiscent of those of Catalonian Gothic churches, and there are traces, notably in the western rose window, of that French Gothic, which was so felicitously domiciled in Spain as at Leon Cathedral. The tower is extremely Spanish, and there are decorative details that are almost Mudéjar.

This elegant church is certainly an ornament to its neighborhood, and it must be preserved.

STONE ARCH BRIDGES
Washington Boulevard below Frankstown Avenue
William H. Brown, Chief Engineer, P.R.R.   1902-03
Roman
Stone   ——————   very good

These great stone arches, roughly coeval with the Pennsylvania's famous and now vanished station in New York City, represent the Roman habiliments, the imperial epoch of the Pennsylvania Rail Road. In these dim days of the railroad's eclipse, these splendid viaducts, the triumph of the engineers, remain as monuments to those vanished refulgent days.

The railroad's portion of this interweaving complex of bridges was part of a project that provided a connective link, known as the Brilliant Cutoff, between its lines, The Allegheny Valley and the West Penn (in the Allegheny River Valley) and the main line tracks at Fifth Avenue. This considerable engineering feat was carried through in 1901-02. Other structures in the scheme were a smaller stone-arched viaduct, a great through-truss bridge across the Allegheny at Aspinwall and an elevated through-truss span at Fifth Avenue (the latter now demolished).

At about the same time the City of Pittsburgh constructed its own bridge with arches of much wider span to carry Lincoln Avenue across Washington Boulevard (it was opened in 1906). The railroad bridge crossed a small body of water known as Silver Lake, which at one time served both as an ice pond and a skating rink, but which is now filled with a drive-in theatre, a tawdry note of modernity made even more petty by these massive structures.

LARIMER AVENUE BRIDGE
Larimer Avenue
——————   1912
Concrete   ——————   good

This graceful concrete structure at the time it was opened in July 1912 broke the previous record for the size of concrete bridge arches. It was begun in 1911. There are a number of these concrete arch bridges spanning the ravines of Pittsburgh and this is perhaps the most representative of the type.

MEADO'COTS
Rosedale and Madeira Streets
Apartments
Frederick G. Scheibler, Jr.   1912
Early Modern
Brick   2 stories   poor

This is perhaps the earliest of Scheibler's groups of houses arranged around a court, although he had already had some experience in handling a complex of buildings in his Old Heidelberg commission (q.v.) which was done in two parts.

118

Here he has deserted stucco for a kind of rough buff brick, and his roof-lines have become a little softer than they were in his earlier work. Here are also on display some of the arresting "modern" features like the corner windows and the exposed steel beam lintels, which had become, rather startlingly, in Pittsburgh, his trademarks. This group of small houses has real distinction even in its present rather dim and fallen state, and it should be preserved.

HOUSE
8415 Frankstown Avenue
——————— c. 1850
Late Greek Revival
Brick   2 stories   fair
This is a five bay house; it is one room deep and it has an interesting central door-way. Much of the detailing seems to be late Greek Revival. The windows have straight lintels with simple corner blocks.

THE HARTER HOUSE
2557 Beechwood Boulevard
Frederick G. Scheibler, Jr.   1923
Early Modern-Romantic
Stone and stucco   2 stories   good
This house, which has been somewhat changed since it was built, is like the Park-stone Dwellings done in Scheibler's late rich-textured Romantic manner. Scheibler did not often get an opportunity to design a house of this size, and he has, on the whole, handled it very creditably. Since it has been difficult to gain entrance to the house in the past, it is hard to say how much of the architect's original interior fittings have survived.

Greenfield

HOUSE
Kaercher Street and Greenfield Avenue
Original use: Tavern (?)   Present use: house
——————— c. 1800-1850
Western Pennsylvania Vernacular
Frame or log   3 stories   good
This house faces the corner diagonally, and may at one time have functioned as

119

a tavern with a double verandah, but the first floor porch has been enclosed. The third floor windows are quite small and there must not be much headroom. There is only one chimney at the side. The house now has modern clapboarding.

Hazelwood

HOUSE
Hazelwood and Bray Streets
—————————— c. 1850
Greek Revival
Clapboard   1½ stories   good
A five bay house, two rooms deep, with double chimneys, transom and sidelight doorway, the house is Greek Revival in style although it has been modernized.

WOODS HOUSE
4604 Monongahela Street
—————————— Before 1800
Western Pennsylvania Vernacular
Stone   2 stories and attic   poor
That this fine three bay house has managed to survive in the dreary industrial wasteland of Hazelwood is almost miraculous. It was recorded by Stotz in the 1930's as being built by George John Woods before 1800.

There is a high basement in front because the house is built on steeply sloping land. The windows are multi-paned and there are stone voussoirs over the front door, which opens out on mid-air since there is no verandah. There is a chimney at either gable end. At the back there is an assymmetrical wooden addition that looks as if it might date from around 1850 or a little later—about the time that Hazelwood was still a "good" residential suburb. The condition of the house is poor and its preservation might be a difficult matter. Preserved nevertheless it should be.

CHURCH OF THE GOOD SHEPHERD
Second and Johnston Streets
———————— 1891
Late 19th Century Picturesque
Stone, brick and shingle   1 story   very good
This congregation was formed in 1871. This asymmetrical and rather fantastic structure with its frilled shingle tower recalls very pleasantly the rugged, stylish "natural" contours of those late nineteenth century suburban churches boldly designed by a small number of "original" architects, a group that might be described as the "boulder and shingle" school.

Certainly this charming and rather amusing little building does mitigate the rigors of the present industrial Hazelwood; it is difficult to remember now that Hazelwood once had some pretensions as a residential suburb. The church should be preserved as a unique local representative of its type.

FIRST HUNGARIAN REFORMED CHURCH
221 Johnston Street
Titus de Bobula   1903-04
Art-Nouveau
Brick and stone   1 story   good
The first building of the congregation was built on Bates Street about 1891, but the present brick and stone building was begun in 1903 and dedicated in 1904. This interesting and rather "original" structure has fantastic almost Art-Nouveau windows on the main facade at either side of the central tower. The architect also designed the Cathedral of St. John Baptist of the Byzantine Catholic Diocese at Munhall, Pa. (q.v.).

East End

HOUSE
7215 Witherspoon Street
———————— c. 1860
Vernacular
Brick   1½ stories   good
This house is four bay with bracketed cornice, two dormers and two chimneys, and it rises to two stories in the rear.

VILSACK ROW
1659-1693 Jancey Street
Row houses
Frederick G. Scheibler, Jr.   1912
Early Modern
Brick   2 stories   poor
Vilsack comprises three rows—one of six units, one of eight units and one of four units—built on a terrace. Brick and stucco with wood trim, these are the most interesting of Scheibler's row houses, a building type in which he rather extensively excelled. The contrast of the glass areas and the coved stucco cornices with the brick surfaces of the entrance sections is notable. In the dull suburban area in which they were constructed, these quite sophisticated structures seem almost totally improbable. Certainly they constitute a kind of descent of grace that was far ahead of its time, not only in Pittsburgh but in much of America as well.

As a voice going before, Scheibler's Vilsack Row represents perhaps the peak of his prophetic achievement. They might well be considered today the product of a contemporary architect. Here the corner entrance pavilions, representative of older volumetric shapes, contrast with the open areas and the slab roofs, which

suggest the intersection and the interplay of planes enclosing spaces. These buildings, now rather decayed and in a poor state of preservation, must have been almost unique in America in their day. Their preservation is certainly to be hoped for.

BAYWOOD
1251 North Negley Avenue
Original use: house   Present use: art gallery and offices
————————   c. 1880
Second Empire-Italianate
Brick   3 stories   poor

Originally part of a grant made to William Heth of Henrico County, Virginia in 1789, the land on which this house stands was bought in 1856 by Alexander King (1816-1890), a Pittsburgh business man. The original house on the property burned in 1879 and the present structure was built soon after.

Following the death of Robert King, Alexander's son, in 1954, the estate became the property of the City of Pittsburgh, who gave possession of the house to the Zoological Society of Pittsburgh, who assigned quarters to various cultural societies, including the Pittsburgh Plan for Art.

It is a five bay house with wood trim and in the center of the facade is an Italian villa tower with a mansard. The porch is late-Victorian Classical, and the side elevations are rather asymmetrical, with bay windows. A two story section has been added to one side roughly approximating the same style.

The house, which looks like a great but clumsy ship, is deteriorating badly and the city should take prompt action.

KING'S FOLLY
1252 North Negley Avenue
Garden ornament
————————   1898
"Gothick" Castellated
Stone   ————————   poor

Constructed by Robert King (1875-1954) as a kind of sham castle or garden ornament in 1898 on a hillside overlooking a ravine at one side of the King house (q.v.), this structure is unique in Pittsburgh; the castle is in the tradition of the English folly or ornamental garden structure, some seventeenth and eighteenth century examples of which were constructions of real architectural character.

As first built, the King sham castle consisted of four towers connected by low battlemented walls. Against the hillside was a house constructed of brick, also part of the "castle", which served as a garden tool house. The Folly has not been well maintained and part of it has been demolished. In December 1965 only two of the towers were left and the remaining ones are not in good condition. It is questionable if the Folly can survive since there seems to be no attempt at maintenance. It

is incumbent upon the city, now custodian, to preserve and rebuild this ornament for Highland Park.

HOUSE
5636 Elgin Street
_____ c. 1865-70
Vernacular
Frame   2 stories   good
This is a three bay white frame house with a verandah and curlicued cornice, a side light and transom front door.

BENDET HOUSE
1321 Cordova Road
_____ c. 1927
Early Twentieth Century Medievalistic Picturesque
Brick   1 story and attic   very good
This house is superlatively the image of the small "cottage orné" of the 1920's,

that is, the "Norman French" farmhouse as fashionable suburban villa. Almost all the vagaries of that vanished medievalism are concentrated here—the crazy-patch brick work, the small pointed Mother Goose turret, the sunken ridge-pole of the roof. This is the very quintessence, the final end result of the antiquarianism of the nineteenth century.

Here reproduction is not merely a matter of imitating the forms of the past but also the very process and texture of the physical process of aging. It is interesting that this type of patination, if one may call it so, reached this peak of intensity just before it disappeared from the architectural scene.

HOUSE
6349 Jackson Street
Frederick G. Scheibler, Jr.   1921
Early Modern
Stucco on tile   2 stories   very good

Built for Mrs. Clara E. Johnston in 1921, this is a detached private house with verandah and sun porch. It is constructed of stucco on tile with wood trim, and it is a good example of Scheibler's incipient later Romantic manner applied to the medium-sized detached house. Here are also his standard modern mannerisms like the corner window and the exposed steel beam lintel above windows.

ALLEN M. KLAGES HOUSE
5525 Beverly Place
Frederick G. Scheibler, Jr.   1923
Romantic-Medievalistic
Stone and stucco   2½ stories   very good

A schist stone with wood trim house done in Scheibler's later Romantic manner of the 1920's. The drawings for this house are dated March 1923. Allen Klages, who commissioned the house, is still (1965) living there; he knew Scheibler personally and apparently was one of those clients who was willing to indulge the wishes of a talented and demanding architect.

Scheibler had become fond of the Philadelphia schist stone and had to have it from a certain quarry in eastern Pennsylvania and he also had to have a certain kind of mahogany for the living room. Klages, according to his own account, was not only willing to have these items but he was willing to pay for them.

The Klages house is related to the Parkstone Dwellings (q.v.) of 1922 and the Harter House on Beechwood Boulevard (q.v.) in its heavy texture, rich density of Romantic imagery and variety of materials.

WEST PENN HOSPITAL
4800 Friendship Avenue
John L. Beatty; Alfred D. Reid Associates
     1908-12; 1926-27; 1956
Classical
Brick over steel frame   various stories   very good

This hospital was chartered in 1848 and the first building was constructed in 1850 after designs by Joseph W. Kerr. This was a four story building in the Greek Revival style located at 28th Street and the Pennsylvania Railroad tracks. Although this structure was added to extensively in succeeding years, by the end of the century it had become both inconvenient and over-crowded. A competition was held for a new hospital to be erected on a site on Friendship Avenue, East End. The building was begun in 1909 and on 2 January 1912 it was opened to the public. This building also has been added to over the years. In 1923 the Nurses' Home was erected on one side of the hospital. John L. Beatty was the architect of the new hospital and the laboratory extension of 1926-27. A new service wing, designed by Alfred D. Reid Associates, was added in 1956. The original part of West Penn is roughly star-shaped with pavilions radiating from a central core, and it is an interesting

124

variation of the nineteenth century pavilion system that Samuel Sloan, the Philadelphia hospital architect, so notably advanced.

NIEMANN-BILLINGS HOUSE
1212 North Negley Avenue
Alden & Harlow   1906
Classical
Brick   2 stories and attic   very good

This is a good example of the Edwardian burgher house, Pittsburgh-style, as well as an evidence of the sober, if rather heavy-handed manner of Alden & Harlow, the most prominent local architectural firm of the turn of the century. Executed in red brick and red sandstone and in a vaguely Georgian style, the house achieves a heavy suavity both of tone and form. Discreetly reworked architecturally and much decorated in its interior, the place now has the adroit glamour of a stage setting.

The building is well maintained but its future as a dwelling house is uncertain. Part of it is now let as flats. John Billings, the owner, has installed in this house the music room from the Armstrong Mansion, also designed by Alden & Harlow shortly after the turn of the century, and which was demolished in the 1950's.

EAST LIBERTY PRESBYTERIAN CHURCH
Highland Avenue, Penn Avenue at Baum Boulevard
Ralph Adams Cram (Cram and Ferguson)   1931-35
Gothic
Stone   1 story   very good

This is the fifth church on the site at Penn and Highland. There were others built in 1819, 1834, 1864, and 1888, running through many of the styles in which a nineteenth century Protestant church could be built. This edifice, the last great structure erected by the Cram firm, was as Cram said himself in his autobiography the kind of commission of which an architect dreams but rarely gets.

The donors, Mr. and Mrs. R. B. Mellon, had conceived of it as a great memorial church and they had desired the very best ecclesiastical structure that could be got according to the standards of the time. Cram was given carte blanche to design a church of cathedral dimensions, using the finest building materials.

The church itself consists of a nave of five bays, transepts, a wide and deep sanctuary, and a great central tower. Stylistically the Gothic of East Liberty is much in debt to Spain. It is interesting that Cram, like Richardson before him, had been attracted to Spain and his later manner was much influenced by the Spanish

125

Gothic. It is interesting, also, to compare Cram's much earlier East Liberty Church
—Calvary Episcopal—with his late work. Since, residentially at least, a good segment of Pittsburgh's wealth was concentrated in East Liberty, one can see why
Cram's authoritative image of ecclesiastical architecture was so thoroughly pervasive
early and late.

All the furnishings and appointments of the church were executed at the time
of its erection, an unusually fortunate procedure, which makes the building almost
a perfect document of its period. There is much fine carving in both wood and
stone, including John Angel's well-known Last Supper above the high altar, and
much handsome stained glass done by most of the prominent stained glass artists
of the time. The profusion and elaboration of the parish buildings foreshadow the
large "plants" of present day suburban Protestant churches. The concept of the
church as a social center has been growing in importance since the beginning of
this century. Both the large urban institutional churches and their suburban "community" counterparts now seem like large circles of organized social activity revolv-
ing around a religious core.

Since the church was built, the East Liberty district has changed greatly and
much of it has been subject to "urban redevelopment". However, the church is
sufficiently well established and sufficiently important that there is no question about
the preservation and maintenance of the building.

MOTOR SQUARE GARDEN
Centre Avenue at Baum Boulevard
Original use: market house   Present use: automobile showroom
Peabody & Stearns   1898-1900
Classical
Brick   1 story   very good
Along with the large addition done for Joseph Horne's department store, this was
Peabody and Stearns' largest commission in Pittsburgh. It was designed at a time

when Boston was still much to the fore as a center of influence on this city's architecture. Here the great market shed, a familiar structure in nineteenth century America, aspired to both Roman and Renaissance forms signaled in the one case by the repeated gables reminiscent of the Baths of Caracalla, and the dome and the Italianate detailing in the other.

This was not the last of the big market houses erected in Pittsburgh; the Diamond Market designed by Rutan and Russell was erected in 1915-16. At least it did not suffer the same fate as the latter building (which was demolished in 1962), but it did not long remain dedicated to its original function. In 1915 it was converted to a "sports arena" and occasionally in later years it was used for trade shows. It is now used as an automobile showroom and miraculously, it has managed to remain standing in an area that has been subject to heavy redevelopment. We are of the belief that it continues to have considerable visual value in its context, and as long as it continues to perform some function, it should be preserved.

Some changes have occurred over the years, and the interior space has been subdivided, but the exterior has not been much changed.

Since this structure by its form and size is an East Liberty landmark, an effort should be made to preserve it.

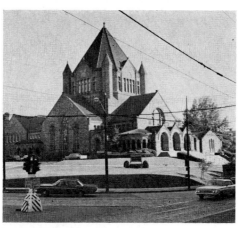

FIRST METHODIST CHURCH
Centre & Aiken Avenues & Baum Boulevard
Weary & Kramer   1893-95
Richardsonian Romanesque
Stone   1 story   very good

This congregation originally occupied a Gothic Revival church designed by J. W. Kerr at Penn Avenue and 8th Street, downtown; when the building burned in 1891, the congregation elected to sell its property and like many other downtown churches, moved farther out. Part of the congregation took half of the sum realized from the sale and built a new church on the North Side—Calvary M.E. (q.v.), and

127

the other (most of whom were resident in the East End) took the rest and constructed the present church.

The great domed church is a large, rugged, and salient example of the centrally-planned Romanesque lantern church so much identified with Richardsonian practice and so notably continued in Shepley, Rutan and Coolidge's Shadyside Presbyterian Church of 1889 (q.v.). The chancel was remodeled in 1952 by Harold Wagoner of Philadelphia, who also was architect for the recreation building at one side of the church. George W. Kramer (1847-1938) was especially noted for his churches, of which this is one of the most outstanding. The church has a flourishing congregation and the building is in an excellent state of preservation.

HIGHLAND TOWERS APARTMENTS
340 South Highland Avenue
Frederick G. Scheibler, Jr.   1913
Early Modern
Brick   4 stories   very good

Very striking in concept and design, this is one of Scheibler's outstanding works. A four story brick apartment house designed around three sides of an open court, this building has, despite the lavish use of "art" glass and the diaper treatment of the spandrels, a very modern feeling. The wide areas of banded fenestration contrasting with the plain wall surfaces, the round concrete columns, the long vertical windows and the turrets of the corner towers, all contribute to the contemporary effect.

The floor plan of the apartments (which have today been sub-divided) are (or were) ingenious. Of special note are the cleverly planned public staircases, which rise partly against a semi-circular wall of rough brick. This building recalls particularly the work of Frank Lloyd Wright (with which Scheibler was familiar) both in character of ornament and disposition.

The interior of the Highland Towers exhibits as well the pervasive influence of Japan, which is also noticeable in the work of Wright. Scheibler was directly motivated by the Japanese through his association with the Japanese-American artist Kentaro Kato (1889-1926), who sometimes collaborated with him in his decorative schemes. The architect, however, whatever his models, was always interested in the visual aspects of his work; sculpture, color, decoration, and landscaping were an integral part of his buildings.

Architecturally, the Highland Towers is one of the most beautiful buildings in Pittsburgh and every effort should be made to preserve it.

128

North Side

ALLEGHENY LIBRARY
East Ohio at Federal Street
Smithmeyer and Pelz   1888-89
Richardsonian Romanesque
Granite   2 stories   fair
In May 1886, a committee of the Allegheny City Council was appointed on Andrew Carnegie's intimation that he would give $240,000.00 for a library if a site were donated. The City of Allegheny donated the Third Ward square. A public architectural competition was held in 1887, and eighteen sets of plans were submitted.

The commission was awarded to the firm of Smithmeyer and Pelz of Washington, the architects of the Library of Congress in Washington, D. C. As well as a library, the building was planned to house a music hall and lecture hall; this structure was apparently a trial run for the much larger Carnegie Library, art gallery, museum, and music hall erected in the Oakland district of Pittsburgh a few years later (See Carnegie Institute). The building was completed in 1889 and dedicated in 1890.

Designed in a rather bold but unimaginative version of the Richardsonian Romanesque then at the height of its popularity, its rather undistinguished tower with its lighted clock faces has dominated the center of Allegheny. The central library section of the building is ill-planned, heavy, and inept; the best part of the structure is the music hall. Like the then recently completed Allegheny County Court House, the building is of granite.

BUHL PLANETARIUM
West Ohio and Federal Streets
Ingham, Pratt and Boyd   1939
Classical
Stone   5 stories   very good
This building, aside from its obvious importance in the cultural life of Pittsburgh, is also interesting as one of the first attempts to arrest the blight that had come upon the North Side in full force by the early 1930's. Demolished to make way for it was Allegheny City's old City Hall, which had been built in the 1860's.

It was built by The Buhl Foundation of Popular Science and dedicated in 1939 to the City of Pittsburgh. It is now leased and operated by the Board of Trustees of the Buhl Planetarium and the Institute of Popular Science.

Even more than the Mellon Institute, and more appropriately, granted the building's use, is the use of the stripped Classical manner of the 1930's. In this low domed building the "grammar" of Classical ornament and detailing has almost disappeared. The ebullience and Quattrocento stylishness of the nearby North Side Post Office (1897) forms an instructive contrast to our building. Unfortunately the Post Office, which is visually much more interesting than the Planetarium, is due to be demolished.

ST. PETERS ROMAN CATHOLIC CHURCH
West Ohio Street at Sherman Avenue
──────────── 1872-74
Gothic
Stone ──────────── very good

Although the interior is disappointing, the stone exterior is a very agreeable example of the Gothic parish church of the 1860's and 1870's. The basement was occupied for church services in 1872 but the entire structure was not completed until 1874. The tower of the church has unfortunately lost its spire, but the large traceried window in the front gable is quite effective.

NORTH SIDE POST OFFICE
Allegheny Center
A. W. Aiken, architect of the
      Treasury Dept. 1897
Early Italian Renaissance
Stone   1 story   good

This delightful building with its dome and its chaste early Italian Renaissance detailing reminds one of those smaller little-known structures—churches particularly—that the traveler encounters in the cities and towns of Italy. Of all the public buildings of the North Side, this is the best designed and most graceful.

At this time the owners of Allegheny Center intend to demolish the building to make way for a high-rise apartment. However, it is hoped that the authorities will recognize the unique contribution that the structure makes to the complex and will reconsider their decision.

ARCHIBALD MARSHALL HOUSE
807 Ridge Avenue
──────────── c. 1850
Greek Revival
Brick   2 stories   poor

A late Greek Revival five bay, center hall house with Doric portico, that is the only proticoed Greek Revival house still standing in Pittsburgh. Architecturally this house is an extremely interesting example of time lag, since by the time it was built the Greek Revival had ceased to be fashionable, although it was still evident in small details sometimes into the 1860's.

This portico is a salient and rather grand survival of the older Classical order and like a passage from one of the great Greek authors, it prefaces the pompous architectural platitudes and the coarse Second Empire pretensions of the Victorian prose behind it. Those Doric columns are at once a majestic valediction and a rebuke.

The late Carroll Fitzhugh, the Pittsburgh bon vivant and litterateur, lived here for some years. He was a grandson of Archibald Marshall.

130

The house, which is said to have figured in the film *Valley of Decision,* is in bad condition and it is doubtful if it would still be salvageable unless something is done to repair it in the near future. This section of Ridge Avenue is now the domain of the new Community College of Allegheny County, which intends to demolish this house.

B. F. JONES, JR. HOUSE
808 Ridge Avenue
Original use: house   Present use: college offices
Rutan and Russell   c. 1908-10
Tudor
Brick and terra cotta   3 stories   good

This is a good example (Pittsburgh version) of the large millionaire townhouse of the turn of the century. Built on a narrow lot, its back premises are rather dark, but its front and side elevations admit sufficient light. Like many other Edwardian "great" houses in Pittsburgh, the Jones house is amply, if not always felicitously laid out; the composition of the main facade is, however, gauche, and the detail pedestrian. Despite its faults, the house is a good example of its type and serving as it will now as the administration quarters of the new Community College of Allegheny County, it will bestow on that institution an aura of tradition and history.

The house cost $375,000 to build, contained forty-two rooms but was abandoned by the family for "Fairacres", their house in Sewickley. The latter was demolished in 1964.

MEMORIAL HALL
809 Ridge Avenue
Original use: Western Theological Seminary dormitory
    Present use: college classrooms
Thomas Hannah   1911-1912
Collegiate Tudor
Brick and terra cotta   4 stories   good

This building, formerly the Dormitory Building of the Western Theological Seminary, is still extant but the Library (Swift Hall) further east on the street has recently been demolished. The latter was and Memorial Hall still is a pleasant if not important local example of the Collegiate Tudor style, which had been popularized by the Philadelphia architectural firm of Cope and Stewardson with their Dormitories for the University of Pennsylvania. The style became enormously popular in America during the first two decades of this century, but it was later ousted from public favor by the Collegiate Georgian, which is still with us today. The present Pittsburgh Theological Seminary buildings in the East End are in that style.

The building is now being renovated for the new Community College of Allegheny County. Its general form and detail are interesting and it could well be the central element in a "restored" 800 block of Ridge Avenue, which would also include the Snyder, Marshall, Denny, Jones, and Oliver houses (q.v.). This complex of buildings would provide the College with a variety of architectural forms and an aura of local tradition, were it inclined to retain them.

HARMAR DENNY HOUSE
811 Ridge Avenue
————————   c. 1890
Richardsonian Romanesque
Stone   2 stories and attic   good

Done in the "Richardsonian Romanesque" style of the late 1880's and early 1890's, this house had a parlor decorated in the 1890's by Tiffany. Née Elizabeth Marshall, Mrs. Denny had been born next door. She lingered in the house long after her neighbors were gone, but moved to the East End during the Depression. This solid, gray dwelling is a sturdy example of its type and must be allowed to remain.

HENRY W. OLIVER HOUSE
845 Ridge Avenue
Original use: house   Present use: offices
Remodelling: Shepley, Rutan and Coolidge
     1871, remodelled c. 1891
15th Century Italianate
Stone   3 stories   fair

This house was built by A. H. English in 1871, who sold it to Henry W. Oliver in 1879. Oliver commissioned Shepley, Rutan and Coolidge (Boston) to remodel it. They did it very handsomely in the neo-Quattrocento manner of the 1880's. Oliver (1840-1904) was active in developing the Mesabi iron ore in Minnesota and joined in Carnegie Steel, finally selling his holdings in 1901 for $17,000,000.00. The house was a scene of much social activity when Oliver's daughter became Mrs. Henry R. Rea. It was well preserved by Instruments Publishing Company, but now has fallen into the hands of the Community College of Allegheny County. It should be preserved perhaps as a faculty club or library.

This house is the best example in Pittsburgh of the 15th century Italianate style made popular in the late 1880's by the new firm of McKim, Mead and White. Shepley, Rutan and Coolidge, who also used the new manner extensively, were, at the same time, the heirs of Henry Hobson Richardson, and there is visible in the house a fascinating blend of the Richardsonian Romanesque and the new "smart" Italian style. Shepley, Rutan and Coolidge owed their Pittsburgh fame to the fact that they had finished the Allegheny County Court House and Jail after Richardson's death.

The Oliver house also presents an intriguing double image because the new grandeur is laid over the shell of a "bracketed" Victorian house of a simpler and earlier day. The essence of the first house is felt in the rather tight, unimaginative plan and layout, which apparently was little changed by the remodeling architects. The particular importance of the house lies in the amplitude and the sophistication of its rich decoration, which will bear comparison with anything else produced in America at the same period.

Of particular interest, among the interior fittings, are the splendidly carved oaken main staircase, the richly inlaid paneling of the dining room and the superb Tiffany windows above the stairs.

Shepley, Rutan and Coolidge did another Pittsburgh "remodeling" of about the same period; the recasting of the Greek Revival Asa Childs house on Halket Street for C. L. Magee has recently been demolished, so the remaining Oliver house is doubly important.

133

WILLIAM PENN SNYDER HOUSE
852 Ridge Avenue
Original use: house   Present use: offices
George Orth and Brother   1911
Late French Renaissance
Stone   3 stories   very good

This house is particularly interesting for Pittsburgh as the city's sole and very late example of the small town palace, built closely and ingeniously on a tight city lot. The inspiration and the tone are so evidently "New York", and this architectural provenance is not only evident in the tightly-contained elevations rising directly from the pavement, but also in the automobile entrance underneath the house and the self-contained garage. The latter feature abundantly admits that the motor age is now far advanced, and it also signalizes the demise of the large urban mansion. This house begins to be the *machine à habiter* and is therefore a transitional architectural document of the present day; here the machinery has not quite taken over and diminished the old image. The rich over-lay of interior detail merely adds poignancy to that change which here literally takes place before one's eyes.

It is interesting as well, in the light of the above, how admirably the house has been adapted to commercial uses and here again we may behold the transitional plane very largely demonstrated.

The latest of the Allegheny millionaire palaces, this house is vaguely French eighteenth century in style and is faced in Hummelstown brownstone. The "grand" staircase and "state" rooms are renditions of the English Renaissance styles from the Elizabethian to early Georgian. The treatment of the basement with its automobile entrance and French ballroom is extremely interesting.

William Penn Snyder (1862-1920) was associated with Henry W. Oliver in developing the Lake Superior iron ore area, and he also owned the Shenango Furnace Company.

The house cost some $450,000. Now in good state of preservation under the ownership of the American General Life Insurance Company, this house should, at all costs, continue to be preserved as a social, even a commercial, if not as an artistic document, preferably as part of a small millionaire enclave.

BYERS-LYONS HOUSE
901 Ridge Avenue
Original use: house   Present use: offices
Alden and Harlow   1898
Renaissance
Brick and brownstone   3 stories   fair

This is a double house masquerading as a nobleman's Renaissance town palace in the Flemish and French manner. Alexander M. Byers, who built the structure, was a well-known Pittsburgh industrialist; his daughter married J. Denniston Lyons,

134

banking and brokerage house president. The Byers' house interior has a heavy, tenebrous quality; the Lyons' house feature is a handsome drawing room in the early Georgian style. The house cost $500,000 to build plus $90,000 for the lot, and sold in 1941 for $15,000. It is now sublet for offices.

This, the millonaire palace with a courtyard, is almost unique in Pittsburgh; the structure is built on two sides of a corner lot, and the "court" is really only a front lawn or "yard", adorned with arcades that are also, in the end, nothing but Victorian verandahs. The fine wrought metal gates in the French manner are notable for their execution.

The exterior walls are of brown Pompeian brick and brownstone but the latter has spalled badly. Another extremely interesting feature of the building is the ingenuity with which the service areas of the two houses are fitted together.

The large back buildings on the property will soon be leveled for the new North Side Expressway.

HOUSE
915 Ridge Avenue
——————— c. 1900

Italianate
Brick   3 stories   fair
Of Pompeian brick and stone with a stone Ionic porch, this center-hall house is three bays wide and is set on a high stone-walled terrace. Now a nursing home, it has suffered because of its isolation due to demolition and unsympathetic industrial construction on both sides.

JOHN MOORHEAD, JR. HOUSE
928 Ridge Avenue
Alden and Harlow   c. 1890
Richardsonian Romanesque
Stone   3 stories   good
This slightly awkward but handsome stone Richardsonian-R. M. Hunt Chateau, one of the few survivors of the 900 block on Ridge Avenue, is related both temporally and stylistically to the Boggs house (q.v.) still extant on North Avenue. Now let out in offices, it stands like a forlorn child's castle on some forgotten and desolate nursery floor. Even so, it would be pleasant if it were allowed to survive.

GARRISON-RICKETSON-RIMBACH HOUSES
929, 931, 933 Ridge Avenue
——————— 1871

Italianate—Second Empire
Brick and stone   4 stories   good
These three houses whose fronts are faced in stone and which were designed in the French-Italian manner of the 1860's are town houses of the Classical urban pattern—party wall constructions with back buildings of varying form and outline. However the facades are not flush with the sidewalks, but are set well back with

green lawns in front, a kind of mid-western compromise with the Classical urban order on the exterior, at least. These are probably the grandest examples of the millionaire row house still extant in Pittsburgh and should be preserved as the only examples of their type. However, the new North Side Expressway planners have ignored their virtues and intend to demolish them.

NORTH PRESBYTERIAN CHURCH
Galveston at Lincoln Avenues
Original use: church   Now vacant
Vrydaugh and Wolfe   1896
Renaissance
Brick   1 story   poor
This building is of no particular importance in itself but interesting from a neighborhood viewpoint. Stylistically a variant of the centrally planned Romanesque lantern church, an especially Pittsburgh type that evolved from Shepley, Rutan and Coolidge's Shadyside Church, its scale and tone are similar to that of some of the millionaire palaces on Ridge Avenue. It exhibits a highly eclectic style combining Georgian details, the Flemish curlicued gables of the Byers' house, and some Italianate features. If the church were to be preserved it might be restored as a community center for the Ridge-Lincoln Avenue area.

DARLINGTON HOUSE
Brighton Road at Lincoln Avenue
——————   c. 1890
Richardsonian Romanesque
Brick   3 stories   good
This is a good example of the long, narrow town-house that takes up the entire width of a long narrow lot. Here we have a definite attempt to emulate the grid pattern of such plots found in Manhattan or London. Since the house is built on a corner lot, the interior would not only have more light but in accordance with the owner's wealth, the side elevation on the intersecting street would afford, as it does here, an opportunity for considerable ostentation of treatment.

The form, if such a long narrow slab can be said to have any distinctive form, is vaguely that of the early French Renaissance or late medieval city dwelling. The style is Richardsonian Romanesque, probably dating from the early 1890's. There is on the side elevation considerable carved "Romanesque" detail.

The interior is of an intense narrowness, so much so we can only wonder at the ingenuity that could fit the functions of a late nineteenth century millionaire house into such a thin attenuated space. Here again one is aware of that elaborate carpentry and joinery in which the age abounded. On this score the main staircase is especially interesting.

The house was once owned by Harry Darlington, a businessman (railroads) and philanthropist who was involved in organizing the Allegheny Preparatory school.

136

HOUSE
836 Western Avenue
────────────── c. 1890
Richardsonian Romanesque
Brick   2 stories and attic   good

A two bay house influenced from Emmanuel Church (q.v.), this is an extremely nice small townhouse related to the stone front house at 838 Lincoln Avenue as well as a brick double dwelling across the street from the latter.

The windows on the second floor have wide brick voussoirs again reminiscent of Emmanuel. There are also evidences of the new interest in the Italianate Renaissance, particularly the egg and dart moulding; the big window of the living room is interesting with its rather arresting detail in the leaded glass of the upper sash.

BOGGS HOUSE
604 West North Avenue
Longfellow, Alden and Harlow   c. 1890-1896
Richardsonian Romanesque
Stone   2 stories and attic   good

This stone city mansion, which has managed to survive in a rapidly deteriorating neighborhood, is typical in its rugged simplicity and breadth of design of those large houses designed by the firm of Alden and Harlow (before 1896, Longfellow, Alden and Harlow) for Pittsburgh millionaires in the decade before and the decade after the turn of the century.

This house in general style and detail is Richardsonian Romanesque, but in form it is early French Renaissance, a common amalgam used in the late nineteenth century. Related stylistically to the Moorhead house (q.v.) on Ridge Avenue, it is generally speaking a better piece of design. It still seems to be fairly well maintained and it should be preserved, particularly as part of the area whose streets commemorate the battles of the Mexican War (q.v.).

It is well sited on the broad avenue overlooking the park.

EMMANUEL EPISCOPAL CHURCH
North Avenue and Allegheny Avenue
Henry Hobson Richardson   1885-86
Romanesque
Brick   1 story   good

After the Allegheny County Court House and Jail, this is Pittsburgh's only other claim to having an architectural monument of national importance. H. R. Hitchcock, the authority on Richardson, considers this church to be the work of Richardson himself rather than his office, and it is related in form to certain English churches of the time. Known familiarly as the "bake oven" church, it has a rugged elemental simplicity of form that is quite beyond "period" and which gives it a serene timeless quality.

This little building influenced much Pittsburgh Romanesque "school work" of its period, and it has been influential even in modern times.

This is a building of national importance, and its preservation is mandatory. It is to be hoped that its immediate neighborhood which is now much decayed can also be made worthy of the church.

LINCOLN-BEECH STREETS PRESERVATION AREA
(See under Preservation Areas)

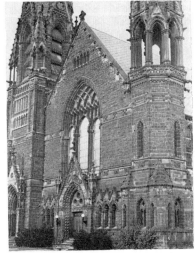

CALVARY METHODIST CHURCH
Allegheny at Beech Avenues
Vrydaugh and Shepherd and T. B. Wolfe   1892-93
Late Victorian Gothic
Stone   1 story   good

This wild, gaunt building in richly carved stone is the eccleciastical counterpart of the great millionaire palaces on Ridge Avenue in the North Side. It has two stone spires (of varying height), unusual in a Protestant "auditorium" church of the period in America.

The towers, whose disposition and form in a crazy, cross-eyed way, recall those of Chartres, preside awkwardly over an amplitude of sloping slate roof and a facade crackling and bristling with fantastic leafage, somber masks, and rampant gargoyles. The carving in its crisp, primitive way has a definite "folk" quality, nearly allied to European provincial sculpture of the early Gothic period. It is Gothic seen through a glass darkly.

The interior with its wealth of golden oak, all richly carved, its brass and mosaic and its mullioned bays is like a huge drawing room devoted to the discreet worship of a safe nineteenth century Deity. The three large "Gothic" picture windows were done by Tiffany of New York, and before they were installed, they were exhibited at the World Columbian Exposition of 1893 in Chicago.

The firm of Vrydaugh and Shepherd of Kansas City were the architects, with T. B. Wolfe as associate. Emil Vrydaugh as a result of this commission came to Pittsburgh and formed a partnership with Wolfe. One of their first commissions was the North Presbyterian Church (q.v.).

This church, which forms a notable anchor for the Lincoln-Beech area (q.v.), is such a curiously and handsomely executed example of its type that it should be preserved. The congregation that was once numerous and wealthy has dwindled, but there has been enough money here of recent years to keep it in good repair.

138

MANCHESTER PRESERVATION AREA
(See under Preservation Areas).

HOUSING
1300-1335 Liverpool Street
Housing
——————— 1880's
Victorian
Mostly brick   generally 3 stories   poor to good
This street was probably laid out sometime in the 1870's (formerly it was called Locust Street), but the houses in this block were not constructed until after 1880.

Most of them were built in the decade 1880-90 and a few after 1890. The north side of the block is entirely composed of a number of double houses so constructed as to give the impression of a long row, a homogeneity of effect not often found in Pittsburgh. The southern side contains, as a kind of centerpiece, the block's only mansion, the Langenheim house, and it is flanked by both single dwellings and row housing. This was not a quarter inhabited by the rich, and the housing varies from middle to upper-middle class, but in its way this is the finest surviving Victorian residential block in Pittsburgh and as such should be preserved. Its rehabilitation is a key to the renewal of the Manchester area.

REGINA COELI CHURCH
1434 Juniata Street
———————— 1865
Romanesque Vernacular
Brick   2 stories   good
A large gabled red brick building, this church has handsome blind arcading.

NEW ZION BAPTIST CHURCH
    (formerly Union Methodist Church)
1304 Manhattan Street
Barr and Moser   1866-67
Vernacular Romanesque Classical
Brick   1 story   good
The Union Methodist congregation was formed in 1846 and the present church was built after the design of Barr and Moser, one of the leading Pittsburgh architectural firms of the mid-nineteenth century. This is an interesting mid-Victorian city church having its brick walls adorned with blind arcading and it is related stylistically to the old North Side Market House and the Allegheny City Hall. In 1961 the building was bought by the New Zion Baptist Church.

ST. MARY'S R. C. CHURCH
Pressley Street at Nash
Fr. John Stibiel   1853-54
Classical
Brick   1 story   good

The parish was formed in 1848 by German Redemptorists Fathers from St. Philomena's at Twelfth and Liberty. In the same year a small frame church was built on the present site, which was later replaced by the present structure begun in the spring of 1853. The architect is reputedly the second pastor of the parish, Fr. John Stibiel, but it is not known if he recruited any professional help.

Fr. A. A. Lambing in his *History of the Diocese of Pittsburgh* describes the structure in a passage that although not always accurate in its architectural terminology has the merit of being Victorian. "The church, which is of brick, is 150 feet in length by 65 feet in width (with a seating capacity of about 900) and has a small 'Byzantine' dome on each corner in front and between these is a porch supported by columns. The nave and aisles are arched with the tunnel or barrel vault and supported by two rows of massive pillars with cushioned capitals. A transverse arch crosses the ceiling in the middle and at the point of intersection with the nave a small dome is erected. In 1882, 'M. Lambart of New York' decorated the interior of the church with large mural paintings depicting scenes from the life of the Blessed Virgin."

Architecturally the church is of considerable interest since it represents the Italianate Classical style, which was not often used for churches in Pittsburgh in the middle of the nineteenth century.

Since the demolition of St. Patrick's R. C. Church built in 1864 at Seventeenth and Penn, St. Mary's is the sole important example of the type surviving in the Pittsburgh area.

The exterior is marked by great simplicity of treatment reminiscent of the work of such men as Latrobe and Sloane, but without their fine sense of scale and proportion. The effect is unlike that of the mid-century Greek Revival, which was in the 1850's becoming increasingly unfashionable, nor is it like the High Victorian Italianate of the 1860's and 1870's. It harks back to the turn of the nineteenth century and is thus rather pleasantly, if startlingly *retardataire*. The most intriguing features of the church were the two bulbous timber bonnets of exotic shape that crowned the two towers; these, however, were removed some years ago and the present diminished finials quite lack the Central European Baroque character of the earlier ones. (These were Fr. Lambing's "Byzantine domes.")

The interior, which employs the colossal Corinthian order although it does not make use of the fine materials of its European prototypes, has a certain distinction.

The structure is in good condition, but there is some question as to its preservation because it lies within an area where much highway "improvement" is projected.

OLD WIDOWS HOME
614 Armandale Street
_____   c. 1860-1903
Late Greek Revival and Vernacular
Brick and stone   2 stories and others   very good

"An Eden that is quite Adamless is the Widows' Home on Northside." The unique little settlement goes by the modest but not quite accurate name of the Widows' Home; it is really a little village in itself occupying parts of Taylor, Sherman, and Arlington Avenues and Atlanta Street of the twenty second ward.

The legislative act incorporating the Allegheny Widows' Home Association was approved in the Pennsylvania House of Representatives on 11 April 1860. First Clause: "Whereas a number of benevolent ladies of Allegheny City have associated themselves for the establishment and management of an institution for respectable widows, elderly maidens and aged maimed people who by sickness or misfortune have

been reduced to poverty, the design being to alleviate their sorrowful lot by affording them shelter and a home at a merely nominal cost."

The initial step was really taken in behalf of poor women deprived of their main support by the Civil War, and the first appeal of the organization, which was the growth of the Allegheny Ladies' Relief Society, was for those "made widows by the sacrifices of the war." It met with immediate success—$11,000 being subscribed. "From the beginning to the present day, its sacred precincts have remained unsullied by the steps of man, except tradesmen."

The original home was the old Allegheny Protestant Orphan Asylum, which was purchased for $15,000 about the time the orphans were removed to their new building. After repair it was opened to receive tenants in 1866. It was soon filled and promoters felt need of more space. Sufficient money was donated for the building of a row of five brick houses on Sherman Avenue in 1873 and later three additional ones on Dawson Street. In 1872, the city opened Taylor Avenue through the property, paying over $5,000 for the privilege. With this amount as a basis, a row of seven houses was built on Taylor Avenue. In 1903 a lot 40' x 100' was purchased on Arlington Avenue, where in the following year was erected a house three stories in height, forty feet wide with center hall and twelve rooms. Again a little later on the rear of the ground facing Atlanta Street was built a house in all respects similar but thirty-seven feet in width. A paved court 30' x 40' and a side entrance three feet in width from the rear, separate the houses and at the same time provide ample space and air. With the exception of those women with children, each tenant is limited to a single room. Although the rents were and are very low, almost nominal for some rooms, the institution has been self-supporting from the beginning.

This complex of buildings is an extremely interesting late nineteenth century American version of the old Christian tradition of benevolent housing dating back to the medieval English almshouses. The central building, the old orphan asylum, is a pleasant example of the late Greek Revival style. The rows of houses, although they have no particular style, have a certain trim, old-fashioned symmetry and homogeneity, rather refreshing in a neighborhood that by now has become more than a little dim and tarnished. This complex could serve as a kind of anchor for a general regeneration of the neighborhood since Taylor Avenue abuts on the Mexican War streets (q.v.), and it could well figure in any large scale rehabilitation.

ALLEGHENY GENERAL HOSPITAL
320 East North Avenue
York and Sawyer   1928-36
Romanesque
Brick, stone, and terra cotta over steel frame   17 stories   very good
Allegheny General Hospital was incorporated in 1882 and occupied some old mansions on Stockton Avenue. After the turn of the century, a Classical building was erected that did duty until the present high-rise structure in the Romanesque manner of the 1920's was opened in 1936.

143

The new building, designed by York and Sawyer, had been begun in 1928, but like many construction projects of the late twenties it was much delayed by the Depression. Although its exterior was completed in 1930, the interior was not finished until several years later. The five story east wing designed by Schell and Deeter was begun in 1958 and finished in 1960.

Like other great general hospitals in the city, its structure is subject to constant change but the building retains overwhelmingly its character as a structure of the 1920's.

ST. BONIFACE R. C. CHURCH
2208 East Street
A. F. Link   1925-26
Romanesque Byzantine
Limestone   1 story   very good

This large church has a three bay nave, a rather shallow apse and a dome on pendentives. The stone pillars have carved caps and the exterior is cased in limestone with some carving.

The dome and all interior vaulting was done in the Guastavino tile system, and the concrete ribs of the great nave arches are faced with tiles and filled in with tiles.

This handsome church should be preserved, particularly for the rather spectacular tile roof system, but the state highways department plans to demolish it for the new East Street Expressway. The highway, if it must be built at all, should be placed on the hillside above East Street rather than through it at the cost of dislocating 1300 families and destroying all of its buildings.

144

AVERY INSTITUTE
Avery and Nash Street
Original use: school   Present use: church
———————— 1849
Greek Revival
Brick   3 stories   poor

This college was founded in 1849 by the local philanthropist Charles Avery (1784-1858) as the Allegheny Institute and Mission Church to provide the traditional classical education for negro youths. According to Erasmus Wilson, "A new building was erected in Allegheny, consisting of three stories, the first and second devoted to education, and the upper to religious exercises." The school, now used simply as a church and meeting building, was the local educational center for many negroes, a number of whom became prominent in the community.

Stylistically the structure is the standard late Greek Revival gabled temple form which had been used so extensively for two decades prior to mid-century. It is a simple building without much architectural pretention, but important in local negro history.

It is now in extremely bad condition and very possibly beyond repair. But this is rather irrelevant because the new North Side Expressway will, as plans stand, pass through it.

HOUSES
900, 902, 904 Canal Street
———— ———— c. 1835
Greek Revival
Brick   2 and 3 stories   poor

These three bay red-brick structures appear to be the only surviving early Greek Revival row houses in the city. Built along the route of the Pennsylvania Canal, they stand on high stone walled terraces approached by steps. At the top of the walls are fragments of Greek Revival ornamental cast-iron fences. All of the houses have multi-paned windows and side light and transom doors. Two of the houses have Doric columns on the verandahs that stretch completely across the facades of all three.

The house on the corner is three stories high because the basement on the Chestnut Street side is treated architecturally, producing a monumental effect unusual in the surviving row housing of Pittsburgh. The structures are in very poor condition and will probably before long join the long list of Greek Revival casualties in the Pittsburgh area. If at all possible, however, an effort should be made to preserve them.

Spring   Garden

MILLER-WIND HOUSE
910 South Side Avenue
————————   c. 1870
Second Empire Italianate
Frame   2 stories and attic   very good
This is a large frame house with vertical siding painted green and white, rather Second Empire-Italianate in style with an Italian villa tower. It was probably built around 1870 by Andrew Miller, who is reported to have been a riverboat captain. John Wind bought it in 1924 from the children of Mr. Miller. Situated as it is on its ample green lawn, it provides a charming picture of the mid-nineteenth century country seat.

Troy   Hill

OBER-GUEHL HOUSE
1501 Lowrie Street
Original use: house   Present use: funeral home
————————   c. 1870
Italian Villa "Stick-style"
Frame   2 stories and attic   very good
This interesting frame house was apparently built about 1870 by a family named Hayworth. After a year it was purchased by a member of the Ober family, of Eberhardt and Ober, the brewers whose establishment was located at the foot of Troy Hill. It is now occupied by the Guehl Funeral Home. There has been some remodel-

ing inside the house, but the exterior has not been greatly changed. Part of its visual effectiveness comes from its location at the top of the Troy Hill Road.

CHURCH OF THE MOST HOLY NAME OF JESUS (ROMAN CATHOLIC)
Harpster and Froman Streets
1868-88

Gothic
Brick   1 story   good

This parish was formed in 1868, one of three German parishes on the North Side, the others being St. Mary's (1848) at Pressley and Lockhart Streets (q.v.) and St. Joseph's, Liverpool Street, Manchester. Troy Hill, with its ancient mythological name, is one of those isolated Pittsburgh hilltop communities that has managed to retain something of its nineteenth century Teutonic character despite the passage of years.

"Progress" has notably passed it by, possibly because there was never any reason for progress coming there. Its narrow streets lined with low Victorian houses seem to dream remotely on their lofty ridge between the wide valley of the Allegheny and the sharp ravine of East Street. The church towers of the Most Holy Name of Jesus, the sharp slate needles of the shrine of St. Anthony of Padua (in this sorcerer's climate, if they had been dedicated to St. Anthony of Egypt we would not have been surprised), and the gaunt surrealist turrets of the Convent of the Good Shepherd (1887), now demolished, give this quarter something of the aspect of a German "burg". Perhaps only at Pittsburgh or Cincinnati would these transplantations have been possible. And at Pittsburgh, only does Troy Hill appear at a distance as if it belonged in the Rhineland or in an illustration to the Brothers Grimm.

Most particularly does the sharp spire of the Most Holy Name of Jesus recall the brick medieval architecture of Germany, and we should be able to identify it even without the German signature stone in the ruddy brick of its facade. The main body of the church was built in 1868. In 1888 the spire and main facade as well as the sacristy and sanctuary at the back were added. The interior of the church is undistinguished in its plaster ornateness, but the whole building seems to be the anchor and aspiration of the dim nineteenth century streets of Troy Hill, and as such it should be preserved.

RECTORY OF CHURCH OF MOST HOLY NAME OF JESUS
1700 Harpster Street
Original use: house   Present use: rectory
c. 1875

Second-Empire-Italianate
Brick and stone   2 stories and mansard   fair

This ornate brick and stone *hôtel particulier* looks rather out of place in the back streets of Troy Hill. It belonged to the Eberhart family (of the Eberhart and Ober brewery) and it was bought in the 1890's by Father Duffner, pastor of the Church of the Most Holy Name of Jesus as the rectory of that church. It is a notable contribution to the fantastic agglomeration of nineteenth century structures that makes Troy Hill the equivalent of a Victorian china closet.

SHRINE OF ST. ANTHONY OF PADUA
(ROMAN CATHOLIC)
Harpster Street

_____ 1880; towers added 1890-91

Vernacular Romanesque

Stone and brick   1 story   good

This extraordinary building was constructed at the wish of the first pastor of the Church of the Most Holy Name of Jesus, who came from a wealthy family. The shrine seems to have been his private whim and when he died intestate in 1892, the parish had to buy it from his heirs. The vaguely Romanesque stone front with its two sharp Germanic needle spires contribute to the general fantastic tone of Troy Hill. The almost oppressively ornate interior with its theatrical gilded and painted fittings, its richly attired plaster martyrs in glass cases, and its cases of saints' relics and ex votos is rather like some fabulous ecclesiastical _nouveau riche_ drawing-room of Victorian curiosities. It is all a little faded and dusty but in fairly good condition.

Fineview

HENDERSON-METZ HOUSE
1516 Warren Street

_____ c. 1860

Medievalistic Gothic Manor House

Stone   2 stories and attic   fair

This large stone structure in the "Gothic" manner is stylistically closely related to the Singer house (q.v.). The barge boards and painted windows and the general sharpness and elongation of its mass testify to the popularity of the medieval domestic silhouette in mid-nineteenth century Pittsburgh. Unfortunately no house of its type

148

has managed to survive in its early "pure" state; most of them have been demolished or remodeled and all of those remaining are poor. This house is no exception.

HENDERSON COTTAGE
Lee and Warren Streets
——————— c. 1865-70

Gothic Revival
Board and batten   2 stories   very good
This in its way is almost as charming as the cottage orné "Heathside" (q.v.), in this area, even if it has not been treated quite so well by time. Formerly, a double house, it pleasantly illustrates the use of the Gothic style in the ornamentation of small picturesque cottages. If possible, it should be preserved as it is among the last survivors of the Gothic Revival house in the city.

"HEATHSIDE COTTAGE"
416 Catoma Street
——————— c. 1855-60

Gothic Revival
Brick   1 story with attic   very good
This little Gothic Revival cottage is of brick with slate roof, latticed Gothic windows,

149

barge boards, and Tudor chimneys. The bay facing on Catoma Street has a signature stone bearing the name "Heathside Cottage."

Hidden away on the Fineview hilltop, this charming little cottage orné with its latticed windows is the very type of the Romantic villa with strong "literary" associations *á la* Washington Irving. It seems all the more exotic, even dreamlike, perched above the Pittsburgh hills. Possibly there was at one time more of this kind of thing in the city, but one wonders if there could ever have been anything quite so intensely and essentially *Moyen Age* in the manner of the 1840's and 1850's in any large numbers. To come upon it now rather bowls one over, as must all rather forceful and sudden confrontations with the past, in dosages, if one might say it, of such "purity". This is like a three dimensional engraved vignette or an architectural enlargement of one of those Staffordshire cottages that used to be placed on cottage mantelpieces. It could have been built anywhere between 1840-1860; much further research is needed. Does "Heathside Cottage" argue a British builder or an anglophile? Although we should like to know more, this small vision is so delightful that the dream is sufficient to the day.

Woods Run

McCLURE AVENUE PRESBYTERIAN CHURCH
3128 McClure Avenue

——————— 1888

Romanesque
Brick and terra cotta   1 story   good
This is a large Richardsonian Romanesque church done in red brick and red terra-cotta. The church auditorium has large gables on three sides with huge wheel

windows. There is an awkward truncated Romanesque tower at one corner. This gaunt, lividly-red structure looks like some prehistoric monster surviving from an earlier time.

The congregation was organized in 1860 and built a frame church in 1867. The present church was built in 1888. The brick was recently cleaned.

ALL SAINTS EPISCOPAL CHURCH
3577 McClure Avenue
Ingham and Boyd   1930-31
Gothic
Stone   1 story   good
This church, constructed in 1931, is a very good example of the Gothic suburban church of the 1920's. The stone structure is quite simple with a long nave (in which the chancel is included) and a parish building at the side. There is a timber roof on corbels. The original church building, formerly on California Avenue, was razed when the Ohio River Boulevard was built.

Perry Hilltop and Northwest

GATE LODGE OF HIGHWOOD CEMETERY
2800 Brighton Road
Gate Lodge and administration office
———————   c. 1860
Gothic Revival
Frame   2 stories   very good
A frame clapboard Gothic Revival cottage with a verandah laced with Gothic-detail and "barge board" ornaments, this is definitely the type of house popularized by Andrew Jackson Downing and the handbooks of the mid-nineteenth century. This looks like a later variation on the theme; the density of Romantic detail has rather disappeared, and we are verging toward the later eclecticism of style heralded by

the bracketed cornice. This is a rather agreeable, one almost might say a "stripped version" of the cotttage orné.

ALLEGHENY OBSERVATORY
159 Riverview Avenue
T. E. Billquist   1900-1912
Classical
Brick, stone, and terra cotta   various stories   very good
The first observatory in this area was built in 1860 on land just off Perrysville Avenue, the architects being Barr and Moser. In 1865 the Allegheny Observatory was transferred to the Western University of Pennsylvania (now the University of Pittsburgh).

When a larger building and a better site was needed, the institution was removed to the present location in Riverview Park. The cornerstone of the present structure was laid in 1900 and it was dedicated in 1912, but Billquist won the competition for the projected building in 1896, the year after the site was donated by David E. Parks to the City of Allegheny along with Riverview Park.

The Allegheny Observatory is a handsome Classical structure of its type and it should be preserved. Its domed silhouette is also a familiar part of the wooded hills above the north bank of the Ohio River.

There had been reports that the University intended to "phase out" the Observatory, but we feel that every effort should be made to retain so pleasing an example of this building type if it can still perform a useful function in the community. Since Pittsburgh would not seem to have at the moment any other observatory facilities, there would also appear to be no doubt as to its being useful.

WATSON CABIN
Riverview Park
Original use: house   Present use: picnic shelter
——————————   before 1850 (?)
Log   ——————————   good
This is the house now known as the Watson Cabin. Only the actual log framing of the cabin would seem to be original. There is a great stone chimney at one side that seems to be modern and also a small stone extension at the rear. The roof also appears modern. It would seem to serve as a kind of adjunct to a small picnic area as is sometimes the case with houses of this sort.

HOUSE
Clayton Avenue
——————————   c. 1850 (?)
Greek Revival
Brick   2½ stories   fair
This is an exceptionally large Greek Revival farmhouse in bad condition. It is five bays wide with a center hall.

South Side

SOUTH SIDE PRESERVATION AREA
(See under Preservation Areas)

EMPLOYMENT OFFICE, A. M. BYERS COMPANY
South Sixth & Bingham Streets
—————— c. 1864
Vernacular Romanesque
Brick   1 story   good

This small red brick gabled structure with round arched windows represents very agreeably the subsidiary industrial building of the mid-nineteenth century. The A. M. Byers Company was founded in 1864 as Messrs. Graff, Byers & Company, and it may well be that the building dates from that period.

OFFICE OF E. W. BLISS COMPANY
901 Bingham Street
—————— 1890-1907
Italianate
Brick   2 stories   good

This stylish building with its tapestry brick, heavy overhanging eaves and its blind arcades in which the windows are recessed, is a nice example of the Italianate manner applied to an industrial building.

ST. JOHN BAPTIST'S UKRAINIAN CATHOLIC CHURCH
109 South Carson Street
—————— 1895; addition of 1919
Edwardian-Classical-Byzantine
Brick   1 story   good

In the variegated vistas of the Monongahela River valley near the Point, the turquoise colored Byzantine domes of this exotic structure add a note of remote and Eastern fantasy to the commercial *longueurs* and the green hills of the Pittsburgh landscape. The juxtaposition of these onion domes with factory chimneys and the roofs of mills is almost startling, but by no means uncommon in our Western Pennsylvania valleys. These domes are important as well because they bear historical witness

153

to the presence of immigrant groups that helped to form the past image of Pittsburgh as one of the great workshops of the world. Visually they not only lend variety to a sometimes excessively utilitarian and industrial scene, but they contribute a necessary note of the mysterious and the other-worldly. They belong essentially to the world of fable and the land of dreams. This church should by all means be preserved and the current aspirations of the congregation to remodel the interior in the modern manner should be reconsidered.

SOUTH SIDE MARKET BUILDING
12th and Bingham Streets
Original use: market   Present use: recreation center
————————   1915
Modified Richardsonian Romanesque
Brick   2 stories   good
The building is interestingly sited in the center of the South Side's Old Market Square, and it would be an act of piety to preserve it because it is one of the last two nineteenth century market houses extant in Pittsburgh; the other is the East Liberty Market (q.v.), now the Hufstader Cadillac Company (1898-9).
     The present building opened in 1893. It burned in 1914 (?) and was rebuilt probably on the old lines and opened in 1915. It became a recreation center in 1950.

BEDFORD PUBLIC SCHOOL
South 10th at Bingham Streets
Original use: school   Present use: warehouse
————————   1850
Greek Revival
Brick   3 stories   good
This large red brick building is a good example of the mid-nineteenth century urban public school building in the Greek Revival style. An inscription on the wall of the main facade bears the date 1850. When it was opened in the autumn of that year,

154

it was known as Birmingham No. 1 since it was situated in the town of that name. When the town became part of the city of Pittsburgh in 1873, it was renamed in honor of Dr. Nathaniel Bedford. In 1960 the school was bought for commercial purposes and turned into a warehouse.

NINTH UNITED PRESBYTERIAN CHURCH
Bingham & South 14th Street
——————— 1854
Greek Revival
Brick   2 stories   good

This is a good example of the urban Greek Revival brick church on a high basement. A signature stone in the pediment of the front gable gives the building date "1854" and the name "First A. R. [Associate Reformed] Presbyterian Church."

There are Gothic windows on the main facade and a Gothic doorway, but the windows on the side are rectangular as befits a building of Greek Revival inspiration. The cornice is also Classical and the side windows of the basement are multi-paned. This is a good example of the mixture of styles sometimes found in these eclectic hall churches of the mid-nineteenth century.

BRADY STREET BRIDGE
Brady Street (South 22nd Street)
Albert Louis Schultz   1895-96
Steel and stone   ———————   fair

Designed by Albert Louis Schultz, this bridge of the through cantilever type was the first city-erected river bridge that was toll free. This great trussed web of steel seems to be the proper visual companion of the steel mills on either side of the Monongahela. If possible it should be preserved, but preliminary highway planning suggests that it will not be.

ST. JOSAPHAT ROMAN CATHOLIC CHURCH
2314 Mission Street
John T. Comes   1913-1917
Romanesque-Renaissance
Brick and cast stone   ———————   very good

This is another of Comes' interesting churches; its brick flanks and exotic-looking tower are visually quite effective against the steep hillside rising above the Monongahela valley and its smoking chimneys. The high central domed tower has a copper roof and a cast stone Romanesque porch.

ST. MICHAEL'S ROMAN CATHOLIC CHURCH
15th & Pius Street
——————— 1857-1861
Vernacular-Romanesque
Brick and stone   1 story   very good

In 1846 the Redemptorist Fathers founded St. Michael's German Church in Birmingham; in 1848 Bishop O'Connor dedicated the church; the Redemptorist Fathers having withdrawn from the parish, the Passionist Fathers were given charge of it in 1853. In 1857 erection of a larger church began. In 1861 on the Feast of St. Michael the church was dedicated by Bishop Domenec.

Architecturally this building is a brick vernacular version of the South German "Rundbogenstil", and it also has a very interesting tower with four quasi-Baroque consoles at the belfry stage, an evidence of that stylistic eclecticism that was more and more coming to be a factor in nineteenth century design. The building is magnificently situated halfway up a steep hillside that looms above the Monongahela valley. The landscape here has a definite Rhineland quality that imparts another dimension to the Western Pennsylvania landscape. At times the church resembles one of

155

those toy German buildings that one used to see in Christmas tree "gardens". The building should be preserved not only for itself, but for its visual importance in the local cityscape.

Mt. Washington

MONONGAHELA INCLINE
Grandview Avenue at Wyoming Avenue
J. S. Kirk and John J. Endus   1869; rebuilt 1882
                              very good

The Monongahela Incline runs from Carson Street near the Smithfield Street Bridge to Grandview Avenue on Mt. Washington. Chartered in 1867 it was the first incline in Pittsburgh. Plans for it were drawn by a Pittsburgh engineer, J. S. Kirk, but they proved unworkable; in 1869 it was redesigned by John J. Endus, of Cincinnati, and the following year it was completed. It was constructed of wood with wire cables made by John Roebling. In 1882 it was entirely reconstructed of metal as a safety measure. The plane is 640 feet in height.

Together with the nearby P. & L. E. Station, the Smithfield Street Bridge, and the trolley car tunnel under Mt. Washington, this incline constitutes an elaborate document on late Victorian transportation.

CHATHAM VILLAGE
Virginia Avenue
Housing
Ingham & Boyd   1932; 1936
Brick   various stories   very good

Chatham Village is a 45 acre tract of land on Mt. Washington that contains a planned residential suburb established by the Buhl Foundation, which described it as the "first large-scale planned residential community built from the ground up in one operation to be retained in single ownership and managed as a long term investment". In recent years, however, the Foundation has withdrawn from the

156

venture, and the houses have been sold to individual owners. There are 197 houses in the plan, of which 129 were finished in 1932 and 68 in 1936. The residents have "four acres of playfields and twenty-five acres of woodland devoted to recreation." Clarence S. Stein and Henry Wright planned the site and Charles T. Ingham and William Boyd were the architects. As a planned community, Chatham Village has far more than local fame and every attempt should be made to preserve its best features.

BIGHAM HOUSE
Chatham Village
Original use: house   Present use: community center
———————— 1844
Greek Revival
Brick   2 stories   very good

Major Abraham Kirkpatrick purchased land in this area in 1794 from the Penns. In 1817, one of his daughters, Maria Louisa inherited a portion on which the house was built by Thomas James Bigham in 1843-44.

A nice Greek Revival structure of brick consisting of a center hall house with an ell in back, it has been considerably changed over the years. Stotz illustrates one of the Greek Revival marble fireplaces. Now known as Chatham Hall, it serves as the community center for Chatham Village.

DUQUESNE INCLINE
1220 Grandview Avenue
Samuel Diescher   1877 (?); rebuilt 1888
————————   ————————   very good

Samuel Diescher designed and built this incline which ascends from West Carson

157

Street west of the Point Bridge to Grandview Avenue. Some claim it was completed in 1873, others say 1877. It was the fourth incline in the city and cost $47,000. The original structure was partly of wood and partly of iron, but in 1888 it was rebuilt entirely of iron.

When the Port Authority of Allegheny County took possession of the incline in 1963, it had only recently been purchased and renovated by the Society for the Preservation of the Duquesne Heights Incline, who had taken it over when the Duquesne Incline Company decided in 1962 that needed repairs were too expensive.

The Authority leases the incline back to the Society for $1.00 a year and the Society has undertaken to restore it to its original condition and keep it operating.

These funiculars, which formed so interesting and picturesque a part of the Pittsburgh scene, were definitely an absorbing local chapter in the history of nineteenth century transportation. The small red enclosed cars of the Duquesne incline moving up and down the steep planes enliven the somber hillside near the Point and the Society is to be commended for its efforts to save this fascinating portion of the past. Of nearly two dozen inclines Pittsburgh once possessed, only two remain.

Beechview

HOVERMAN HOUSE
1200 Westfield Street
House
——————   1825
Vernacular
Stone   2½ stories   poor

This is an interesting example of a Western Pennsylvania stone vernacular house built on a steep hillside. Five bay, it has two stories on the lower side and one on the upper; there is also an attic. The windows are multi-paned and there is a chimney at either end; the fenestration on the lower side is interesting because it includes two asymetrically placed staircase windows.

The remote and rural situation of the house on a thickly wooded hillside facing the entrance to the Liberty Tubes is typical of Pittsburgh, where city and country sometimes alternate with startling abruptness due to the rugged character of the topography.

The structure is of sufficient quality to warrant renovation.

West End

WEST END BRIDGE
Western Avenue and Carson Street
——————   1930-32
Steel and stone   ——————   very good

One of the most beautiful bridges in Pittsburgh, this is a "tied arch" structure in which the thrust of the arch is resisted by the bottom chord of the truss itself (similar to the string of a bow) instead of by masses of masonry.

Here we have a modern version of the poetry of engineers; this great semi-circular web, which appears at a distance to be as light as gossamer, also represents the first and greatest application of pre-stressed hangers in a bridge. The floor of the structure is suspended from the trussed arch by pre-stressed wire cables.

OLD STONE OR COATES TAVERN
434 Greentree Road
_____ 1793-1816
Western Pennsylvania Stone Vernacular
Stone   2 stories   fair
One of the earliest surviving local taverns, this one has a facade of five bays and is built of stone with large chimneys at each end. There are two doors almost side by side and a small front porch; a large frame addition is attached at the back. A datestone on the side would seem to be a later attempt to establish historicity. This tavern must be preserved, but it stands in an area that is decaying. Nearby is a large brick building with gable curtains.

CHURCH
Sanctus & Steuben Streets
_____ 1864
Ecletic
Brick   1 story   good
This is a German church with a signature stone in German in the gable showing the date 1864. A pleasant little building in a deteriorating neighborhood, it is built of red brick with corbeling near the roof line and a small cupola above the front gable end.

Carrick

ST. BASIL'S ROMAN CATHOLIC CHURCH
Brownsville Road
Herman J. Lang   1922-23
Romanesque
Brick   1 story   very good
This handsome church of the early 1920's continues very agreeably the ecclesiastical image established so notably at Pittsburgh by John Comes. The interior with its wooden roof is especially interesting.

Aspinwall Borough

SAUER BUILDINGS
Center Avenue
Housing
Fred C. Sauer   1900-1940
Stone, brick and terra cotta   various stories   very good
This fantastic group of buildings constructed by a local architect in the later years
of his life is possibly unique in Pittsburgh. Our age, which has so often been labeled

as one of conformity, has a marked predilection for manifestations of the unusual, the "original" and the fantastic. The architect has often to consider the wishes of his client, and it is rare that, as an artist, he can afford to build only as he wishes. In this case the designer and builder Fred C. Sauer (1860-1942), after a lifetime of conforming to the wishes of his public, constructed a group of buildings for his own amusement.

Sauer bought his hillside tract of land in 1898 and built himself a house on it not long thereafter. This house does not partake of the fantastic quality of the other—and later—structures on the property. Beside the mansion, there are two more houses and an apartment house called "Heidelberg" (that was remodeled about 1928-30 from his former chicken house). The procession of spaces between these structures seems to be almost medieval and accidental, but the houses themselves defy any close stylistic analysis. It is evident also that Sauer used both building material and carved details rescued from demolished structures.

Even as "dream" structures there is about them something a little pedestrian, awkward, and fumbling. There is something here of the old-time amusement park, more than a seasoning of the frantic romanticism of the 1920 real estate sub-division, a touch of the cinema landscape of Rudolph Valentino. In the end the hillside is Sauer's own private Disneyland with profits at six percent. But having said that, there is a charm and an interest about the place that is irreducible. It is a minor, but still valid document of humanity's primal love of fantasy and legend.

Braddock Borough

CARNEGIE FREE LIBRARY OF BRADDOCK
419 Library Street
William Halsey Wood   1888-89; 1893
Richardsonian Romanesque
Stone   2 and 3 stories   good

This building by William Halsey Wood, who had also entered the competition for the Pittsburgh and Allegheny Carnegie Libraries, is executed in his early Richardsonian Romanesque manner. The building, although it is no masterpiece of architecture, is a good example of Wood's early work. It also has a certain historical importance as the first Carnegie library to be built.

The building was constructed in two sections, that which has an angle turret of four stories in front for the library; the one in back, erected in 1893, has an inscription over its portal "Carnegie Hall". The structure was thus intended to be a social center for the workmen in Carnegie's mills.

161

FIRST METHODIST CHURCH OF BRADDOCK
Library Street and Parker Avenue
—————————   1890
Richardsonian Romanesque
Brick   1 story   **very good**
This is an engaging image of the small Protestant city church in the Richardsonian Romanesque manner. It supports very agreeably the heavier massing of Halsey Wood's Braddock Library (q.v.) across the street.

ROMAN CATHOLIC CHURCH OF THE SACRED HEART
Sixth and Talbot Streets
John Comes   1904
Spanish Renaissance
Brick and terra cotta   1 story   **very good**
An early example of Comes' work in the Spanish Renaissance manner, here as elsewhere in the architecture of the early twentieth century, terra cotta cheaply and easily provided an entire ornamental grammar, in this case Spanish. Again, a church of this type definitely adds a note of grace and interest in an otherwise drab industrial environment.

162

ROMAN CATHOLIC CHURCH OF ST. MICHAEL THE ARCHANGEL
Frazier Street and Braddock Avenue
Carlton Strong   1930
Romanesque-Byzantine
Brick and stone   1 story   good
This highly interesting church of the central plan in the Romanesque-Byzantine style is one of the last as it is one of the best works of Carlton Strong. The building which is rather tall for its site, has little ornament on the exterior; the octagonal dome on the interior is carried on squinches. There are some sculptured plaques of exceptional quality in the vestibule.

The congregation bought the church site in 1891. The present church took the place of an earlier frame one.

Braddock Hills Borough

HARRISON HOUSE
657 Illinois Avenue
———————   1850-1900
Late Vernacular Greek Revival
Brick   2 stories and attic   fair
A photo in the Braddock Bicennential pamphlet shows this as the oldest house standing in Braddock Hills. The photo shows a double porch with door above, but this has been changed.

This is a five bay house with a low pitched roof and bracketed cornice. It is two rooms deep with double chimneys and a brick wing in back. The main door has the transom and side light pattern. The building is quite large and it may owe its preservation to its distance from present day traffic flow.

163

Brentwood Borough

JORDAN HOUSE
538 Becks Run Road
——————— c. 1800
Vernacular
Stone   2 stories   good
This early stone house, now modernized, has thick walls and small ashlar chimneys.

Bridgeville Borough

MURRAY HOUSE
423 Washington Road
——————— c. 1828 and later
Greek Revival
Brick   2 stories   good
This pleasant little vernacular Greek Revival brick house was apparently built in two sections and there is a 13 inch wall between them. Part of the house was a brick shop, which later became an undertaker's establishment. The house has five bays on the facade with multi-paned windows and a classical gabled porch that may be original. There are two chimneys—one at either end—and a simple cornice. Although the house has two stories, the roof slopes down to the first floor in back, rather in the manner of a salt box house.

MIDDLESWART-MURRAY HOUSE
745 Washington Avenue
——————— c. 1828
Vernacular Classical
Frame   1 story and attic   very good
This structure is a double frame house, each of which is three bay, with clapboard walls. The windows are multi-paned, there is a simple Classical cornice, and there are three brick chimneys. The structure is a very agreeable example of the simple frame vernacular stemming from the late Classical style of the eighteenth century.

This lot and several others next to it were purchased in 1803 and 1828 by Moses Middleswart. He built the house now owned by Mrs. A. B. Murray in 1828 (q.v.) and since this is of the same style, it was probably built at the same time. It is said also to have been once a toll house for a bridge across the Chartiers Creek.

MANSFIELD BROWN HOUSE
602 Poplar Way
———————— Before 1830 (?)
Western Pennsylvania Vernacular
Stone   2 stories and attic   very good

This is a five bay, finely dressed stone house of ample proportions with large chimneys and an annex to the rear. A Victorian porch and three shingled dormers are late additions. The house has been remodeled inside and is well maintained. A cavern about eight feet wide and lined with stone runs into the back hillside from the first floor. A stone springhouse on the property still functions.

HOUSE
221 Doolittle Street and 400 Fifth Avenue
——————— 1850-1880 (?)
Second Empire-Italianate
Brick   2 stories   good
A five bay house with verandah and porte cochere and bracketed cornice, it has a wing in back. The building has a commanding site overlooking Carnegie.

Cheswick Borough

BESSEMER & LAKE ERIE RAILROAD BRIDGE
——————— 1918, Built by American Bridge Company
Steel truss and stone   ———————   very good

Erected in 1918 by the American Bridge Company to replace one built in 1896, this bridge occupied 29 months in building. This is a bridge of the decktruss type, 2327 feet in length, with the rails 165 feet above pool level. One end, the north, emerges onto a high embankment, the south end disappears into a cut; between are eight spans from 60 to 520 feet in length resting on stone piers.

The effect of this bridge has been somewhat spoiled by the erection of the rather pedestrian Pennsylvania Turnpike bridge beside it. Prior to this intrusion, the B. & L. E. Bridge constituted a notable example of the poetry of the engineers. The valley of the river is rather wide at this point and the bridge seemed to span the

166

valley like a huge primeval filigree dragon. There is a subtle consonance between the complex forest of trusses, and the branching verdure of the trees on the hillsides.

It is curious how these trussed railway bridges, seemingly so utilitarian and rigid, merged with the intricate greenery of hill and riverbank. Not only is there a rich complexity of structure here, but also a kind of mystery, for the entrances to this steel web are at least from below, hidden from the beholder's eye.

Churchill Borough

BEULAH PRESBYTERIAN CHURCH
Beulah & McCready Roads
1837
Late Vernacular Classical Georgian
Brick   1 story   good

This is another example of the large one-room brick church with gabled end and low-pitched roof. The absolute simplicity of the form itself with no blind arcading or pilasters would seem to argue here a memory of the Western Pennsylvania frontier version of the Georgian manner rather than any dependence on the newer Greek Revival.

A new church has been built to the east of the old one, which has now assumed a subsidiary position, but the "elder statesman" still bears a sort of pioneer witness to those early nineteenth century days when rural congregations in Western Pennsylvania, who were very often not familiar with the latest architectural styles, would build in the mode of an earlier time. Once their buildings were constructed, they might use them for long periods of time, much as their Sunday go-to-meeting clothes might also be made in sturdy independence of the latest fashion. The strait simplicity of this structure has an almost timeless quality.

Collier Township

NEVILLE HOUSE "WOODVILLE"
Rt. 50 (Washington Pike)

—————— 1785

Virginian Vernacular Georgian
Frame   1½ stories   very good

This house is one of the important early houses of Western Pennsylvania. It was built in 1785 by John Neville (1731-1803), a Virginian, and the house definitely shows the influence of Virginian architectural precedent notably in the wide trellised verandahs and the great sloping roof. A few years later General John Neville built another house for himself nearby called Bower Hill, and the earlier house came into the possession of his son, Colonel Presley Neville. Bower Hill was burned during the Whiskey Insurrection of 1794. The house has always remained in the family and it is now in the possession of Mrs. Joseph H. Fauset, a great-great-great grandniece of John Neville.

The plan is interesting. The house is bisected by an entrance hall that contains the stairs; on one side of it is a large living room with two small bedrooms at the back and on the other two irregularly shaped rooms. The interior contains some good late eighteenth century woodwork.

The highway has been steadily encroaching on land in front of the house, but

the building must be preserved as one of the few remaining eighteenth century houses in Allegheny County. It is also historically important through its connection with the Nevilles.

HOUSE
l. r. 02022 east of 02043

———————— c. 1850-1860

Late Vernacular Greek Revival

Brick   2 stories   good

This house has some Classical detailing, although ornament is sparse. It is five bays wide with a side light and transomed doorway, multi-paned windows, and a bracketed cornice. One room deep, it has chimneys at each end and a frame extension at the rear.

EWING FARM
Noblestown Road, east of Pinkerton's Creek (l. r. 02246)
——————— pre-1840 (?)
Log   2 stories   good
This is a log house with a board and batten gable end. Much modernized, it stands across the valley from the Nike installations as a rather feeble symbol of times past

GABRIEL WALKER HOUSE
Noblestown Road at Rennerdale
——————— 1849
Vernacular
Brick   2 stories   fair
This house, said by the owner to have been built in 1849, has a six bay facade and is one room deep. It is constructed of brick painted white and has three chimneys.

Coraoplis Borough

CORAOPLIS-NEVILLE ISLAND BRIDGE
Theodore Cooper   1892
Steel and stone   ———————   good
Designed by Theodore Cooper (1839-1919) and completed in 1892 as the Sixth Street Bridge in Pittsburgh, it was lowered on barges in 1927, towed down-river and re-erected at the present site.

Crafton Borough

FREW-GORAN & McFALL HOUSE
105 Sterrett Place
Stone section before 1800, brick c. 1840
Stone is late Eighteenth Century Vernacular
Brick is Vernacular Greek Revival
Stone and brick   2 stories   very good

The earlier three bay house is constructed of stone and its corners were strengthened by bonding with larger stones. The original plan was elementary; there is but one room in the basement and on the first floor and two on the second. All woodwork is quite simple and in much of it wooden pegs were used instead of nails.

Attached to this stone portion is a five bay, one story and attic brick house with a transverse center hall having at either end a good side light and transom doorway. A long verandah with simple pillars and railings runs the length of each side elevation. In each case the porch roof is cantilevered out from the main roof and the slim pillars are not supporting members. All windows are multi-paned. Some of the rooms in this section have been reworked, always sympathetically, but much of the original simple woodwork remains.

The house stands quite close to the street but there is a large garden in back.

CREIGHTON-DAVIS HOUSE
51 Noble Avenue
Eli Crum   c. 1871
Greek Revival and Mid-Century Eclectic
Stone and brick   1 story and attic   very good

This five bay house is essentially Greek Revival in form with a Classical gabled porch in front and a typical side light and transom central doorway. There are Second Empire touches in the detailing and echoes of the cottage orné in the Tudor chimney stacks. With its blackened stone walls, said to have come from a railroad tunnel in the neighborhood, this little house is a charming exercise in the midwestern Eclectic manner of the mid-nineteenth century.

ST. PHILIP'S CHURCH
Steuben Street
William Ginther   1906
Late Victorian High Gothic
Stone   1 story   good

Although erected after the turn of the century, this is a large and expansive example of the late Victorian stone parish church complete with elaborate tower and spire.

    The first church, a brick structure, was dedicated in 1839 and it did duty until the present building was finished. The latter is in good condition, and the interior was renovated in 1955.

Edgewood Borough

GARDNER-BAILEY HOUSE
124 West Swissvale Avenue
————————   c. 1864
Victorian
Frame   1 story   very good

This is an extremely charming frame mid-Victorian suburban house of a type never very common in the Pittsburgh area, and we do not recall any other surviving examples. It is heavily bracketed and ginger-breaded with long windows and a balustrade on the roof of the verandah. The cupola in the center also has a balustraded "widow's walk". The house was built c. 1864 by a Mr. Gardner; it was bought by George C. Bailey in 1944 after several other changes in ownership.

GRUBBS-KERR HOUSE
235 West Swissvale Avenue
—————— 1835-1865 (?)
Frame, board and batten, brick   2½ stories   very good
This is a very pleasant example of a mid-century suburban villa with window hoods and a fancy jigsaw verandah. The dining room, which is of brick, may have been built in 1835. A Dr. King purchased the property from the Swisshelm estate, but there is no mention of a house in the deed so the exact date cannot be determined.

Edgeworth Borough

NICHOLAS WAY-JONES-HALL HOUSE
108 Beaver Road
—————— 1838
Greek Revival
Brick   1 story and attic   very good
This house on a high basement is one of the most elegant Classical domestic structures still extant in the Pittsburgh district. Both in plan and elevation it is quite similar to the slightly earlier Lightner house (q.v.). In form the Way house is also late Georgian interpreted in the broad Classical idiom of the Greek Revival of the 1830's. As Stotz says, the portico with one story order as expressed in the Way and Lightner houses was not common in this area. The bull's eye window in the porch gable of the Way house is much more graceful than the window of that of the

Lightner place; both, however, have central transomed doorways, rather different in treatment, but equally fine.

The Way house, although it still preserves its essential form and character, has been much modernized and aggressively, although pleasantly, interior decorated; a large living room addition has also been recently added to the rear. It is in excellent condition and its preservation is mandatory.

The house was built by Nicholas Way and remained in the possession of the Way family until it was bought a few years ago by Mrs. W. L. Jones. In 1966 it was purchased by the Campbell Hall family of Sewickley.

OGDEN-THOMPSON HOUSE
424 Beaver Road
_____ c. 1820 and later
Brick   2 stories and attic   very good

This house has been so extensively remodeled that it is difficult to assess its merits as an old building. Part of the structure is said to date to 1820 but there are no documents to prove it. Some old photographs of the house show it to have been a provincial version of the asymmetrical mid-nineteenth century American cottage orné. Charles Stotz remodeled it in 1939 in the Georgian manner. Anthony Wolfe designed the den and the porch about 1956. The gardens were done by Ralph Griswold.

The house and grounds, both in excellent condition, together make a charming suburban ensemble.

STINSON HOUSE
420 Oliver Road
Original use: school   Present use: house
_____ 1835-1900
Greek Revival-Edwardian Georgian
Brick   3 stories   very good

The Edgeworth Female Seminary was established in 1825 by an Englishwoman Mrs. Mary Oliver, who named it for the novelist Maria Edgeworth. It was first located in Pittsburgh, but soon afterward removed to Braddock's Field and in

174

1836 to the Sewickley valley, where it occupied a brick building to the south of the Beaver Road on property that had been part of the Shields estate. The central part of this building was three stories in height with a portico, and the frame wings at either side were of two stories. A school hall adjoined one of these wings. On Mrs. Oliver's death in 1842, the Seminary was closed but it was re-opened in 1846. In 1865 the career of the school came to a close with the destruction by fire of the two wings. The central section then became a house and the Hon. Morrison Foster, brother of Stephen C. Foster, lived there for many years.

In 1903 the house became the property of J. Wilkinson Elliott, an architect who enlarged and remodeled it. It was he who added the large portico with Tuscan columns that faces the Beaver Road.

One enters a wide hall with a staircase that is also Edwardian Georgian with fancy balusters and ramped balustrades. At one side are two "parlors" divided by a huge square opening. The trim and mantels in these rooms look as if they might have belonged to the original Seminary building. The upper floors also have some original mantelpieces.

The exterior of the house seems now rather Edwardian in character and there has been much modernization both inside and out, but with all the changes and accretions it is still an important suburban house and should be preserved.

WAY-WALKER HOUSE
Beaver Road
Original use: house, then inn   Present use: house
———————   1810-1820
Early Western Pennsylvania Stone-Brick Vernacular
Stone and brick   2 stories   very good
This is a good example—it is notably manicured, barbered, bathed, and custom tailored—of the old Pittsburgh tavern that has fallen into "good hands", in this case into the very heart of old Sewickley.

The house is in two sections, each with its own hall-way; two-story and attic, the house has later additions. The interior has been much made over to accommo-

175

date modern suburban living. The staircases have nice handrails, and there is some original wood trim in the house. Everything is quite well kept and in excellent condition, the exterior painted white and with black trim. The grounds are beautifully maintained with a very small stream in a stone walled channel running through.

Charles M. Stotz, says that it was built as a private house, became an inn, and was enlarged in 1820. He also has an illustration (*The Early Architecture of Western Pennsylvania,* p. 183) of the part nearest the road.

THOMAS LEET SHIELDS HOUSE
436 Beaver Road
Joseph W. Kerr   1850-54
Greek Revival
Brick   2 stories and attic   very good

Built by the son of David Shields, this house is a good example of the late Greek Revival brick dwelling house that was fairly common in Western Pennsylvania during the middle of the nineteenth century. This example is chiefly interesting because we know the name of the architect. It is in excellent shape and there should be no question about its preservation.

SHIELDS PRESBYTERIAN CHURCH

Church Lane and Beaver Road
J. W. Kerr (?)   1868-69
Gothic
Stone   1 story   very good

The congregation of this church was formed in 1864, and a frame church was built on the present site shortly thereafter. The present building, rectangular in shape, is of dressed stone laid in regular courses with a steeply pitched roof. On the main facade are three large lancet windows and the nave is lit by smaller ones on the side walls, none of them have any tracery. There is a small rose window above the choir loft at the rear of the church. At each corner of the building there are four small crenellated turrets, one of which serves as a chimney. The interior plan is quite simple, much ornamentation and stained glass not being added until nearly the turn of the century.

The structure is undeniably handsome in a restrained way and late as it is, it is probably one of the best surviving examples of the archaeological phase of the Gothic Revival in Western Pennsylvania. The congregation is to be commended for its respectful handling of the church building since they have resisted any impulse to remodel it in accordance with modern taste. The church together with the Shields' Mausoleum (q.v.) and the adjacent parsonage make an interesting, if stylistically disparate, group of buildings.

SHIELDS FAMILY MAUSOLEUM

Church Lane and Beaver Road
Frank E. Rutan (?)   1893-94
Richardsonian Romanesque
Stone   1 story   very good

Although this structure is a rugged and powerful example of the style associated with the name of Richardson, it is chiefly interesting as an example of a building type not very numerous in America, the large family churchyard mausoleum. In Western Pennsylvania it may well be unique. Since the Shields family no longer intends to use it as a place of burial, perhaps a new use can be found for the superstructure. The structure does warrant preservation.

SHIELDS SCHOOL HOUSE
Beaver Road
Original use: school   Present use: none
Vernacular   1826
Brick   1 story   poor
Built in 1826 by David Shields on high ground directly across the Beaver Road from his residence, "Newington" (q.v.), this simple school building was intended for the use of his tenants and neighbors. It was used for school, prayer meetings, and general church purposes. Mrs. Shields started here in 1835 an afternoon Sabbath School that she personally superintended until 1844.

After the building of the Shields Presbyterian Church in 1868, the Sunday School was discontinued. The structure is now in bad condition, but if a use could be found, it would not come amiss to preserve it.

NEWINGTON
Shields Lane
House
————   1816-1823
Greek Revival
Brick   2 stories and attic   very good
This house was built by David Shields on land (part of the so-called Depreciation Lands) that was acquired by his wife's father, Daniel Leet, who was a major in the Revolutionary War, as payment for his military services. In 1825 the house became the Post Office of Sewickley Bottom, which was that portion of the valley lying in the vicinity of the Little Sewickley Creek; there was also a mill on the property. Since David Shields was a factor for the Economy Settlement farther down the Ohio River, it is possible that there is some connection between the design and construction of those buildings and Newington.

For the long, rather low, two storied original portion of the house, Stotz gives the date 1816; it later became a wing of the much larger five bay, two story house that David Shields and his wife occupied in October 1823. The latter is a large center-halled structure with four rooms on each floor and a full attic under a hipped roof. There are two chimneys at each end with gable curtains between. On the west side of the house is a large filigree cast-iron verandah whose workmanship is exceptionally fine, and there is a smaller one on the east side. Two small quasi-oriental looking turrets—ventilators of a sort—on the roof were added some time in the mid-nineteenth century. The large lunette window in the gable of the Beaver Road facade was added about 1900 when a kind of study or "den" was made in the attic; at about the time the broad terrace below replaced another cast-iron porch. The house was modernized to some degree and put in a thorough state of repair in 1959 when the present owner, J. Judson Brooks, who is a descendant of David Shields, took possession of the house and the eleven acres of grounds.

It is the grounds and gardens of Newington that contribute very notably to its large and ample air of accrued elegance and aristocratic foundation, an air that seems oddly at variance with the unremittingly industrial Pittsburgh tone. In these green pleasances, one feels more conscious of the Hudson than of the Ohio Valley, and it is the (one might almost say) exotic quality of the place that gives it its special charm.

The present owners believe that the grounds were laid out in the English Romantic landscape manner by the landscape architect Samuel Parsons in the 1870's. About 1910 Bryant Fleming designed the formal garden in the southern part of the grounds.

"Estates" of this kind were never exactly common during the nineteenth century in the Pittsburgh area, and Newington would seem to be the sole grand survivor of those that were established; the great millionaire estates of the period 1890-1929 are another story. Both the house and grounds should certainly be preserved as a unique document of their era in this part of the country.

179

VINEACRE
413 Woodland Road
House

———————— c. 1850; remodeled 1916
As remodeled—1916 Pseudo-Vernacular
Brick   2 stories and attic   very good

Although Vineacre is famous as the birthplace of Ethelbert W. Nevin (1862-1901), the house was so extensively remodeled about 1916 by the Doyles that it now little resembles its original appearance. There is a poorly reproduced pencil sketch of the old Vineacre in Vance Thompson's *Ethelbert Nevin,* page 10. Parts of the interior remember the Nevin regime, notably the room to the right as one enters the house from the front verandah. It is still the home of Mrs. C. L. Doyle.

Elizabeth Borough

ELIZABETH BOROUGH PRESERVATION AREA
(See under Preservation Areas)

Elizabeth Township

HAYDEN LOG HOUSE
Route 51 south of Elizabeth and on the eastern side
Original use: house   Now abandoned

———————— c. 1800-1840
Log   2 stories   derelict and rapidly decaying

This abandoned house screened by some ragged conifers from the roaring ribbon of Route 51 rather shouts the dereliction and disregard of our early Western Pennsylvania heritage. This house in its broad valley, back from the main river

180

valley, shows forth the essence of what our grandfathers were—and that it should have been reduced to such a desolation is our shame. It is a double log house, each unit two bay with two stories, parts of which have been sided; there is a central chimney and two frame additions in the rear.

ROUND HILL PRESBYTERIAN CHURCH
Round Hill Road at Route 48
———————— 1884-85

Eclectic Vernacular
Brick   1 story   very good
This is a square brick gabled church with simple corbeling and a small wooden peaked cupola at the apex of the front gable. There is brick corbeling on the front gable, and the building is interesting in its simplicity for this date.

VAN KIRK HOUSE
Round Hill Road at Route 48
———————— c. 1854

Late Greek Revival
Brick   1 story and attic   good
This is a very handsome five-bay late Greek Revival house with Doric pillars, good (but late) sidelight and transom doorway; and a very simple cornice with deep eaves. It is two rooms deep with double chimneys. On the main facade are very large multi-paned windows with green shutters. There is a curiously awkward, but rather nice cornice on one porch and a low stone terrace in front has now been

white-washed. At the back there is a two-story ell. This house must be preserved because of its exceptional architectural quality.

HOUSE
Round Hill Road at Route 51
——————————— c. 1850 (?)
Vernacular Greek Revival
Brick 2 stories good
A five bay red brick house, two rooms deep and with attic, it has double chimneys, a double porch in the center of the front wall with door above, and multi-paned windows with shutters. The cornice is heavily bracketed. This is an important house in the area and must be preserved.

HARMONY SCHOOL HOUSE
Round Hill Regional Park
Original use: School Now abandoned
——————————— 1870-80 (?)
Vernacular
Brick 3 stories poor
This interesting little building is a one-room rectangular red brick rural school house —a familiar American type. The date of its construction is not known, but it had apparently been disused as a school house for some years prior to its purchase by the County, since it had been made over as a dwelling house.

The exterior is quite simple with three windows on each long side and a door at one end. The interior has now been stripped and the partitions of the dwelling-house phase removed. The construction of the central chimney is interesting because it is hung by iron rods from the ceiling beams and the flue of the now vanished stove was attached to it.

Those in charge of the Regional Park are considering restoring this little structure as a representative rural nineteenth century American school house and we strongly endorse the project. The structure is basically sound and its rehabilitation would provide for present and future generations of the County a three-dimensional document of the manner in which many of our forefathers got their education.

MT. VERNON COMMUNITY PRESBYTERIAN CHURCH
Buena Vista at Greenock Road
——————————— 1868
Greek Revival
Frame 1 story very good
Established in 1868, this white frame hall-church with gabled ends and an un-bracketed cornice is a simple late Greek Revival building. There is an awkward, Second Empire doorway on the facade. It was moved some years ago to this location and has additions from the 1930's.

182

HOUSE
Route 48 at Pitt Street
_____ Before 1850 (?)
Western Pennsylvania Vernacular
Frame and stone or log   2 stories   good
This house possibly is log under the frame siding. The stone section, which is probably the older, has huge quoins, and the frame portion has a stone chimney. It is known as the old Logan place.

HOUSE
Buena Vista-Industry Road near Rock Run Road
Original use: house   Present use: abandoned
_____ c. 1850
Greek Revival
Brick   2 stories   poor
This is a huge five bay, red brick house, two rooms deep, with a double porch, and sidelight and transom doorways on both floors. The cornice is bracketed, and the small gables have fanlights. It has a hipped roof, not frequently found locally, and multi-paned windows. The site overlooks the Youghiogheny River and the house is becoming a rather spectacular ruin.

HOUSE
Route 51 and West Newton Pike
———————— 1850-1900 (?)
Vernacular-Victorian
Brick   2 stories   good
This is a large brick house of five bays with an elaborate Victorian verandah on one side.

BOSTON PRESERVATION AREA
(See under Preservation Areas)

Etna Borough

CHALFANT HOUSE
89 Locust Street
Original use: house   Present use: Chalfant House Women's Club
———————— c. 1840-50
Greek Revival
Frame   2 stories and attic   good
This five bay Greek Revival house is of excellent, if not exceptional quality. It is said to have belonged to the Chalfant family and that it was moved from another location at some time in the past. The history of the house needs more study; we can do no more here than record its architectural features as a house worthy of preservation.

The walls are probably frame, but they have been covered with aluminum siding. The windows are multi-paned and they are floor length on the first floor. The verandah cornice and roof are Greek Revival in style but it is supported by modern concrete posts. The central doorway is of the sidelight and transom type, with a shouldered architrave around the reveal of the recess.

The house is also two rooms deep on either side of a central hall; the rooms are large and the long windows give the house a great sense of spaciousness. At the back of the hall there is a good, simple staircase with a slightly curving line at the landing. The dining room still has a good plain marble Greek Revival mantelpiece. On the other side of the hall is a large double parlor with two chimneys (having ugly late Victorian mantelpieces) between which are two doors giving access to a large five-sided bay window. This latter feature is unusual and we do not remember seeing anything like it elsewhere in the County. All the doors and windows on the first floor have shouldered architraves. On the second floor the windows are not shouldered but have panels below them. The interior has seen fewer changes than the exterior.

HOUSE
11 Vine Street
_____ c. 1850-60 (?)

Vernacular
Board and Batten 3 stories very good
This high, five bay house stands on a prominent location against a hill and at the head of a narrow street that climbs precipitiously up the grade. A frame extension is at the rear of the house. The site and a bright yellow paint contribute to the dominance of this otherwise inauspicious but tidy construction.

HOUSE
66 Walnut Street
_____ c. 1850-60 (?)

Vernacular
Board and Batten 2 stories good
This is a pleasant worker's house tucked into a narrow, crowded street. It has a three bayed facade, a doorway with a transom, and multi-paned windows. Board and batten houses are now only infrequently found in the County, and when they are in such good condition, no matter how unpretentious or simple, they contribute to the visual pleasure of a neighborhood and should be preserved as a vanishing type.

HOUSE
151 Mt. Royal Boulevard
_____ c. 1850

Late Vernacular Greek Revival
Brick 1 story and attic fair
This is a five bay house on a high basement and perched on a steep hill above Mt. Royal Boulevard. There is a double verandah on which transomed doorways open. The structure is one room deep with an ell in back.

HOUSE
Boggs Road, l. r. 02014
——————— c. 1850

Greek Revival
Brick   2 stories   poor
A five bay house with a fine fan-light door and what appears to be an original Classical porch, this is an exceptionally fine house of its type. The windows are multi-paned.

McADAMS HOUSE
——————— pre-1850 (?)
Log   2 stories   fair
Only a portion of the original log fabric can be seen because part of the structure is inselbricked.

McELHANEY HOUSE
l. r. 02009 west of 02023
——————— 1824

Early Western Pennsylvania Stone Vernacular
Stone   2 stories   very good
This fine stone house rests on a high basement and has a stone chimney at one side

with a fireplace in both the basement and first floor. There is a modern dormer.

The present occupants possess some documentation on the house and have kept it in good condition. It still reflects an earlier and more rural way of life. To the rear of the property is a barn with splendid stone pillars.

The owners claim that the conestoga wagon in Carnegie Museum came from this property. They also own a painting that shows the house as it originally appeared.

BYERS-NEELY HOUSE
c. 1850
Vernacular Greek Revival
Brick   2 stories   good

This long brick house, painted red, has on its main facade two doors, one of which has a transom and good paneling. The cornice is very plain and the windows are multi-paned. The house is one room deep.

Also on the property is a small outbuilding cabin in fair condition, built of board and battan with a large outside stone chimney.

Forest Hills Borough

THE WESTINGHOUSE ATOM SMASHER
Forest Hills at Westinghouse Plant
1937

Original Use—Atom smasher; now decommissioned

Undoubtedly one of the more important buildings in this book, the Westinghouse atom smasher was begun in the summer of 1937 and largely completed by the fall of 1938. It was in full operation at least by December 1939.

At the time it was built the structure was the world's largest unit for conducting experiments in the field of nuclear physics. It consists of a huge pear-shaped tank, thirty feet in diameter and forty-seven feet high which housed an electrostatic direct current generator and other required parts including a forty foot vacuum tube through which particles were shot in the bombarding of certain types of targets. The structure, including a two story brick building, is sixty-five feet high. It was decommissioned on the 20th of October 1958 and has not been in use since that time.

The steel shell of the atom smasher was erected by the Chicago Bridge and Iron Company; it is probable that no specific architect was concerned with it (none is mentioned in the records), but Dr. William H. Wells, head of the Westinghouse nuclear physics program at that time, is mentioned as instrumental in its design.

This instrument was the first atom-smasher to be installed by the industry and it made a number of significant contributions to knowledge in nuclear physics at

187

a time when such knowledge was sketchy and yet extremely necessary to the accomplishment of nuclear fission on a practical scale. If Pittsburgh today may be called the "Atomic Capitol of the World" it is due to Dr. William E. Shoupp, after 1940 director of the nuclear program, the atom smasher staff, and the work that was done there.

The structure is extremely important, historically speaking, and it certainly should be preserved, even if it is no longer in use. Looming above the Western Pennsylvania hilltops, it is still a landmark in the fate of mankind.

Forward Township

HOUSE
Monongahela and Elizabeth Road
———————— 1850-1860
Vernacular Greek Revival
Brick   2 stories   good
A five bay farmhouse with single wide chimneys and an ell, the structure has two fanlights in each gable end.

SUTTON-WUNDERLICH HOUSE
Mentor Road, l. r. 02036
———————— c. 1860
Vernacular Greek Revival
Brick   2 stories   good
A five bay brick house with an attic and a double porch recessed at one end, it is now painted yellow.

KING-STRACELSKY HOUSE
Mentor Road, l. r. 02036
———————— c. 1830-1850
Greek Revival
Brick   2 stories and attic   very good but much changed
This Greek Revival house with its large multi-paned windows and its gable curtains has been so much changed on the interior that it is difficult to reconstruct the original appearance. Only a handsome newel post and balustrade on the main staircase survive.

ALLEN-RAISNER HOUSE
Mentor Road, l. r. 02036
———————— Between 1819-23
Late Georgian
Brick   2 stories and attic   fair
This is a house of exceptional interest and unusual quality for Allegheny County, where little remains that recalls so forcefully the eighteenth century and the archi-

tectural amenities of the Georgian eastern seaboard. One has pervasively the sense that he is actually examining a house from the Philadelphia region in a wavering western mirror where the image of the "fine" Georgian house of eastern Pennsylvania has been subtly transmitted into a new "free" provincial version.

The house is splendidly situated on a high hill looking in the direction of the Monongahela Valley, although the river itself cannot be seen. It is a large rectangle of brick laid in Flemish bond, on an exceptionally solid projecting stone foundation. The main facade is five bay, with a central doorway in the Georgian manner. The provincial carpenter has attempted a curved pediment that, although it is unsuccessful, has a charming ineptitude. The fanlight below it is, however, unusually good. The multi-paned windows are large but they are Georgian rather than Greek Revival in feeling and their voussoirs are also eighteenth century. There is an agreeable provincial Classical cornice.

At one side is the one story remnant of a brick two story wing. The roof of the main house is gabled, and apparently part of it had been replaced after damage in a wind storm. The house is two rooms deep and there was originally a fireplace in each one, but at the gable walls both the flues at each end are brought together into a single flue. Some of the partition walls are brick and they are carried up from the basement through the upper floors. The stone foundations generally are enormously solid.

The interior is even more interesting than the exterior. An extremely good stairway rises at the back of the central hall; it is treated architecturally rather in the manner of the middle-Georgian staircases of the Philadelphia region. The balustrades are ramped and along the wall an attempt has been made at a ramped dado with small pilasters at the landings. Granted its provincial quality, the effect is so remarkably in the seaboard tradition that one wonders if the craftsman who executed it could not have had his training in the East.

The three remaining mantelpieces in the first floor rooms are quite tall with the thin reedy Adamesque carving so common to this type of fixture in Western Pennsylvania. All the rooms have paneled cupboards on one side of the fireplace; these are quite simple, but that in one of the rooms at the front of the house is very elaborate. The mantels on the second floor are excellent—simple, well proportioned Classical fittings.

The structure was probably built by David Allen between 1819 and 1822-23. The house is only in fair condition but it could easily be restored. Because of its quality and its interesting construction every effort should be made to preserve it in spite of its remote location.

Fox Chapel Borough

LA TOURELLE
La Tourelle Lane
Janssen and Cocken   1924-25
Medievalistic-Romantic
Brick   2 stories   very good
This is the superlative image of the Romantic suburban villa or country house of the 1920's, done with great sophistication and élan by one of the most talented of Pittsburgh architects of the later Eclectic period, Benno Janssen. Of brick with high-pitched slate roof, the rather exaggerated forms, the insistent gables, and sharp turrets testify to the persistence of the Romantic domestic tradition of the revived vernacular of the nineteenth century. There is little period detail in the house (built originally by Edgar J. Kaufmann) ; the composition is mostly an exercise in varied forms.

Franklin Township

GERMAN EVANGELICAL LUTHERAN CHURCH
Brandt School Road
——————   1868
Mid-Nineteenth Century Eclectic Vernacular
Brick   1 story   very good
This is a red brick gabled structure with white trim. It is a hall church and has

round topped windows, brick corbeling, pilasters, and a modern Classical porch. There is small white cupola on the front gable.

HOUSE
1591 Arendt Road, l. r. 02100
Outbuilding
_____ pre-1850 (?)
Log   1 story   fair
This log house is only one room in size with a door on one side.

Greentree

HOUSE
892 Greentree Road
_____ 1850-1880 (?)
Vernacular Greek Revival
Brick   2 stories   good
A five bay red brick house, one room deep, it has multi-paned windows and a nice fanlight doorway.

Hampton Township

HOUSE
Mt. Royal Boulevard at Ferguson Road
——————————— c. 1850-1860 (?)
Greek Revival Modified
Frame   2 stories   fair

This five bay house has a simple bracketed cornice and pilasters at the end. The verandah also reflects a simple Classical treatment and there is a sidelight and transomed door. Smooth-finished board siding covers the walls, and the house is just one room deep with an ell in the back. There is a single chimney at each end.

FERGUSON-EARLY HOUSE
Ferguson Road
——————————— 1860-61; frame ell 1890
Greek Revival
Brick   2 stories and attic   very good

This is a handsome vernacular Greek Revival, five bay farm house. There is a fine Greek Revival side light and transom doorway and all the windows are multi-paned with shutters. The main section of the house is one room deep. All the doors and windows on the lower floor interior are architecturally treated with rudimentary pilasters and simple pedimental cornices. There is a plain but well proportioned mantelpiece in the living room and a good staircase in the center hall. Some of the rooms have been done over in the modern manner and the house is well maintained.

ANDERSON-MILLER HOUSE
4554 William Flynn Highway, Allison Park
————————— c. 1820-30

Greek Revival
Brick   2 stories   very good

This is a large house of five bays, having a very simple bracketed cornice and two chimneys at each end. Although the front verandah has been removed, there is a porch at the back. This is a very sturdy well-preserved example of the Greek Revival.

CALVARY INDEPENDENT BAPTIST CHURCH
Wildwood Road near Route 8
————————— c. 1860

Vernacular Greek Revival
Brick   1 story   fair

This structure was built by the Covenanter Presbyterian Church, which was organized in 1805. In 1837 the church bought the site; Stotz gives 1860 as the date of erection of the building. In 1925 the church was vacant, and in 1948 it was bought by the Episcopal Church of St. Thomas in the Fields. In 1963 the Baptist Church acquired the structure when St. Thomas moved into its new building.

The church is a small brick gabled building with a low pitched roof and a returned cornice. It has been recently repaired and "restored".

CALVERT HOUSE
2538 Middle Road
Original use: house   Present use: apartments
Janssen & Abbott   c. 1910
Edwardian Picturesque
Stone, slate, and timber   2 stories   good

Built of stone, slate, and timber, this is a structure of dispersed, rambling forms that

194

foreshadows Janssen's later country-house manner. It was burned out during the Depression, but was later rebuilt.

Harmar Township

HARMARVILLE UNITED PRESBYTERIAN CHURCH
521 Indianola Road
——————— 1851

Greek Revival
Brick   1 story   very good
This congregation was founded in 1838, and in 1851 erected this red brick Greek Revival building with pilasters, pediment, and multi-paned windows with shutters. This charming provincial building that pleasantly, if remotely recalls the antique temple form, is very nicely sited among its rural greenery.

Harrison Township

PENN SALT COMPANY HOUSING
——————— c. 1850

Board and batten and other   2 stories   fair to good
This group comprises about eighteen small detached workers cottages, some of them board and batten and many of them still displaying the unmistakable Romantic forms of the 1840's. They were apparently built about 1850 by the Penn Salt Company to house its workers. This community was the nucleus of the town called Natrona—after Natron or natural soda. The Penn Salt Company, formed by a group of Philadelphia investors for the purpose of manufacturing chemicals, also erected

195

buildings where they might carry on their business. Most of these structures, which were interesting documents of mid-nineteenth century industrial architecture, have been demolished since the Penn Salt land was acquired by the Allegheny Ludlum Steel Corporation. The workers' cottages should be studied as examples of such early Victorian housing while they still survive.

BURTNER HOUSE
Burtner Road off Route 28
───────────── 1821
Western Pennsylvania Vernacular
Stone   2 stories   fair

This is a fine old Western Pennsylvania stone house, built in 1821 by Philip Burtner and his wife born Anna Negley. It has always remained in the same family, until it was recently sold. The facade has four bays and there are three in back. Great stone chimneys adorn the gable ends. The house is in basically good condition, but for the front verandah. The surrounding landscape has rather suffered with time and provides a very dim setting, but the house is a must for preservation.

HARBISON HOUSE
Harbison at Stewart Streets, Saxonburg Road
——————— c. 1830
Western Pennsylvania Vernacular
Stone   2 stories   good
This medium size stone house that is nearly hidden among vines and verdure, has three bays, is one room deep, and has two rooms up and down. A modern porch has been added at the back.

Homestead Borough

HOMESTEAD CARNEGIE LIBRARY
Tenth Avenue
Alden & Harlow   1896-98
French Renaissance
Brick   2 stories   very good
This building, which occupies a commanding site on the Homestead hillside, is one of those large public buildings that Andrew Carnegie erected in some of the steel towns of the Monongahela valley to serve as social and cultural centers for the workers in his mills. It is constructed of buff Pompeian brick with stone trim and has a high-pitched red-tiled roof. The library occupies the center section, and there is a music hall in the eastern end and an athletic clubhouse in the western wing; the structure has two stories and a basement and is 226 feet long by 98 feet wide. Except for its large scale, it bears a marked resemblance to the millionaire mansions of the time.

The architects were Alden & Harlow, the contractors William Miller and Sons of Pittsburgh. The contract was let in November 1896 and it was completed in August 1898.

The building is in good condition and should be preserved.

ST. JOHN'S GREEK CATHOLIC CHURCH
Tenth and Dickson Streets
Titus de Bobula   1903
Art Nouveau
Brick and stone   1 story   very good
Stylistically this church (which should be compared with the same architect's Hungarian Reformed Church at Hazlewood q.v.) displays a very interesting turn of the century "moderne" manner combined with freely used Classical elements. Constructed of stone and brick, the structure has twin towers of a rather startling

form. There is also a parish house in the same style. With the Hungarian Reformed Church across the street, it makes an interesting study in architectural forms.

Indiana Township

CROSS KEYS HOTEL
Dorseyville Road
——————— c. 1850
Vernacular Greek Revival
Brick   1 story   very poor

Typical of small country taverns through much of the nineteenth century this five-bay building is a good example of the simplest provincial Greek Revival style. There is a doorway with side lights and transom.

Jefferson Township

JEFFERSON MEMORIAL PARK HISTORICAL BUILDINGS
Jefferson Memorial Park
Original use: houses   Present use: miscellaneous
——————   1782 1800
Log, stone and log   ——————   good
The John Work stone and log house, built in 1800, is still standing, but the log section is now inselbricked. Four bay in front with a low ell in back, this structure needs restoration, but its condition is good.

The Jacob Beam log cabin, built 1782, and now memorialized by a replica, was originally farther down the hill from the present reconstruction. The replica contains only eight of the original logs. A plaque marks and explains this building.

LARGE HOUSE
Route 51 at Railroad
Original use: house   Present use: offices
——————   1838
Greek Revival
Brick   2½ stories   very good
This big house stands prominently in the flat valley at Large. The facade is five bays wide with a large side light and transom doorway, and there are two fanlight windows in the side elevations at the third story. There is a central door at the second story and there are multi-paned windows throughout the house. A frame annex stands to one side at the back of the house and a brick ell to the other. A porch of probably later date with Doric columns is in front of the house. A plaque in the gable reads "J & E Large 1838." This is one of the largest and best preserved of our brick Greek Revival houses in the County.

To the south of the house is a smaller two story brick house with multi-paned windows and a wooden-sided annex to one side. It is reputed to be older than the Large house and to have been used as a headquarters for government bonding agents.

BEDELL FARM AND DISTILLERY
Cherry Road
——————   c. 1820
Greek Revival
Brick, stone, and frame   various stories   fair to poor
Here we see the remnants of a once prosperous farm and business. The house is

very large, of red brick, and has a facade of five bays, with multi-paned windows, side light and transom Greek Revival doorway, and a porch in the same style. It has two stories and an attic and four chimneys. This is the best preserved structure of the group, but it lacks its earlier luster.

Near the house is a small three bay, one story, one room brick structure with a chimney at one side, and behind the house stands an old brick shed.

Deep in thickening verdure rests the vestigial hulk of the Bedell distillery. This huge frame building that seems to be a cross between a covered bridge and ship riding the crest of a wave is sited on a hillside and built on a stone foundation. However, it has been long disused, and at present it is disintegrating rapidly. Parts of the walls and roof have already collapsed and its final demise is imminent. The surrounding trees have now almost entangled it, submerging its aging wooden bones in fresh leaves.

The farm is situated on land given over to ore storage and weeds. Some years ago the area was stripped for coal, and all about the property rise great ugly hills of arid, lifeless shale. Certainly in its day one of the most successful of such establishments, the Bedell place now is a symbol of the brevity of all things.

CASTOR FARM
Castor Lane, off l. r. 02206
——————————— c. 1800-1830

Stone, log, frame   various stories   poor to fair

This cluster of buildings includes a house of clapboard with two recessed porches, one in the original section of one story and one in the later section of two stories, as well as a loghouse of one story with a huge stone chimney and a derelict frame addition, and a combination springhouse and smokehouse of two stories built of narrow fieldstone. The complex overlooks a great ravine that has been strip-mined ruthlessly in past years and now serves to store ore for the Federal Government. It is a valley of ashes.

200

HARTWOOD FARMS
Saxonburg Road
Alfred Hopkins and Associates   1929
Tudor
Stone and concrete block   various stories   very good

This fabulous domain of the 1920's located on a large tract in the rolling country near Pittsburgh is a good local example of the great millionaire country estate which was such a feature of the American landscape before the Depression of 1929 which latter, in essence, signaled the end of the way of life these ephemeral "seats" represented.

The manor house, superbly sited at the top of a high wooded eminence, and much chimneyed, gabled, and mullioned, is finely executed in that suave and archaeological Tudor style so dear to fashionable American architects of the earlier part of this century. Architecturally it represents a grammar of form and ornament as effortlessly and pleasantly commanded as it was prevalent. This house, if it does not transcend stylistically the general mold, at least very eminently and intensely represents the type.

The large, rambling stable complex which lies in a valley below the house is just as intricately Romantic in form and silhouette as the manor house, but much of it is constructed in more prosaic material—concrete block. Possibly its overriding tower, the abounding and variegated gables, the elaborately contrived Gothic passageways and courts, form a corpus of Romantic reference more appropriate

to the novel and the cinema, but for that reason we would not deny the essential validity of this pleasant medievalistic vision. The concrete block was then sufficient to the architectural day; there is no reason why it should not be so for ours.

But to hope that this fairytale domain could be preserved is nowadays perhaps to dream too much.

NEESON LOG HOUSE
825 Dorseyville Road

Log   1 story   very good

This two room log house is something of a puzzle. At the moment both its builder and its date of erection are unknown. Nothing remains of it now but the walls of tough ancient red oak logs and the stone foundations. A second story has been added and a kitchen has replaced the former lean-to at the back of the house. Everything has been encased in clapboard siding and the present exterior of the entire house is entirely anonymous and nondescript, although the sloping site is pleasant. A large modern living room has been added to the back of the kitchen wing.

The chief mystery of the house is a set of three openings in the back wall of the original structure. These square holes are symmetrically placed, the middle one being rather larger than those at either side of it. They have been tentatively identified as gun ports; perhaps with an excess of romantic historical zeal, and in tenuous support of this theory the openings seem at the right height for a man to sight a musket against stealthily advancing Indians. Nowadays one has merely a good view of the kitchen from these mysterious embrasures.

They really seem much too large for gun ports, and there may well be some simple and less dramatic reason for their existence.

The log walls have for the most part been exposed on the interior and they are now quite well maintained.

Leet Township

LARK INN
634 Beaver Road
Original use: tavern   Present use: house
——————— 1800
Western Pennsylvania Vernacular
Stone   2 stories and attic   good

Many western Pennsylvania taverns, as Stotz remarks, without their signs and porches, are scarcely distinguishable from dwelling houses of the period. This three bay house must have had at one time a front verandah and a sign. The rather well-proportioned center door gives access to a large room on one side of the house that must have served as a taproom; there are two smaller rooms on the first floor, both having fireplaces, and the kitchen is in an ell at the back. The present owners have made a passage at one end of these rooms. There is also a handsome spring-house at one side of the property.

This house is an especially good example of rugged Western Pennsylvania vernacular stone architecture; it is well maintained and seems to be in sympathetic hands, although there has been some unfortunate refurbishing.

Marshall Township

SHENOT FARMHOUSE
Route 856
——————— 1800-1890 (?)
Log   2 stories   very good

The owners claim that the earliest part of this rather long log house is 150 years old. The Shenots settled here in 1860, and at that time the first section was standing. They subsequently added other sections, the latest about 70 years ago. It is now entirely covered with aluminum siding. The land was originally part of the Bradford acreage.

BRIDGE
Brown Road at Warrendale-Ambridge
———————— 1891

Stone ———————— very good

This is one of many such bridges across creeks and streams in Allegheny County, and it is included here as one of the best examples of its type. It is a large stone arch bridge, very rugged and durable. More and more these bridges are disappearing as roadbeds are changed.

Charles Davis was the engineer and William Dickson the builder.

MILLER'S FARM
Route 856 at Warrendale-Bayne Road (l. r. 02227)
———————— pre-1850 (?)

Log 2 stories very good

This is a log house of three bays with a one story addition at the back and a modern brick wall at one side.

DAVIS-McCALLEN HOUSE
Route 856, Meadow Vue Drive
———————— c. 1860

Italianate-Medievalistic-Eclectic

Frame 2 stories very good

Built c. 1860 by a Dr. Davis, this interesting white frame house is an Italian villa-cottage orné with very elaborate verandahs and barge boards. Once called Olive Grange, it is very similar in style and general character to the Evergreen Hamlet houses (q.v.). There have been some changes in the interior and the house generally is in process of renovation.

HOUSE
Route 856
Outbuilding
_____ pre-1850 (?)
Log   1 story   good
A one room log house now used as outbuilding but kept in good condition.

McCandless Township

STRANG LOG HOUSE
Grubbs Road
Outbuilding
_____ c. 1820-30
Log   1 story   very good
This building consists of a one story log construction on a stone basement; a functioning spring-house is located in the basement section and the upper portion is now used as an outbuilding for storage.

HOUSE
272 Ingomar Road
_____ c. 1850
Vernacular Greek Revival
Brick   2 stories   very good
A five bay, red brick house, this one has white trim, multi-paned windows, and is one room deep. The doorway has side lights and transom.

Franklin Park Township

PIERCE HOUSE
Grosick Road
_____ pre-1850
Western Pennsylvania Vernacular
Stone   2 stories   very good
This house is built of dressed stone with a small modern porch in the front and a springhouse at one side. It is nestled down in a valley behind a grove of pines. Its charm and its architectural quality warrant preservation.

"THIS OLE HOUSE"
Old Kummer Road
—————————— pre-1850 (?)
Log   2 stories   good
This log house has several frame additions and a modern porch. There is a small one story log addition in the rear and a modern picture window has been opened into the side wall. "This Ole House" is only a dim reminder of the original.

WILLOUGHBY CABIN
9457 Highland Road
—————————— Before 1823
Log   2 stories   good
This log house is now sided and it is difficult to tell what it originally was like.

City of McKeesport

McKEESPORT WATER WORKS
Beside the Youghiogheny River at 15th Street Bridge
Alexander Potter, designing engineer   1907-08
Romanesque
Brick   1 story   good
This circular building with its dome-like central roof is certainly the most interesting structure of its type in the County. In form it resembles an early Christian or Romanesque "round" church of the central plan type. It is still well maintained and it should be preserved as an unusual example of water works architecture.

MUSE HOUSE
4222 Third Street
—————————— 1820
Vernacular
Stone   2 stories   very good
This is an unusually fine and large house in two sections, one three bay with a door

at the side and the other two bay. There is a low pitched roof now covered with metal and dormers that are probably modern. The windows are multi-paned.

HOUSE
4232 Walnut Street
———————— 1810-1830 (?)
Vernacular
Stone   1 story   very good

A small stone house with two windows on each side elevation, this structure has a modern classical porch and pilasters at the corners.

McKEESPORT PUBLIC LIBRARY
Library, Carnegie, and Union Streets
——————— 1900-1902
Richardsonian-Romanesque
Stone   3 stories   good
This building is an agreeable, if rather late, version of the Richardsonian-Romanesque manner. Changes have been made in the interior.

McKees Rocks Borough

McKEES ROCKS BRIDGE
——————— 1929-31
Steel and masonry   ———————   very good
5500 feet in length, this is the longest bridge in the County. Its main span is known as the Hell Gate type, because it was used in the Hell Gate Bridge across the East River at New York. In this type of structure the thrust of the arch is resisted by the masonry of the piers. Frank Vittor did the sculptural work on the main pylons.

ST. MARY'S ROMAN CATHOLIC CHURCH
1011 Church Avenue
William Ginther   1900-05
Gothic
Brick, limestone and cast stone   1 story   very good
This is the third church building of this congregation, the earlier ones dating from

208

1854 and 1870. The architect did a number of large Roman Catholic churches in the Pittsburgh area around the turn of the century.

Constructed in the Gothic style, the church is unusual in having three spires, two on the main facade and a smaller one at the crossing. The great serrated bulk of the church is visually quite imposing in the flat-lands of the Chartiers Valley. Although the congregation is no longer so numerous as it once was, the church still seems to be well maintained.

Millvale Borough

WILKINS HOUSE
144 Evergreen Street
_____ Before 1826
Western Pennsylvania Vernacular
Stone   2 stories   very good

This five bay house is a good example of early Western Pennsylvania stone architecture and is especially noteworthy because it has retained its late Georgian fanlighted door. There is a frame addition in the rear.

The house was on part of a 230 acre tract of land marked No. 1 of the Jones District of Depreciation Land granted to John Wilkins. A deed of 24 April 1826 says that there were two dwelling houses standing on the property at that time, of which this must be one.

209

SAMPLE-BUMMER HOUSE
Lawrence Avenue
——————— Said to be 1794
Stone   2 stories and attic   much changed

This three bay house bears little resemblance to its original state. The blank-walled sides on which there are no windows were apparently stuccoed at some time during the nineteenth century, but the stucco is in bad condition. The front has been perma-stoned and the frame addition at the back would appear to be late Victorian or Edwardian. Again in the interior hardly a vestige remains of the original fittings of the house. This structure is little more than a phantom and we include it merely for the historical record.

ST. NICHOLAS ROMAN CATHOLIC CHURCH
24 Maryland Avenue
Fred C. Sauer   1900
Edwardian Classical
Brick   1 story   very good

Architecturally this church—not a very good example of Sauer's pedestrian talents —scarcely merits inclusion in this book, but it does possess considerable interest because of the murals by Maximilian Vanka that decorate its interior.

The church was built by a Croatian-speaking Catholic parish in 1900 on the site of the Salt mansion. In 1921 the structure was destroyed by fire and rebuilt, again after the design of Fred Sauer, in 1922. In April 1937 Vanka, who had been a professor of fine arts in the University of Zagreb in Yugoslavia, began to paint the murals, or rather frescoes, since they were painted in tempera on wet plaster. The paintings are intended to memorialize the contributions of Croatian immigrants to American industry and there are also mordantly satirical passages attacking the capitalists that caused some stir in the socially conscious climate of the 1930's.

The frescoes, at once exotic and powerful, modern in style and yet influenced by medieval Yugoslav paintings, "make" the interior which seems to have a vitality of its own quite independent of the architecture. For this reason alone this church is a "must" for preservation.

Moon Township

BEGGS HOUSE
Route 51 at the P.&L.E. Railroad
——————— 1835
Stone   1½ stories   good

This small stone house is four bays wide. The dressed stone is old, but the roof, windows, and doors have been modernized. Nevertheless, the house, as a lone survivor in the area, should be preserved.

ST. ANTHONY ROMAN CATHOLIC CHURCH
Howard Street
John T. Comes   1914-15
Spanish Renaissance
Brick   1 story   very good

Another of Comes' large brick churches not infrequently found in the large industrial towns of the Pittsburgh area, this one favors the Spanish Renaissance style. The two Spanish towers on the main facade are rather effective. Very few changes have been made to the structure.

STOOPS FERRY RAILROAD STATION
Route 51 at the P.&L.E. Railroad
Original use: station   Present use: office
Joseph L. Neal   1908
Stone   1 story   good

A rustic stone building with overhanging eaves, this little, romantic, suburban railway structure should be preserved (although its usefulness as a station would seem to be finished) as a good example of Edwardian naturalistic architecture. Since the station was designed to serve the fashionable suburb of Sewickley, it has a porte-cochere for the carriage trade. The site is interesting as the building stands at the mouth of a broad, wooded valley, facing out toward the Ohio River.

It was built by the Pittsburgh and Lake Erie Railroad, but it now belongs to the Tri-State Plastics, Inc.

Monroeville Borough

GRAHAM LOG HOUSE
Ramsey Road
———————   c. 1800-1830
Log   2 stories   very good

The owner of this house claims a building date of 1805. It is a log structure with the original chimney of brick and stone and an original and fine fireplace on the first floor that has a stone arch.

There is both a stone foundation and cellar as well as an attic. The second floor fireplace is now covered as are some of the first floor walls, but restoration is very possible.

Situated high over the Turtle Creek Valley and deep in a forested hillside, the house has managed to remain extant and it should be preserved.

WALLACE-NASOR HOUSE
Mosside Boulevard (l. r. 02251)
—————— c. 1790-1830
Western Pennsylvania Vernacular
Stone   2 stories with attic   poor

This three bay house has a one-story sloping later addition at one side. There is also a stone springhouse on the property. The house contains six rooms and its facade originally had double porches, one above the other, now removed. The property seems originally to have been a part of two estates of James Irwin called "Veron" and "Newry" of 232 acres deeded by James Irwin to George Miller in 1805 in what was then Versailles Township. George Miller was a private in the Revolutionary Army who signed his name by mark. The property was willed to the descendant James Michael who passed the property to William Wallace, who in turn deeded it to his daughter Mary M. Lang of Irwin. It came to have the name "Pickup Farm" and at present is owned by Fred Nasor. The land was warranted in 1787, surveyed in 1789, and patented in 1824.

A farmhouse to this day, it stands far down a hillside quite alone, but from the house there is a spectacular view down through the Turtle Creek Valley. A house of this type is a rarity in the district and its deteriorating condition demands immediate attention.

Mt. Lebanon Township

ST. BERNARD'S ROMAN CATHOLIC CHURCH AND SCHOOL
311 Washington Road
Comes, Perry & McMullen   1933-1947
French Gothic
Stone   1 story   very good

The congregation was formed in 1919 and occupied temporary quarters of various kinds until in January 1926 the basement of the completed school building began to be used as a church. This function was transferred to the substructure of the

church building proper, which was begun in 1933 and finished in 1934. In 1942 the construction of the church superstructure was begun; it was delayed, however, because of the Second War, and the first Mass was not heard in the completed structure until 1947.

The large rugged mass of the building, which stylistically favors the early French Transitional Gothic of the twelfth century, is a dominant note in the Mount Lebanon skyline. It is definitely a design document of the 1920's. Its walls of granite and limestone and its roof of Spanish tiles abundantly reinforce its image as one of the last constructions of the Eclectic period.

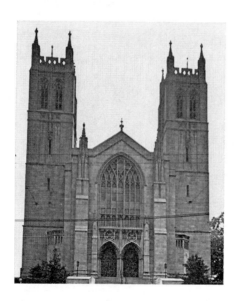

MT. LEBANON UNITED PRESBYTERIAN CHURCH
255 Washington Road
Lou Beatty, O. M. Topp   1927
Gothic
Stone   1 story   very good

This church with its twin English Gothic towers standing on elevated land has for a number of years been visually a landmark in Mt. Lebanon. The form of the church illustrates an attempt, not extraordinarily successful in the present instance to combine the Protestant auditorium church with the nineteenth century ritualistic

213

chancel church. The Gothic style has also been agreeably used here, but with no great verve or originality of handling.

BOCKSTOCE-FULTON HOUSE
Off Shady Drive East near Alfred Street
—————— 1835-50

Greek Revival

Brick   1½ stories   very good

This five bay house occupies a very secluded position next to the Mt. Lebanon Cemetery. It belonged originally to Henry Bockstoce, whose farm became the cemetery; the house is now owned by Congressman James G. Fulton.

The ground slopes away to the back and one side, so that in effect the house has another story. The windows are multi-paned and there is a side light and transom central doorway on the main facade; the house has four chimneys and a bracketed cornice. This little oasis of early nineteenth century Western Pennsylvania is all the more refreshing for being embedded in the spreading suburban acres of Mt. Lebanon. The place is obviously now in very sympathetic hands and for the present, at least, there is no question as to its preservation.

214

Munhall Borough

HAYS MANSION
Off Whitaker Avenue
——————— c. 1870
Second Empire-Italianate
Brick   2 stories and attic   poor
This great gaunt Italianate-Second Empire house, weather-stained and shorn of its porches, stands starkly on its bare hillside above the Monongahela River, looking rather like a "mansion" in a modern Gothic novel. It was built by Abraham Hays, a riverboat captain, after he had purchased the property from John Munhall in March 1867. The structure has no particular architectural importance, but it is interesting as a riverboat captain's mansion. His son W. S. B. Hays, also a captain of riverboats, added the back section. It is now owned by his grandson, W. S. Hays, who lives in it.

COYNE HOUSE
125 Larkspur Street
——————— Before 1830 (?)
Log   2 stories   good
This structure has been so changed and modernized that the original silhouette of the log house has been quite lost. Only the great thickness of the walls testifies to the ancient construction beneath their modern outer covering.

North Fayette Township

LYNCH HOUSE
Noblestown Road, Noblestown
——————— c. 1850
Vernacular
Brick   2 stories   good
A four bay brick house on a stone foundation, the building is one room deep with a chimney at each end and a modern verandah in front. It is one of the best preserved houses of the Noblestown area.

HOUSE
Noblestown Road, Noblestown
——————— c. 1850
Vernacular
Brick   2 stories   fair
This four bay house abuts on the road. It has a corbeled brick cornice and a tran-

somed doorway that retains its original paneled door. It is but one room deep with a small frame ell in the back.

At the back of the property is a large barn-like structure of frame. It has small windows, two stories, and is unpainted. This building is in use as a kind of work-shop, but is sagging badly.

NOBLE-DE VESSE HOUSE
Noblestown Road, Noblestown
——————— c. 1840-50
Late Vernacular Greek Revival
Brick   2 stories   fair
This is a large, five bay house, two rooms deep and twelve rooms in all with four chimneys, a doorway with a side light and transom and an original paneled door and multi-paned windows. The porch at the doorway has been removed. The cornice has groups of twin brackets.

General Noble is supposed to have built the house, which stands on a commanding hilltop site above Noblestown.

HOUSE
Just off Noblestown Road, west of Noblestown
——————— c. 1860
Vernacular
Brick   1 story   good
This is a small one story house, with six bays plus a one bay frame addition at either end. There is a verandah across the front. The house is rather curious in its narrow elongation and the disposition of its doors and windows.

HOUSE
1. r. 02033 nw of 02246
——————— c. 1850
Vernacular Greek Revival
Frame   2 stories   poor
This is a five bay house with multi-paned windows and appears to consist of a three bay section and a two bay addition. There is a chimney at either end and the house is one room deep.

WALKER-EWING-GLASS HOUSE AND LOG HOUSE
Box 435, Route 02033
——————— 1855

Vernacular Greek Revival
Frame   1 story and attic   very good

A five bay frame house with side light and transom doorway and multi-paned windows, the building has a small wing at one end balanced by a modern garage on the other side. The house is two rooms deep.

There is a two story log house on the same property that may have been built by John Henry, an early settler in the area, in the late eighteenth century. Isaac and Gabriel Walker acquired the land in 1785. Isaac's daughter who married William Ewing next acquired the site in 1816. William's son J. Nelson Ewing brought his bride there in 1843, but ten years later he erected the above house. E. W. Glass, who still lives in the later house, is a grandson of Nelson Ewing. The log house has two stories and at one time was used as a barn, because a large door had been cut in one side of it.

Both houses have now been purchased by the County as part of a new park and the log house is to be restored by Charles M. Stotz.

NORTH STAR HOTEL
Route 22, east of l. r. 02005
——————— 1850-1900

Vernacular
Brick   2 stories   fair

A five bay brick building with a modern Classical verandah and four chimneys, it has a four bay modern addition added to the western side. The brick cornice is corbeled, is not returned, and lacks brackets. This is a large structure standing in a desolate area given over to strip mining.

217

DUNLAVY-CAMPBELL HOUSE
Box 162, Route 978
_____ 1814

Western Pennsylvania Vernacular
Stone   2½ stories   fair

This is a good example of the three bay, two story Western Pennsylvania stone farm house of the early nineteenth century. This rugged structure is located among tall pines on the side of a hill looking into a valley, obviously so placed as to be sheltered from harsh winds; it is hidden from the main road and one approaches it by a winding, rutted track.

Due to the slope of the land the front of the house is almost three stories tall, but it has also lost its verandah and the front door has been made into a window. The main facade is now at the back and there is another entrance at the side. On the opposite side of the house is a chimney from which opens a huge fireplace that heats a room that is now used as a living room but which may once have been a kitchen. Just beneath the chimney in the apex of the gable is an oval signature stone bearing the date 1814.

Parts of the barn are quite old and there is a stone springhouse with a log loft above.

The owner, James E. Campbell, who has lived on the place all his life, still farms it. Enough remains of the original installations to give the visitor an adequate idea of what an early Western Pennsylvania farm was like.

North Versailles Township

GEORGE WESTINGHOUSE MEMORIAL BRIDGE
Route 30 over Turtle Creek
_____ 1930-32

Reinforced concrete   very good

Work began on this bridge 15 May 1930 and was completed 28 December 1931. It opened 10 September 1932.

It spans the Turtle Creek valley at Turtle Creek and is constructed entirely of reinforced concrete; it is a five span bridge of the double-ribbed type. At the time it was built, the center span was the longest reinforced concrete arch in the country. In a city of bridges, this is one of the most handsome.

"The George Westinghouse Bridge claims a place in the select company of other great engineering achievements of recent years, such as the Holland Tunnel, the Hudson River Suspension Bridge, and the Hoover Dam," editorialized *The Engineering News Record* at the time it was opened.

HOUSE
Route 30 west of Route 48 near Deming Way
—————— pre-1850
Log   2 stories   very good

This log house has an exterior stone chimney at one side. It has been much modernized including the addition of modern doors and windows. No historical data is available.

Oakdale Borough

HOUSE
Sturgeon-Noblestown Road
——————— c. 1850

Vernacular
Brick   2 stories   fair
This is a small brick, three bay house located at an intersection. It is now much changed and is painted white.

HOUSE
105 First Street
——————— c. 1850

Vernacular
Brick   2 stories   good
This house comprises two sections, each with three bays. One section has the door located to one side; the other section has a central door. There are pairs of small, delicate brackets under the eaves.

HOUSE
Clinton Avenue
——————— c. 1860 (?)

Vernacular
Brick   2 stories   fair
A typical three bay, brick structure of the period, this house lacks ornamentation of any kind. There is a board and batten addition at the rear. The building stands on a wooded hillside back from the road.

Oakmont Borough

HOUSE
Twelfth Street and Hulton Road
Frederick G. Scheibler, Jr.   c. 1907-08
Early Modern
Stucco   2 stories   very good
This was a house in stucco executed for S. M. Ament. The drawings are dated
December 1907. It was occupied for a time by Mrs. C. F. Blue, Jr. In 1960 it was
occupied by B. F. Fletcher. During the occupancy of Mrs. Blue, a large addition
was made to the house, which much changed its character.

O'Hara Township

FERRY-SCHULTZ HOUSE
403 Dorseyville Road
————————   Early 19th Century
Greek Revival
Brick   1 story   poor
This is an interesting Greek Revival house although we do not know when it was
erected; it may have been built in sections, but, again, we are ignorant of its early
history. It consists of a central section with two projecting wings at either end;
between the front projections is a recessed porch, the whole being covered with a
hipped roof. There is one central chimney between the two rooms that comprise
the middle section. The very simple cornice of the porch roof is supported by two
hollow wooden Doric columns with rudimentary caps. An almost startling element
in the general ensemble is the narrow fan-lighted Georgian doorway at one side
of the back wall of the porch. The execution of the doorway is crudely provincial,
the proportions narrow and thin, but something of the grace of the original model
still inheres in this frontier version. There is also a very good rather tall mantelpiece
in the living room of the middle section. It is carved and incised with the thin,

reedy, late eighteenth century ornament sometimes found in Western Pennsylvania houses of the early nineteenth century.

The rooms in the wings are not very well finished and some of the woodwork looks very primitive, although it is so vernacular, so completely lacking in style, that it is difficult to date.

The house is in poor condition and a sympathetic restoration might prove not only interesting but productive of some more exact information on its construction.

GREENWOOD CEMETERY HOUSE
321 Kittanning Pike
_____ 1838
Vernacular Greek Revival
Brick   2 stories   very good

This is a pleasant five bay house, one room deep with a chimney at each gable end. Only one or two of the original multi-paned windows remain. The rest have been replaced by modern efficient aluminum sashes that are entirely out of character with the house. Otherwise the place has been well maintained.

O'NEILL LOG HOUSE
Mt. Nebo-Roosevelt Road
_____   c. 1830, 1870
Log   2 stories   very good
This is a double log house with siding. According to the owner, the one log section was built in 1830, the other in 1870. The second half may be frame. The central chimney is part of the addition of 1870.

SWEENEY HOUSE
480 Gene Drive off Roosevelt Road
_____   1820
Early Western Pennsylvania Vernacular
Stone   2 stories   very good
A three-bay dressed-stone house, two rooms deep with one chimney at each end, this is another example of the Early Western Pennsylvania stone house.

223

MORROW CABIN
11401 Frankstown Road
———————— 1819
Log and sided   2 stories   good

This log house, which has been sided since it was built, has a stone chimney at one end and a later addition at the rear. The rooms inside, despite their modern finish, are small, low, and cramped, but the exterior of the house, which now fronts very closely on a crowded suburban highway, jostled by encroaching modern dwellings and a not-too-distant shopping center, still preserves something of the primitive bulk and the ground-hugging silhouette of the earliest type of domestic architecture in this area.

BLACKADORE HOUSE
1235 Blackadore Avenue
———————— c. 1860
Second Empire Vernacular
Brick   2 stories and attic   very good

This house with its thin chimneys, front verandah, and latticed side porch represents very forthrightly and agreeably again, the solid mid-century image of the prosperous Western Pennsylvania farm house. It was built by Isaac Blackadore (1819-1896), a farmer who made a specialty of growing fruit.

The house appeared to better advantage when it dominated the little valley in which it lies; at present it is surrounded by a lower-class suburban area. The house seems to be in excellent condition and at present there would appear to be no question about its preservation.

FITZSIMMONS HOUSE
E. Fitzsimmons Road
_____ Early 19th Century (?)
Vernacular
Brick 1½ stories poor
This house was probably five bay but the center door is now gone. It is just one room wide with two end chimneys. Except for one wall, it appears to be nearly original.

SCHILLER HOUSE
123 Faybern Drive
_____ Log c. 1800 Brick c. 1820-60
Vernacular Greek Revival
Brick and log 1½ stories very good
This house of brick with stone foundation has four chimneys with gable curtains between each pair of chimneys. The front is of five bays with central door and there is a simple brick projecting cornice. The original house on the site, a log cabin, now covered with siding, has been attached to the rear of the brick structure, and there have been many changes in the interior of both sections. In the basement is a springhouse with the original spring. Brick or frame houses of this particular form were once common in Western Pennsylvania and those that remain should be preserved wherever feasible. The log section has been so changed that it is difficult to tell what its original appearance may have been.

225

LONGUE VUE COUNTRY CLUB
400 Longue Vue Drive
Janssen & Cocken for original section   1922-26, 1951, 1954
Early Twentieth Century Romantic neo-Vernacular
Stone   3 stories   very good

These buildings with their intensely Romantic massing and silhouette, their field-stone walls and slate roofs that tend to echo the very countryside on which they sit, represent, together with the rolling well-tended golf course and the attendant gardens, the superlative bright image of the American Country Club. The very excellence of its architecture, and not its list of members or its social position in the landscape, entitles it to inclusion in this survey.

The final drawings for the buildings, from the office of Janssen and Cocken (now in the possession of the successor firm of Hoffman, Loeffler and Wolfe) are dated 1922. The central section of the complex was finished and opened in 1926; the building for the men golfers was executed about 1951 and the ball room about 1954.

The site of the buildings is superb; on the river side the trees have not been allowed to encroach, and from the side windows of the ball room or from the

226

terrace one is treated to one of those "sudden" breath-taking Pittsburgh views. This one is a wide panorama up the Allegheny River valley.

The buildings are well maintained and certainly at the moment there is no question as to their preservation.

WYCKOFF-MASON HOUSE
6133 Verona Road
————— 1774-75
Log   2½ stories   good

This land was originally part of land grant from William Penn to three men of whom George Duffield was one. In 1774 Duffield deeded a portion of this land to Isaac Wykoff, who built the present house. The Masons purchased it in 1960.

The house is built of chestnut logs; the section farthest from the road is two bay and the addition toward the front has but a single bay. The back of the house is faced with siding. The original beams are exposed in the living and dining rooms. There are three fire places and two stairways, one leading up from the living room and the other from the dining room.

HOUSE
726 Hamill Road
————— Before 1820 (?)
Log   1½ stories   very good

This log house is in good condition, but it has been much suburbanized in setting and treatment. One room has been added but otherwise no changes to the exterior have occurred.

HOUSE
Arendt Road, l. r. 02100
——————— pre-1850 (?)
Log   2 stories   good
This log house, which has a one room later Victorian addition to one side, is now undergoing restoration.

HOUSE
920 Mt. Nebo Road at Arendt Road
——————— pre-1850 (?)
Log   1 story   fair
This one story log house has a later second story now shingled.

HOUSE
Route 02213
Original use: house   Now abandoned
——————— 1800-1840
Early Western Pennsylvania Vernacular
Stone   2 stories   derelict
Ruined and abandoned, this three bay stone house looks as if it has been burned out. In back of the lot are the stone foundations of what was probably once a barn. Little more than the walls of the house are now standing.

HOUSE
Route 02195 south of Rodi Road
——————— c. 1850 (?)
Brick   2 stories   good
A typical five bay, red brick house with side light and transom doorway. It is only one room deep.

Pine Township

ROSS-TOOKE HOUSE
Old State Road
———————— c. 1835
Vernacular Greek Revival
Brick   2 stories and attic   good
This five bay farmhouse is one room deep and has chimneys at each end; there is an ell at the back. The windows are multi-paned and there is a side light and transom central doorway. This is a very pleasant example of the vernacular Greek Revival farmhouse.

Plum Borough

HOUSE
1831 Hulton Road
———————— Before 1850 (?)
Log   1½ and 2 stories   fair
The 1½ story section has two bays and there is a later frame addition of two stories with two bays.

HOUSE
Route 380 below junction of Unity-Trestle Road
———————— 1850-1880 (?)
Italianate Second Empire
Frame   2 stories   good
Now shingled, this is a frame, Second Empire farmhouse of five bays with a verandah in front.

HOUSE
l. r. 02166 west of 02164
———————— c. 1850
Vernacular Greek Revival
Frame (?)   2 stories   good
A three bay, two story house now covered with grey asbestos shingles, it has a side light and transom doorway, multi-paned windows, as well as a returned cornice.

HOUSE
l. r. 02166 east of 02164
———————— c. 1850
Vernacular
Frame   1½ stories   good
A five bay, one and a half story frame house with side light and transom doorway and multi-paned windows.

HOUSE
l. r. 02164 near 02001
_____ 1850 - 1900 (?)
Vernacular
Brick   2 stories   fair
A red brick, five bay house with an ell at the back, it has a returned cornice.

HOUSE
Route 380 at l. r. 02143
_____ c. 1800 - 1840
Early Western Pennsylvania Vernacular
Stone   2 stories   fair
This is a four bay stone house with big chimneys at each end. There is a stone wing at the rear with a verandah at the back and a small porch in front. Remains of a barn are in front of the property. The house stands at a considerable distance from the road.

PLUM CREEK PRESBYTERIAN CHURCH
550 New Texas Road south of Route 380
_____ 1867-79
Vernacular Romanesque
Brick   1 story   very good
The first place of worship of the Plum Creek congregation was a log "tent"—an open-air pulpit arrangement—from 1791 to c. 1810. About the latter date a log

church was erected and in the 1850's a brick structure. In June 1867 the contract for the present church was given to A. McJunkin and William Miskimins; in 1879 the building was completed. In 1951, 1962 and 1963 further additions were made.

It is the surviving Victorian building that interests us, however. This consists of the familiar rectangular brick, gabled auditorium (really little more than a meeting hall) that during at least three quarters of the nineteenth century was the standard church building form in Western Pennsylvania. This example is placed on a high basement and is vaguely Romanesque in style, with plain pilasters and brick corbeling. There is a wheel window in the front gable.

Richland Township

FIRST PRESBYTERIAN CHURCH OF BAKERSTOWN
Route 8 south of 02273
—————————— 1838
Greek Revival with Gothic detailing
Brick   1 story   very good
This is the usual Western Pennsylvania gabled rectangular meeting house so common through most of the countryside during much of the nineteenth century. A signature stone in the front gable informs us that the structure was built in 1838 and remodeled in 1888 (then the Bakerstown M. P. Church). Possibly at that time the rather severe vernacular Greek detailing of the structure was relieved on the main facade by some pointed Gothic arches. The building is now a subsidiary structure in a large religious complex.

HOUSE
3752 Fisher Road at Lakeside Drive
—————————— c. 1850
Late Vernacular Greek Revival
Frame   2 stories   very good
This is a square, five bay, white frame house with a hipped roof and two square chimneys toward the center. It has a side light and transom doorway in front with a small bracketed porch; it is two rooms deep.

DEER CREEK UNITED PRESBYTERIAN CHURCH
Bairdsford Road
—————————— 1853
Late Greek Revival
Brick   1 story   very good
This congregation was formed in 1802. An outdoor pulpit was built in 1811 and

used until 1817 (similar to the log "tents" of early church-going days in Western Pennsylvania). A replica of this early structure has been erected on the church property. A log church was built in 1834 and was torn down in 1837, its timbers being used to provide lintels for the new brick structure. When this church burned, the present one was built in 1853.

This is the usual late Greek Revival gabled church building, this one adorned with Classical pilasters and blind arcading. There is also a small cupola at the apex of the front gable for a bell. In 1952 a copy of the 1853 building was erected beside the earlier one, and the two were connected by a wing.

Robinson Township

DANIEL ROSS-LACEY AND BURGESS HOUSE
Baldwin Road Extension
——————— Before 1820
Vernacular Greek Revival
Brick   2 stories   very good

This house is exceptionally fine. It is an early Western Pennsylvania farmhouse excellently preserved. It has a double verandah and a splendid entranceway with a fanlight on the second floor.

Water is admitted to the house through a rain drainage system that takes the water from the roof and runs it into a cistern in the hillside, and from there into the lower portion of the house.

An insulation of sorts was achieved by building a false back second foundation wall against the hillside.

An absolute must for preservation, the house is living now on borrowed time because part of Interstate 79 will pass through it. A major campaign by the Pittsburgh History & Landmarks Foundation and private individuals was abortive in persuading the state highways department to relocate that section of the interchange. As is often the case, that bureau seems indifferent to the value of the cultural heritage of the region.

HOUSE
Cleve Road at Elliott Drive
——————— 1850 - 1900 (?)
Vernacular
Brick   2 stories   fair

A three bay house one room deep, this building has chimneys at each end and a returned cornice. The windows are multi-paned and there are double doors in front. A frame addition stands at the back.

HOUSE
19 Silver Lane   (l. r. 02209)
————————   1850 - 1900
Vernacular Greek Revival
Brick   1½ stories   good
This is a late Greek Revival house with multi-paned windows and a nice Classical cornice.

HOUSE
289 Silver Lane (l. r. 02209)
————————   1850 - 1900 (?)
Vernacular
Brick   2 stories   good
A five bay house, this building has a good fanlight doorway with side lights and Victorian sash windows. It is one room deep with a chimney at each end.

HOUSE
McKees Rocks and Forest Grove Road
————————   1850 - 1900
Vernacular
Brick   2 stories   fair
This three bay house has a high basement, a porch front and back, multi-paned windows, and a door into the basement in the middle of the front wall.

HOUSE
Beaver Grade Road at Route 51
————————   Pre-1850 (?)
Vernacular
Log or frame   2 stories   fair
A three bay house with a stone foundation and a large stone chimney at one side, this building is now inselbricked, but it might be log underneath.

HOUSE
Beaver Grade Road (l. r. 02319)
————————   1850-1900 (?)
Vernacular
Brick   2 stories   good
A five bay, two story brick house painted white with an ell in back.

HOUSE
McMichael Road
———————— c. 1850
Vernacular Greek Revival
Brick   2 stories   good
A five bay, two story brick house with a double porch in front and gable curtains.

HOUSE
Glass Road
———————— 1850-1900 (?)
Vernacular Greek Revival
Brick   2 stories   fair
A five bay, two story red brick house with a brick corbeled cornice, side light and transom central doorway and a small portico before the front door.

Ross Township

EVERGREEN HAMLET
Evergreen Hamlet Road
Vying in interest to some degree with the communitarian settlement of Economy at Ambridge, near Pittsburgh, is this small Romantic suburb, one of the first of its kind in America. A refuge from the smoke and clangor of industrial Pittsburgh, it was founded in 1851 by a local lawyer William Shinn, who with a group of other well-to-do citizens formed a community with the purpose of securing to themselves the advantages of both city and country living.

The charter drawn up for this community contains the rights, privileges, and duties of the members, and it is a most interesting document, reflecting as it does some of the idealism of those communal societies that were so much a part of the American social scene before the middle of the nineteenth century. This was definitely a middle-class community, however, and the members retained their property and owned their own houses in the settlement, although there was a communal schoolhouse where the children of the associates were taught by a communal teacher. However, each member contributed to the school in proportion as his family used it.

The tract of 85 acres was surveyed and laid out by Hastings and Preiser, a local firm of surveyors. Work was begun in 1851 in grading and laying out the land in roads, residential areas, and farm plots. Construction was begun on the houses and they were finished in 1852. Four out of five of these are still extant.

This experiment in community living under close rules failed in 1866 as so many others have before.

Simple and unassuming, these Evergreen villas, whose white walls contrast so admirably with the verdure above them, appeal deeply to the American sensibility; this architecture has a youthful freshness about it that is absent from later suburban construction. The houses are listed below.

Kelly House, Evergreen Hamlet

Grove House, Evergreen Hamlet

Views of the Davis House
Beall House

HAMPTON-GILLESPIE-ARENSBERG-KELLY HOUSE
Evergreen Hamlet Road
J. W. Kerr (?)   1851-52
Eclectic Vernacular
Frame, board & batten   2 stories   very good

This house is an excellent example of the upper class suburban dwelling of the mid-nineteenth century when the type, due to the proliferation of the railroads, had become fairly well developed. The basic form of the main section is not very different from that of the standard large farm house of the period, and the long wing at the back with its asymmetrical rambling silhouette is of much the same type as many other nineteenth century back buildings.

The long verandah that runs the length of the main facade with its sturdy, Renaissance-derived pillars and its balustraded deck above seems related to steamboat decks and the porches of the summer hotels that were beginning to be a feature of the American landscape. The verandah turns the corner of the house, and its supports assume a much thinner, latticed quality. French windows open on this porch and on the garden from the chief rooms of the first floor.

The style of the house is highly eclectic. The cornice of the house is heavily bracketed and from those points where the brackets meet the wall, long thin pilaster-like strips descend the length of the wall, forming battens on the board walls. The effect gives a touch of the vernacular Romanesque of the first half of the nineteenth century to the general ensemble. The essentially Greek Revival transom and side light doorway branches out into brackets in its cornice.

The house was built in 1851-52 by Wade Hampton, a Pittsburgh businessman who was also one of the original Evergreen Hamlet colonists. Later it was sold to J. J. Gillespie, who was a well-known Pittsburgh art dealer. In recent years Charles C. Arensberg lived there and it is now occupied by Bernard J. Kelly and his wife, Marie T. Kelly, the painter.

SELLERS-GROVE HOUSE
161 Evergreen Hamlet Road
J. W. Kerr (?)   c. 1851
Eclectic Vernacular
Frame   2 stories   very good

This five bay house whose walls are sheathed in shiplap siding in the front and clapboard elsewhere, has the general form of the Hampton-Kelly house, but the details are different. The main section is two rooms deep with a central hallway. There is a long verandah on which French windows open, running the length of the main facade. This porch is arched and latticed and there is a balustraded deck above; a side light and transom doorway gives access to the central hallway. All the windows have shutters. There is also a long wing in back that contains the kitchens and offices.

The house was built by one of the original colonists named Sellers and it is now occupied by John A. Grove, Jr., the architect.

HILL-McCALLAM-DAVIES HOUSE
Evergreen Hamlet Road
J. W. Kerr   1852
Vernacular "Gothic"
Frame   2 stories and attic   very good

This board and batten house with its pointed windows, Tudor verandahs, and barge boards might be described as vernacular American Gothic—a Middle Western provincial version of the more sophisticated late Medieval *cum* Tudor, *cum* Jacobean house that had been Americanized by Downing and Davis from the English Picturesque cottage orné.

Built in 1852, it came into the hands of the McCallam family in 1871, and it remained in the possession of their descendants until 1953. It is now owned by Dr. T. Harrison Davies.

For all its medieval detailing, the house is symmetrical in mass and the coupled windows with their "Gothic" tracery are rhythmically disposed in the composition. The projecting center pavilion with its Tudor arch is a marked feature of this type of house and the verandahs on either side of it have decks above railed with ornamental cast iron. The dormers in the low hipped roof are a later intrusion.

The plan of the first floor interior is remarkably open and the great space with its three divisions—library, hall, and parlor—is 57 feet in length.

SHINN-BEALL HOUSE
168 Evergreen Hamlet Road
J. W. Kerr (?)   1852
Vernacular "Gothic"
Frame   2 stories and attic   very good

This is a charming local varient of the medieval Gothic cottage orné with a few vaguely Classical tags including the side light and transom main doorway. Its "lattices" are, however, Gothic of the American folkish variety—"steamboat Gothic" if you will. This house was built by William Shinn, the prime mover in the Evergreen Community and it now belongs to Dr. and Mrs. Chester Beall.

Of all the Evergreen houses, this one is the nearest to the asymmetrical forms so often seen in the Romantic cottage orné.

WALTER HAWKER HOUSE
120 Nelson Run Road
———————   c. 1840-1865 (?)
Vernacular Greek Revival
Brick   2 stories   good

This three bay side-hall house has a two story front section with attic. The cornice has pairs of twin brackets, and there are double chimneys at each end. The interior has been considerably changed, but the original stairway is good, as are the doors. No original mantels exist.

The rear section is one room upstairs and down and it has retained its original turned stair. The windows of the second floor are multi-paned.

HOWARD J. HILL HOUSE
231 Nelson Run Road
———————   c. 1835
Vernacular
Brick   3 stories   good

This house, bought by the Hill family in 1923, was erected by the Nelsons, for whom Nelson Run was named. Built of brick, it is five bay wide with three stories, having in front a double Victorian porch, side light and transom doorway, and multi-paned windows.

The foundations are interesting: they are of stone and extremely heavy and

238

thick. The present owner described them as "corbeled" from the hillside against which the house stands, but the elements of the foundation were not sufficiently visible to this recorder to warrant any exact description of the construction. Possibly it would repay more extended investigation.

That the builders of the house wished a sheltered site is evident; even today its position on the side of the Nelson Run ravine seems remote and secluded.

At one time there was also a smaller stone house on the property, but it is now demolished.

JORDAN HOUSE
3392 Evergreen Road
—————————— 1826
Vernacular Greek Revival
Brick   2 stories   very good

This is a five bay house painted white with an elaborate transom and side light front door and later front porch. The central section has a center hall and good staircase; on the first floor the doors and windows are architecturally treated.

HOUSE
203 Crider Lane
——————————   Back ell before 1830   Front c. 1843
Greek Revival
Brick   2 stories   good

This five bay red brick house was built about 1843 and thus falls well within the Greek Revival period; the two story ell containing a kitchen and loft at the back was constructed before 1830. There is a nice doorway also in the style of the Greek Revival and the windows are multi-paned. There is a modern verandah in front that is enclosed on one side. The late Lamont Button, the architect, owned the house for a time. The present owners are restoring the house.

GRAHAM HOUSE
208 Twin Oaks Drive
——————————   c. 1840 (?)
Greek Revival
Brick   2 stories   very good

This is a Greek Revival farmhouse with woodwork of the same style including shouldered architraves over the interior doorways; it has oak floors and cherry balustrades.

STEWART-SCHLAG HOUSE
Sangree Road

_____ 1834

Greek Revival

Brick   2 stories   fair

This is one of the finest Greek Revival houses remaining in the County; like the Lightner and Nicholas Way houses, it retains traces of the Georgian manner of the late eighteenth century, and even the Flemish bond brickwork reinforces this image. The house is five bays wide and one room deep with an ell at the back. There is a fine fan-light doorway with side lights and a front verandah that may be original. The front of the house rests on a rather high basement due to the slope of the land. Windows are multi-paned except in front, where the original lower sash has been replaced by sheets of glass.

Inside, all the door and window casings on the first floor of the front section of the house are architecturally treated with wooden panels below the windows proper. The staircase is exceptionally good with a curving line at the landing.

The house has been kept in good condition by the Schlag family and its exceptional quality makes it a premier candidate for preservation. Aside from its architectural importance, however, the structure is still the center of a working farm. Many of the outbuildings have been preserved and the general ambiance of the place gives some idea of what a prosperous Western Pennsylvania farmstead was like in the earlier nineteenth century. Unfortunately suburban builders have their eye on the property and the present owners should be assisted in their desire to retain at least the immediate surroundings of the farmhouse. The circuitous drive bordered with ancient pine trees, which makes such a fascinating introduction to the domain, is certainly also worthy of preservation.

240

HILAND PRESBYTERIAN CHURCH
845 Perry Highway
Darby & Evans   1836
Classical
Brick   1 story   very good

This is an exceptionally interesting suburban building—mostly interesting, architecturally, for what it once was—a simple gabled rural church of the Classical type.

As the congregation grew, an education building was added in 1914. As the twentieth century advanced, the area surrounding the church became suburban, in 1936 the interior was remodeled, and in 1940 the exterior was remodeled in the Georgian manner complete with spire. The red brick was white-washed so that everything would look more eighteenth century—at a period when such an effect was considered eminently desirable. R. Hensel Fink was the architect of this latest metamorphosis.

Scott Township

ST. LUKE'S EPISCOPAL CHURCH
Original use: church   Now derelict
——————   1852 (cornerstone placed)
Gothic
Stone   one story   poor

Originally a log church built in 1774 by General John Neville, this building was

241

burned by the insurgents during the Whiskey Insurrection of 1794. A frame church took its place which was again replaced in 1852 by the present edifice. The building has a certain vernacular charm, if no great architectural distinction; it is merely a rectangular stone meeting house with Gothic windows. The structure has been derelict and vandalized for several years, and both it and the surrounding grave-yard were in deplorable condition, but the building is now being restored. It is the oldest extant Episcopal church in the diocese.

Sewickley Borough
Sewickley Heights Borough

SEWICKLEY PRESERVATION AREA
(See under Preservation Areas)

SEWICKLEY PRESBYTERIAN CHURCH
Beaver Road
J. W. Kerr   1859-61
Gothic
Stone   1 story   very good

This is a good example of the mid-nineteenth century picturesque parish church formally applied to the needs of a small town Protestant congregation. The fact, however, that the congregation was able to employ Kerr to build it a fashionable stone church showed that the community had already taken on something of the solid quality that has distinguished it for many years. The nave and transepts with their simple lancet windows in triplets are very engaging, but the tower is the weakest part of the composition; there is a notable separation between the rather awkward stone base and the octagonal wooden belfry and spire.

The Sewickley Presbyterian Church was founded at the Edgeworth Seminary in 1838. A brick church was built in 1840 on Beaver Street, which stood until 1883 when it was demolished. It had become too small by the end of the 1850's, however, and in 1858 it was decided to build a new church. Land was purchased across the street, and early in 1859 J. W. Kerr was employed as architect. In 1860 the building was roofed and completed externally in course of the summer. In 1861, the building was finished within and the windows were set. In 1864 Barr & Moser were employed as architects, and rough drawings for a chapel were prepared; it was dedicated 1872. In 1895 the floor of the church, which had been level, was inclined, and new pews were added. In 1914 the firm of Rutan and Russell made designs for a new parish hall to replace the old chapel.

J. Phillips Davis was the architect of the Chapel of the Resurrection constructed in 1953, which is also in the Gothic style.

242

ST. STEPHEN'S EPISCOPAL CHURCH
Broad Street and Frederick Avenue
Bartberger & East   1894
Romanesque & Gothic
Stone   1 story   very good

The parish was organized in 1863, chartered in 1864, and in 1863-64 a small frame board and batten church designed by the rector, William P. Ten Broeck, was built by the new congregation. It was consecrated in May 1864 by the Bishop of Pennsylvania (Pittsburgh did not become a diocese until 1866). In June 1894, a new and larger church building designed by the local firm of Bartberger and East, was begun and the first service was held there in December.

In 1911 the church was enlarged and a new parish house erected after the designs of the local firm of Alden and Harlow. This parish house burned in 1914 and was rebuilt the same year. In 1937 the Mary Colwell Jennings Memorial chapel designed by Boyd and Ingham of Pittsburgh was added to the church. In 1953-54 a church school annex designed by Hoffman and Crumpton was built and occupied. Also during 1953, the church chancel was redesigned and enlarged by Leslie Nobbs of New York.

In toto, this is a very pleasant suburban church of medieval derivation, partaking of both Romanesque form and Gothic detail. There is about extra-urban structures of this type a kind of domestic quality that nearly relates them to contemporary houses of the more prosperous suburbanites of Sewickley, although this phenomenon was not uncommon in the late nineteenth century.

SEWICKLEY PUBLIC LIBRARY
Broad and Thorn Streets
H. D. Gilchrist   1923
Italianate Classical
Stone   1 story   very good

This well designed and gracefully executed building is architecturally one of the best things in Sewickley and should definitely be preserved.

MILLER-ZORN HOUSE
503 Broad Street
————————— c. 1840-50
Vernacular Greek Revival
Stone and brick   2½ stories   very good

This five bay stone house with its double verandah is notable even in a community which possesses many fine houses from all periods of the nineteenth century. Located on a sloping lot the lower or basement story is of stone with a central doorway while the upper portion is of brick. There are two chimneys with gable curtains at each end of the house. The interior has been somewhat changed, but it still retains some of its original woodwork.

LEES LOG CABINS
Various sites
Houses
————————— c. 1810-30
Log   2 stories   very good

These cabins are situated in several locations and are all owned by Justin Lees. On Barberry Road stands the cabin in which the Lees currently live. It has been re-chinked with concrete; the logs originally projected at the corners, but they were cut back because they had rotted.

244

On Audubon Road are two cabins that were put together and therefore have a thick middle wall. They contain seven rooms and also have been re-chinked with concrete.

A two room cabin on Little Sewickley Creek Road has an interesting stone chimney.

Shaler Township

DICK LOG HOUSE
142 Seavey Road
——————————— Before 1850 (?)
Log   1 story   poor
This log house, abutting the road, is in very bad condition. It is now covered with clapboard siding. Preservation of the structure should be investigated.

THOMPSON-DeHAVEN-LEET HOUSE
3201 Mount Royal Boulevard
——————————— 1831 or 1836
Greek Revival
Brick   2 story and attic, 1 story wings on either side   very good
Perhaps the shadow of the formal Virginia house of the eighteenth century—the mansion comprising the central block with dependencies on either side—lingers in this symmetrically disposed structure. Most country houses in the Greek Revival style that the Pittsburgh area possessed have disappeared and this building, which was constructed probably as a farm house—albeit an elegant one—is thus almost unique.

The central block is a two story and attic, five bay structure, two rooms deep and with two chimneys at either end. The central doorway on the front elevation has

245

Greek Revival pilasters and a transom above; the small porch in front of the door looks modern. The walls are of brick, laid in Flemish bond, painted white.

At either side of the main house is a small one-storied wing with a gable roof like the larger structure. There is a large back porch attached to the rear of one of these wings.

The house was built by a man named Thompson; later it was bought by Harmar DeHaven and occupied for two generations by the DeHaven family. The present tenant is Clifford S. Leet.

ISAAC LIGHTNER HOUSE
2407 Mt. Royal Boulevard
———— 1833

Greek Revival
Brick   1 story & attic   very good

This brick house, related to the Nicholas Way House (q.v.) on Beaver Road in Edgeworth (1838), reflects the building practice of the late eighteenth century although the spirit of the Greek Revival has very notably informed, if it has by no means transformed, the structure.

Stylistically the effect is curious; it is as if the rather delicate and refined post-Colonial forms had been invaded by a new style broadening and subtly coarsening the mass of the building; this is especially visible in the gabled porch. The small window in the porch gable is a fanciful vagary of provincial design. The kitchen in a separate building at the back is connected with the main structure by an open but covered passage or porch. The house is also raised on a high basement of stone. In the 1920's or 1930's the house was much modernized in the interior, but its character is still cohesive enough to commend it for preservation.

GLENSHAW VALLEY PRESBYTERIAN CHURCH
Butler Plank Road
—————— 1885
Picturesque frame Richardsonian Romanesque
Frame   1 story   very good
This church was started before the Civil War in the Old Sickle Factory owned by Thomas Wilson Shaw. The present church building was built in 1885. It is a white frame picturesque structure, essentially domestic in form, having a porch with fat turned pillars. Located not far from the Greek Revival Shaw homestead (q.v.), this house complements, with its rural, Romantic masses, the austere simplicity of the house itself.

SHAW-TATOM HOUSE
1526 Butler Plank Road
—————— 1824; 1830-32
Greek Revival
Brick   2 stories   very good
The first section of the house, that forming the ell in back, was built in 1824, the front portion in 1830; both sections are constructed of brick made on the Shaw property and both are five bay and two story with center halls and good staircases.

The interior woodwork is very simple but well designed; some of the rooms have the original mantelpieces. All windows are multi-paned, and those in the front section have Venetian blinds with carved valance boards, installed when the house was built.

The older portion has a certain rugged simplicity that is carried over into the more elegant front section; the form of the latter is that of the classical eighteenth century country house as broadly interpreted in the new century's Greek Revival

247

idiom. The square Doric pillars of the front verandah are nicely scaled to the general mass as is the main doorway with its side lights and transom. There is a single chimney at each end of this section. The walls are painted grey with green trim, but the porch pillars are white.

Built by Thomas Wilson Shaw, the house has always remained in the family and is now the residence of Mrs. Dan E. Tatom and Miss Catherine Shaw. The first school in the area was set up in the house by T. W. Shaw for the children of the neighborhood. The interior is beautifully furnished with old family furniture and oil paintings, including portraits of the builder of the house and his wife.

NICKLE HOUSE
1621-23 Middle Road
—————— c. 1850-1870

Vernacular
Brick   2 stories   poor
A five bay house located very near the road, it has multi-paned windows and a small addition at the side as well as a long ell at the back.

Sharpsburg Borough

MOUNT OLIVE BAPTIST CHURCH
200 Block of Main Street
—————— 1850

Vernacular Romanesque
Brick   2 stories   good
This is a brick mid-century Romanesque church with low pitched roof. The auditorium is raised on a high basement. A signature stone in the front gable reads "First Regular Baptist Church A.D. 1850."

ST. MARY'S ROMAN CATHOLIC CHURCH
211 Garnier Street
Peter Dederichs   1916
Romanesque-Renaissance
Stone over steel frame   very good

The parish, which was founded in 1852, erected this great Romanesque-Renaissance stone building in 1916 on the site of an earlier church. The large boldly modeled masses of this structure perhaps owe something to Abadie's Church of the Sacré-Coeur in Paris, while its two domed towers perhaps recall the shrine of Ste. Anne de Beaupré in Canada. Much of the detailing is Renaissance, but the plate tracery of the rose windows is Romanesque. There is something European about the siting of the church, which dominates the little *place* on which it fronts while its rugged outline competes successfully with the rather stark hills behind it. Like the Immaculate Heart of Mary Church (q.v.) on the other side of the Allegheny, this is an important and salient visual landmark not only in its own neighborhood but in the river valley as well. It is one of those elements in the landscape by which the eye "steers", and it should be preserved.

South Fayette Township

HOUSES
Route 519 South of Bridgeville
————————   c. 1850 (?)
Vernacular
Frame   2 stories   fair

These appear to be range of three small houses of frame clapboard with multi-paned windows in the lower floors and a porch over the center section. It has two chimneys and a stone foundation.

South Park Township

HOUSE
2650 Brownsville Road, l. r. 02329
——————— c. 1830
Greek Revival
Brick   2 stories   poor
This is an exceptional five bay red brick house. It has a fanlight doorway but no chimneys on the gable ends. A brick ell extends outward at the back. This is a very early example of the Western Pennsylvania farmhouse and it should be preserved.

ROWELL HOUSE
3914 Snowden Road, l. r. 02085
——————— c. 1800
Western Pennsylvania Vernacular
Stone   2 and 1 stories   poor
This is a stone house of considerable interest—on the exterior at least. The main

section is two story, three bay with a deeply embrasured central doorway without transom. The roof is gabled with chimneys at either end; the windows are multi-paned with Georgian stone voussoirs above. At one side is a one story, two bay addition with a chimney at the end gable.

The interior has been badly treated and except for the paneled wooden window embrasures not much remains of the original fittings. The structure is in poor condition but its solid silhouette places it among the better examples of early Western Pennsylvania stone construction.

HOUSE
l. r. 02066

——————————— Pre-1860 (?)

Vernacular

Log (?)   2 stories   good

This is small two bay house possibly built of log but now covered with clapboard siding; it has a large stone chimney. There is a porch in front and an addition at the side.

HOUSE
2500 Brownsville Road

——————————— c. 1840 - c. 1870

Late Greek Revival and Italianate Second Empire

Brick   2 stories   good

A five bay house, it comprises a lower floor with multi-paned windows and a fanlight door and an upper floor having windows with Victorian sashes and Italianate window cornices. Chimneys stand at the end, and a porch runs across the front of the house. There is an ell at the back.

HOUSE
Piney Fork Road

——————————— 1850-1900

Vernacular

Frame   2 stories   good

This is a small frame house notable especially for a huge chimney probably built of stone but now plastered. The place is tucked back in an isolated valley.

JAMES MILLER HOUSE

Stone Manse Drive, South Park
Original use: House   Present use: Historic site
——————— c. 1808

Early Western Pennsylvania Vernacular
Stone   2 stories   very good

This house consists of two sections, each two bay and two story, but one section is a little larger than the other. The courses are random with dressed stone corners and a chimney at the gable of each section. The door of the larger half has a transom. The roof is restored with "shakes."

The house, now known as the "Stone Manse", is preserved as an historic site by the County and its future seems secure. A well is also still maintained near the house.

EGGERS HOUSE

Maple Springs Drive, South Park
Original use: House   Present use: Picnic Shelter
——————— Pre-1860 (?)

Greek Revival
Vernacular Greek Revival
Frame   2 stories   very good

A five bay structure, this house has multi-paned windows, a side light and transom doorway, and a porch in front. It is a good representative example of this type of farm house.

Now part of South Park, it is called the "Community House". Certainly it should be preserved, and the County should publicly mark it as an historic building.

Swissvale Borough

RUDOLF E. HELLMUND HOUSE

7510 Trevanion Avenue
Frederick G. Scheibler, Jr.   1915-16
Early Modern
Stucco   2 stories & attic   very good

This small stucco house with a red slate roof is an excellent example of Scheibler's Romantic manner of the mid-teens of this century. Stylistically the German and Austrian "Modernism" of the pre-1914 period, which influenced his earlier work, seems to be tempered here by a new romanticism of approach that owed some-

thing to the English school of Lutyens, *et. al.;* this new manner was to culminate in Scheibler's design for the Parkstone dwellings of 1922. This house is an interesting transitional document in his career. Still inhabited by the widow of R. E. Hellmund, a German engineer who came to this country in 1912, the place should be preserved.

Currently (1967) the house seems to be in considerable danger. Erosion caused by the excavation for a nearby supermarket parking lot is steadily undermining the property.

HOUSE
7506 Trevanion Avenue
Frederick G. Scheibler, Jr.   1906
Early Modern
Concrete   2 stories   good
Constructed of concrete, this is a charming cottage in Scheibler's early manner. The original deed and drawings (the latter dated 1905) are in the possession of the current owner.

Tarentum Borough

HOUSE
215 First Street
——————   c. 1860
Italianate Second Empire
Board and batten frame   2 stories   very good
This pleasant five bay house with its hipped roof is a charming reminder of the riverside residential area of the Tarentum of the mid-nineteenth century. The vernacular Italianate windows with their simple architraves contrast very well with the battened walls. The front verandah—very much a part of such a house—has been partially modernized with concrete block. There is a bracketed cornice. Part of the charm of the house are the trees and shrubs that surround it.

253

ASICK HOUSE
307 First Street
—————————— c. 1860
Italianate Second Empire
Board and batten frame   2 stories   very good
Another five bay house rather similar to No. 215, but the windows have cornices. The eaves of the hipped roof are also much deeper and the cornice is supported by large coupled brackets, a treatment which is echoed on the verandah, which is supported by square posts. There is a side light and transom central doorway.

HOUSE
203 Fourth Avenue
—————————— 1840-50 (?)
Greek Revival
Brick   2 stories   poor
A five bay house with a Greek Revival door and multi-paned windows.

Thornburg Borough

THORNBURG PRESERVATION AREA
(See under Preservation Areas)

Turtle Creek Borough

ST. COLMAN'S ROMAN CATHOLIC CHURCH
128 Shaw Avenue
Fred C. Sauer   1901-03
Gothic
Brick and stone   1 story   good
This church extends the Revived Gothic image of the nineteenth century parish church into the twentieth century, very solidly if not very felicitously. For the most part the work of Fred Sauers was rather pedestrian, and this structure is less so than much of the rest. The chief merit of this type of church is to provide an interesting focal point in the otherwise dull landscape of an industrial suburb.

St. Colman's School nearby is an intriguing example of the medievalistic parish buliding of the 1920's. Designed by Link, Weber and Bowers, it was completed in 1929. Its patterned brick work is notable.

254

Upper St. Clair Township

GILFILLAN FARMHOUSE
1950 Washington Road
——————— 1855-57
Late Greek Revival and Second Empire
Brick   2 stories   very good
A three bay house of red brick, this structure is stylistically a combination of late Greek Revival and Second Empire elements with a side light and transom doorway, coupled windows, and a chimney at each end.

HOUSE
Segar Road
——————— pre-1850 (?)
Early Western Pennsylvania Vernacular
Stone   2 stories   good
This is a four bay house with large chimneys at each end. The stone is dressed but laid in random courses. There is a Victorian porch and shutters on Victorian sash windows. A log outbuilding stands in front of the house.
 Both of these buildings, almost unique in this area, must be preserved.

FULTON LOG HOUSE
Clifton-Bridgeville Road at Route 19 (l. r. 02240)
——————— pre-1850 (?)
Present use: empty
Log   2 stories   good
This old house is now being restored. It stands facing the interchange below Route 19.

255

DeMUTH-HARTMAN HOUSE
121 Hays Road

———————— 1881

Vernacular

Frame   2 stories   good

This is frame house of four bays with a long, five bay wing in the rear. It has a commanding site on a knoll. This house and the Johnson-Pollok house are the earliest extant in the district.

JOHNSON-POLLOK HOUSE
122 Hays Road

———————— 1882

Second Empire

Frame   2 stories   very good

A rather grand building, this house, painted white with green trim, is Second Empire in style. It has a chimney at each end, a small verandah in front and a water cave in the basement. Quite unique to its area, which sports only modern suburban villas, it must be preserved.

HOUSE
McMillan Road (l. r. 02052 north of 02240)

———————— pre-1840 (?)

Vernacular

Stone   1½ stories   very good

This house, sequestered in a valley and surrounded by pines, has modern frame extensions to both the side and rear. Nevertheless, much of its early and rather rough character has been preserved.

256

HOUSE
Morrow Run Road (l. r. 02052 south of 02240)
—————— pre-1850 (?)
Log   1 story   poor
This one story log house with a frame addition in the rear is in bad condition.

BARN
2333 Lesnett Road

—————   —————

Frame   —————   very good
This is an octagonal barn, a lone survivor of the type in the county. It is painted white and is well maintained.
    There is also a log outbuilding well preserved.

257

Verona Borough

BRUNOT HOUSE
729 Brunot Street

——————————— c. 1870

Victorian Medievalistic—Second Empire

Frame   2 stories and attic   good

Felix R. Brunot bought a large farm above the town of Verona in 1870 and presumably built the present house shortly thereafter. It was first occupied by the Brunot family in 1873, after which time they always spent their summers there. Their townhouse—a handsome Greek Revival structure located on the North Side at Stockton and Union Avenue—was recently demolished to make way for the new Allegheny Center.

The Verona house is a rather interesting frame version of the asymmetrically disposed mid-Victorian, medievalistic manor house that was throughout much of the nineteenth century the counterpart and rival in the field of domestic architecture of the Classical symmetrical Greek Revival dwelling. The householder of the mid-century, if he could afford it, could have the Greek in town and the medieval in the country or vice versa. Such eclecticism of residence was not uncommon.

In the Pittsburgh area the medieval manor house was, as one might suppose, often to be found in suburban areas. Most of these houses, have, however, proven quite unacceptable to later generations and they have largely disappeared. The Brunot house may be compared with more solidly built surviving examples—the Singer and Henderson houses (q.v.).

Versailles Borough

BAYARD HOUSE
4232 Third Street
—————————— pre-1850 (?)
Vernacular
Stone 2 stories good
This house is stone on the first story and brick on the second. It has heavy, dressed stone piers at the corners that are rather similar to the small stone house at 4232 Walnut Street in McKeesport (q.v.).

West Deer Township

BULL CREEK PRESBYTERIAN CHURCH
Tarentum-Culmerville Road
—————————— 1853
Vernacular Greek Revival
Brick 1 story fair
The first services here were held out-of-doors in 1796 and the first log church was built in 1801; another smaller one was erected in 1833 because the earlier church was too large to heat in the winter. In 1853 a substantial brick church was constructed; this rectangular gabled meeting-house with its blind arcading now serves as a recreation hall, since a new church has been erected across the road.

MARSHALL HOUSE
Bakerstown-Culmerville Road, two miles east of Bairdsford Road

—————— c. 1860

Stone   2 stories   very good

This house is part of a complex of farm buildings all of which were home-spun constructions and which have a curious crude, almost carrion, quality. The house, which is built of flat narrow stone quarried out of strata right next to it, rests in a declivity directly on a large slab of the formation, and the stone in the hill behind the house serves as one of the cellar walls. It is five bay with multi-paned windows and deep embrasures. The narrow stones, laid almost at random, give the house a primitive, makeshift quality that is both ingeniously original and somewhat grotesque. Inside there are great log beams in the basement but they are currently being consumed by termites.

Two of the most interesting structures on the property are a dry kiln and a corn

crib. The former is a small brick structure with slots in one side for six trays that hold fruits for drying by means of a fire lighted at the front. It is topped with a cupola holding a large bell that used to sound the dinner call.

The corn crib is propped on stones placed vertically in the ground and has a slate roof. It is made of large planks—up to almost twenty inches in width—held by square head nails. An interesting feature is a trough on either side from which corn can be removed when the crib is full. A barn, also with a slate roof, is supported by long hand-hewn logs and wooden pins. There is a two story wagon shed with weathered boards of a shimmering, deep rust color. On the quarry side of the house a large sagging frame building is hovering on a final slump into collapse. An optimistic effort to preclude the inevitable is a chain affixed to the structure and linked to a stone outcrop.

The entire complex far removed from the road and suffering visibly from desuetude, is the work and emblem of five generations of an Irish family that committed their lives to it, and while containing the unique impress of people who "made do" with local materials, it has a raw quality that in total effect is not entirely fortunate.

CHURCH HOUSE
Box 316 Rittman Road off Bakerstown-Culmerville Road
—————————— Before 1850 (?)
Log   1½ stories   fair
A three bay construction with heavy chinking and a frame extension to the rear, this house is located in a remote section near the Republic Steel colliery.

West Mifflin Borough

LEBANON PRESBYTERIAN CHURCH
Lebanon Church Road near County Airport
——————————   1871
Vernacular
Brick   1 story   very good
This church has a long history that might be considered as illustrative of the early building history of the County. The first building was apparently a rudimentary log structure with no windows and no floors, erected between 1776 and 1781. Before 1806 a second log construction was built that had windows and a door on one side. In 1823 the first brick church was constructed, but by the middle of the century this had become inadequate and in 1871 the cornerstone of the present church was laid. It was dedicated in 1872 and in March of the same year the name was officially changed from Lebanon Meeting House to Lebanon Presbyterian Church.

The present church is a simple brick building with plain pilasters and corbeling; it is constructed in the shape of a T with the cross bar at the back. The windows are pointed but lack tracery.

RHODES HOUSE
Ridgeview Drive off Bull Run Road
——————— c. 1850
Vernacular
Brick   2 stories   ———————
This house could not be examined because it lies in a prohibited area owned by the Atomic Energy Commission. Located near the old county airport it is a brick house of five bays painted white.

West View Borough

WEST VIEW BOROUGH HALL
Schwitter Street
Original use: house   Present use: borough hall
——————— c. 1870
Italianate-Second Empire
Brick   2 stories plus mansard   good
A large two-story red brick house originally built by the Schwitter family, it has a variegated slate mansard and a mansarded tower in center. There is also a stable garage, which has an Italian-villa tower.

BORLAND-JONES HOUSE
2683 McClintock Road
—————— 1831
Vernacular Greek Revival
Brick   2 stories   good
This house is one room deep with a single chimney and an extensive overhang at
the eaves. It is five bays wide and has a bracketed porch. There is a signature stone
in one gable end having the inscription "JA & NR 1831".

HOUSE
McClintock Road
Original use: house   Present use: empty
—————— 1850-1900 (?)
Vernacular
Brick   2 stories   good
This red brick, five bay, two story farmhouse with its slightly bracketed porch in
front and porch in rear exemplifies many such farmhouses in this survey and many
not included in it. For this reason, the County of Allegheny should preserve it in
the new park in which it now stands. It, unlike many of the others, would then
receive both protection and maintenance. The house is very well sited on a
knoll.

BAKER HOUSE
1901 Vermont
—————— 1850-1900 (?)
Vernacular
Brick   2 stories   good
This is a five bay house just one room deep with a plain corbeled brick cornice

and two chimneys. The original door is gone, and there is an early brick addition. The porch has been spoiled.

CHERRY LANE FARM
3511 State Street
——————— c. 1850 (?)

Vernacular
Frame   1½ stories   very good
A very pleasant house of five bays, two rooms deep with chimneys, it has a large and intrusive gabled addition to the second story with an addition also at the back containing a bay window and a Victorian porch.

RANKIN HOUSE
Rankin Road off White Oak Level Road
——————— c. 1850

Vernacular
Brick   2 stories   fair
This is a five bay, red brick, two story house with multi-paned windows, a fine doorway with transom and sidelights, and an original panelled door. There are simple mouldings on the cornice. The house is one room deep with an addition at the back. The porch may be original but it could also be a later addition.

Wilkinsburg Borough

COLONY OF ITALIAN VILLA HOUSES
7700 Abbott Street and 7700 block Edgerton Avenue
——————— c. 1875

Italian Villa
Brick   2 stories   good to fair
At the time these houses were built, their situation must have been something

264

rather more than suburban; perhaps rural would be a better word. Most of these houses are high-shouldered, miniature, and very late, versions of the Italian Villa style, although there are also a couple of rather nondescript cottages of the picturesque type. Most of them have villa towers with mansards (which would place them in the 1870's). The detail is rather crude, an instance being the vestigial drip moulds in brick over the windows.

SARVER-LOHR HOUSE
1023 Ross Avenue
—————— 1862

Vernacular
Frame   1½ stories   very good
This charming little four bay house, originally frame but now sided with aluminum,

with a central chimney, was built in 1862. The front and side porches were added in 1932. The structure recalls very gracefully the half-rural aspect of Wilkinsburg in the middle of the nineteenth century.

ROW HOUSES
7800 Inglenook Place
Frederick G. Scheibler, Jr.   1907
Early Modern
Brick   2 stories   fair to good

These simple row houses display Scheibler's early "Modernistic" manner reduced to an almost geometric simplicity. The name of the short "place" so connotative of cottage-like homey-ness, reflects the cozy tradition of the English vernacular in an early twentieth century Pittsburgh street. It is doubtful if these houses are now in very good condition. It would be pleasant, if not mandatory to preserve them.

They consist of three buildings of four units each on the south side in the 7800 block and another section of three units in a different design matched on the north side of the street with two sections of four units above toward Wood Street.

ROW HOUSES
1300 Singer Place
Frederick G. Scheibler, Jr.   1919
Early Modern
Brick   2 stories   good

These houses, very pleasant examples of Scheibler's middle period, are like strata of brick and glass emerging from a wooded hillside in Wilkinsburg. Again they are a tribute to Scheibler's marked talent in dealing with domestic architectural forms.

They consist of three sections, six units to a section, brick with wooden trim and sun porches, and a simple ribbon casement fenestration.

266

JOHN F. SINGER HOUSE
1318 Singer Place

——————— 1865-69

Gothic

Stone   2 stories and attic   poor

This is probably the largest, grandest, and possibly one might just say, the "best" example now surviving in the Pittsburgh area of the medievalistic "Gothic" manor house of the mid-nineteenth century. In this type of house, which was little more than a not very subtle expansion of the English ornamental villa or the cottage orné, the gables were sharp and pointed, the sashed Gothic arched windows were high and narrow and the barge boards and Tudor chimneys ubiquitous. A stone country house—as it was then—of such size and elaboration was unusual in Pittsburgh in the 1860's.

John F. Singer (c. 1834- c. 1880) was a partner in the steel manufacturing firm of Singer, Hartman & Co., which later became Singer, Nimick & Co. He bought, near the small town of Wilkinsburg, in the 1860's an estate of 30 acres which he laid out in the Romantic fashion with a large ornamental lake and

267

shrubberies. At one side of the house is a private chapel (now a garage), which at one time had a flêche as its central feature. This turret was probably removed in the 1930's.

Not only the materials but the carved ornament of the house are extremely rich, much of it partaking of the almost vulgar lavishness of the Second Empire. The interiors are also interesting in their eclectic richness of detail, although some of it has suffered through neglect. There is a particularly interesting "Gothic" staircase hall. Even in its present raddled state, this is still one of the best and the most effective High Victorian buildings extant in Pittsburgh. Every effort must be made to preserve it.

GRAHAM HOUSE
2015 Penn Avenue
——————— c. 1830
Frame   2 stories   very good
This house, which had the good fortune to fall into a "good" suburban enclave, has been perhaps almost too well treated, and it now has a slick neo-Williamsburg glaze, a suburban "woman's magazine" glamour which has, however, not removed it from the historical house category. It is five bays wide.

Wilkins Township

LINHART HOMESTEAD
221 Farnsworth Avenue
——————— c. 1782
Log   2 stories   very good
This is a two cell log house with double chimneys. It is in fine condition, and

is tucked into the side of a hill near the Turtle Creek Valley. The second house, was attached to the original by tie logs twelve years after the first part was built, to accomodate a married daughter. Although the Indians were friendly with the Linharts, "living together" was considered safer for the family. Later there was an Indian attack and the houses in the area were burned with the exception of the Linhart house. The occupants fled to Fort Braddock for safety but returned when danger had passed.

The Linharts owned the local saw mill and presumably used the best logs for their house. The house possesses enormous fireplaces constructed of local stone. It has been said that this is the oldest occupied house in Allegheny County.

Wilmerding Borough

WESTINGHOUSE AIR BRAKE COMPANY
ADMINISTRATION BUILDING
Original building architects unknown; Janssen & Cocken for
    addition   1890; 1896-97; 1928
Richardsonian Romanesque and French Renaissance
Sandstone and brick   4 stories and attic   very good
The first section built in 1890 was destroyed by fire in 1896; it was rebuilt in 1896-97. The new wing, which is early French Renaissance, was added in 1928 after the designs of Janssen and Cocken. The earlier building is rather Richardsonian Romanesque in style, but the later favors the early French Renaissance, and it is carried out in the suave manner for which Janssen was noted. A tall clock tower adds a note of dignity and consequence to the composition. This building dominates the town of Wilmerding and is visually quite important in the landscape.

MAPS

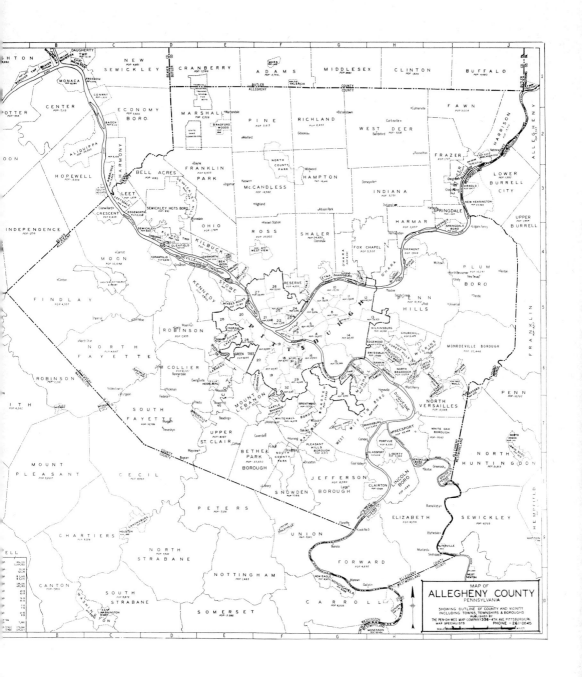

MAP OF
ALLEGHENY COUNTY
PENNSYLVANIA

SHOWING OUTLINE OF COUNTY AND VICINITY
INCLUDING TOWNS, TOWNSHIPS & BOROUGHS
PUBLISHED BY
THE PEN-OH-WES MAP COMPANY 336-4TH AVE PITTSBURGH,PA.
MAP SPECIALISTS   PHONE - 261-0645

271

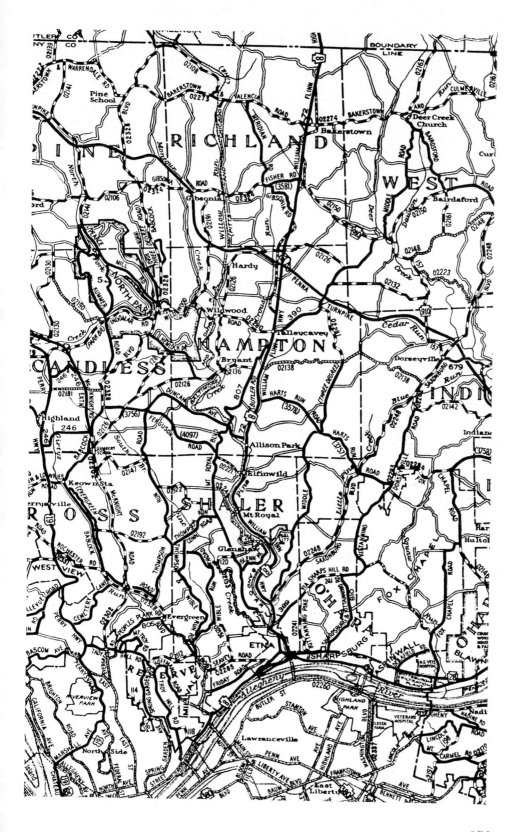

273

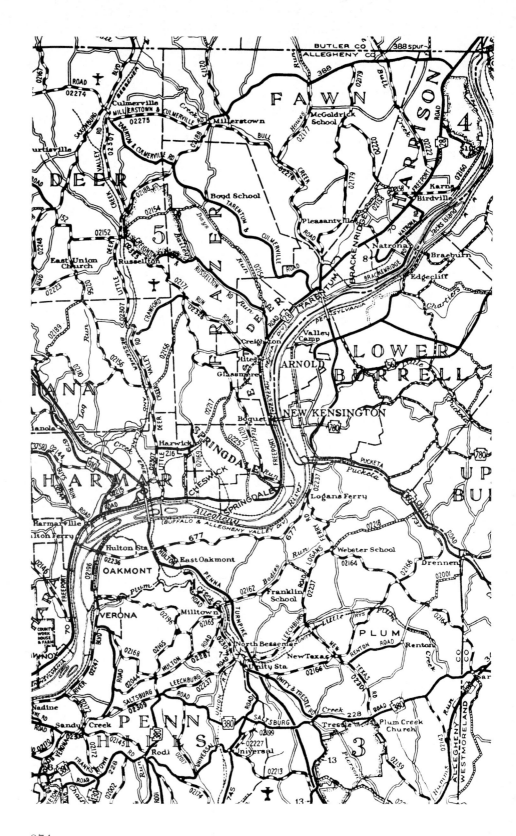

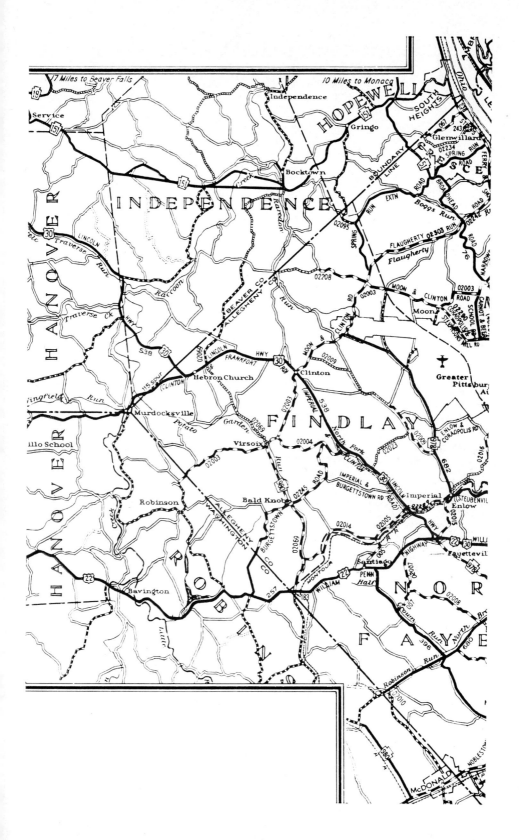

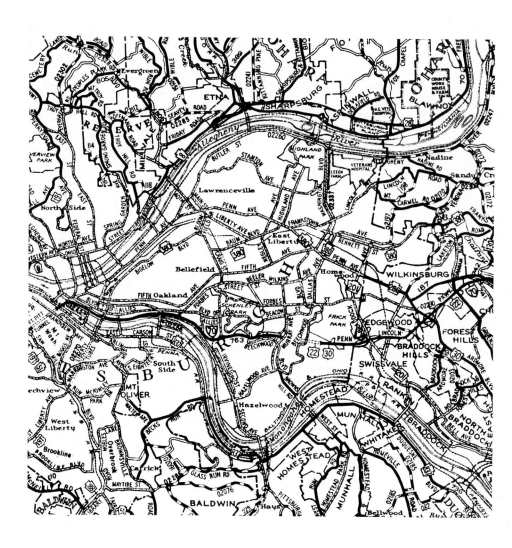

276

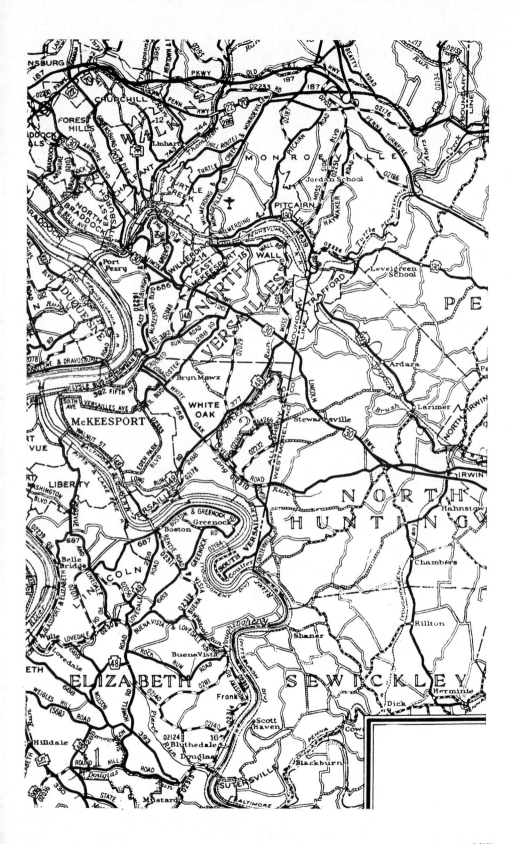

277

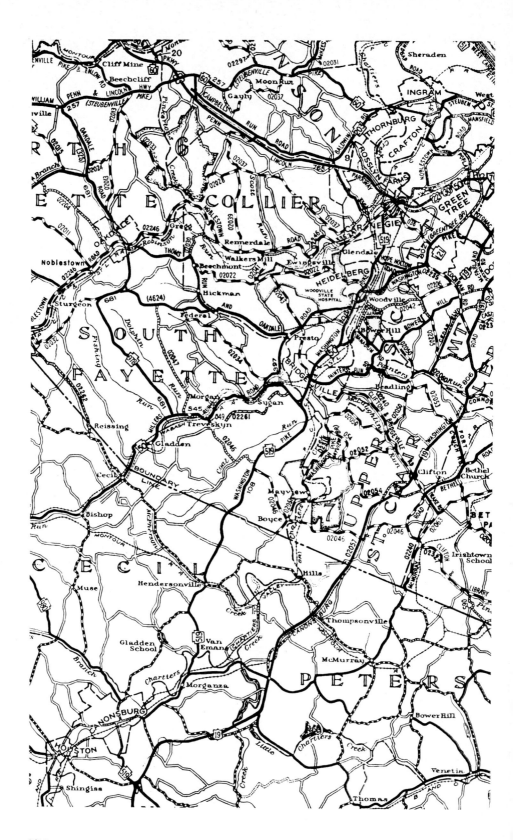

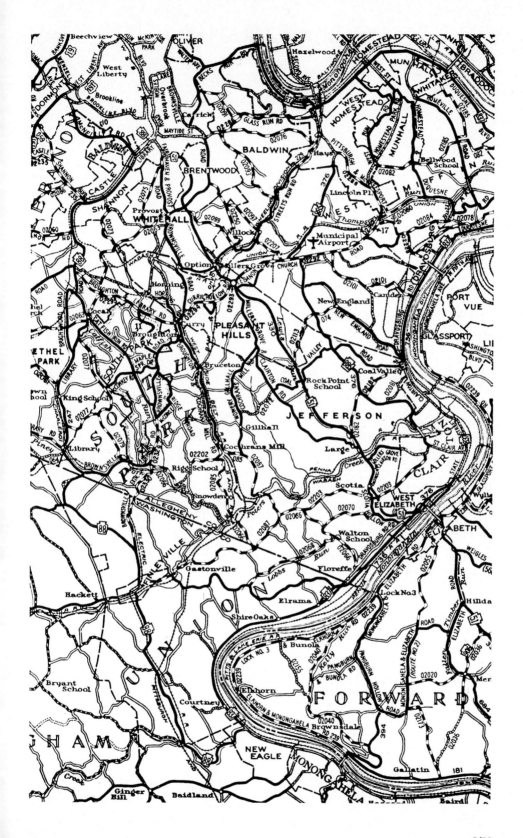

279

BIBLIOGRAPHY

Abbott, Walter D. and William E. Harrison, comp., *First One Hundred Years of McKeesport.* McKeesport: McKeesport Times, 1894

Account of the Work of the Art Commission of Pittsburgh from its Creation in 1911 to January 1st, 1915. Pittsburgh: Pittsburgh Printing Co., 1915

Agnew, Daniel, *Fort McIntosh and its Times: an Historical Sketch.* Pittsburgh: Myers, Shirkle & Co., 1893

Allegheny Cemetery, Pittsburgh. Pittsburgh: Blakewell Marthens, 1873

Allegheny County, Pennsylvania: Illustrated. Pittsburgh: Consolidated Illustrating Co., c. 1896

Allegheny County: miscellaneous historical transcripts from early newspaper files. 19 vols., Pennsylvania Historical Survey, 1942

Allegheny County-County Commissioners, Communication from the Commissioners to the Board of Prison Inspectors of Allegheny County in Relation to the Erection of New County Buildings. Submitted February 19, 1883, Pittsburgh, 1883

Allegheny General Hospital, *Annual Report.* Pittsburgh and Allegheny, 1889-1890, 1892-1906, 1922/23, 1964/65

American Architect and *Architecture.* 1876-February 1938 v. 1-152, no. 2666, 1876-1938

American Competitions. v. 1-3, 1907-13

Andrews, Wayne, *Architecture in America.* New York: Atheneum Publishers, 1960

——————————, *Architecture, Ambition and Americans.* New York: Harper, 1955

Annals of Mt. Lebanon: Commemorating the Twenty-fifth Anniversary of the Founding of Mt Lebanon Township. S. A. Schreiner, chairman. 1937

Archambault, A. Margaretta, ed., *A Guide Book of Art, Architecture and Historic Interests in Pennsylvania.* Philadelphia: John C. Winston Co., 1924

Architectural Forum. 1896-date, (monthly), 1896-1916 title reads, "The Brickbuilder".

The Architectural Record. July 1891-to date, vol. 1-to date

Architectural Review. Boston, November 1891-July 1921, v. 1-28

The Architectural Work of Graham, Anderson, Probst & White, Chicago, and Their Predecessors, D. H. Burnham & Co. and Graham, Burnham & Co. 2 vols., London: B. T. Batsford, Ltd., 1939

Art Work of Pittsburgh. Views of Pittsburgh, Allegheny and vicinity accompanied by a short sketch of the history of the two cities. Chicago: W. H. Parish Publishing Co., 1893

Art Work of Pittsburgh. Views of Pittsburgh and vicinity, preceded by a short description and historical sketch. George E. White Co., 1899

Atlas of the City of Pittsburgh, containing large scale maps of each of the 27 wards of the city, prepared by Lippincott, McNeil, Pittsburgh. Pittsburgh Map Co., 1911

Baldwin, Leland D., *Pittsburgh: The Story of a City.* Pittsburgh: University of Pittsburgh Press, 1937

Banker's Green Book: Official Directory of Financial Institutions (in the Pittsburgh district), Pittsburgh: Banker Publishing Co., 1908-09

Behind These Columns. Mellon Institute. Dedication of the New Building . . . Pittsburgh: Eddy Press Corp., 1937

Belfour, Stanton, *Centennial History of the Shadyside Presbyterian Church.* Pittsburgh: Davis & Warde, 1966

BI, The Bulletin Index. November 9, 1895-February 19, 1949, v. 32-133 no. 8, Pittsburgh, 1895-1949. (This represents the holdings of the Carnegie Library of Pittsburgh).

Bigger, Frederick comp., *Scrapbook of Newspaper Clippings Relative to City Planning (Pittsburgh) . . . and the History of Allegheny County.* 2 vols., vol. 1-1913-18, vol. 2-1924-26

The Blue Book Map of Pittsburgh, Allegheny, and Environs for 1902, published in connection with the *Pittsburgh and Allegheny Blue Book,* Pittsburgh: Elite Publishing Co., 1901

Booth & Flinn Company, Pittsburgh, Pa. *70 Years of General Contracting: A Review of Major Construction Accomplishments of Booth & Flinn Company, General Contractors, Pittsburgh, Pa., 1876-1946.* Pittsburgh, 1946

Boucher, John Newton, *Century and a Half of Pittsburgh and Her People.* 4 vols., Chicago: Lewis Publishing Co., 1908

The Brickbuilder, 1896-1916, architectural periodical, now "Architectural Forum, the magazine of building," (monthly), 1896-date.

Brookline, in manuscript form, n.d.

Buck, Solon J., *The Planting of Civilization in Western Pennsylvania.* Pittsburgh: University of Pittsburgh Press, 1939

Builder (Pittsburgh), v. 20-35, no. 3, April 1904-May 1919. (This represents the holdings of the Carnegie Library of Pittsburgh).

Burchard, John Ely and Albert Bush-Brown, *The Architecture of America: A Social and Cultural History.* Boston: Little, Brown, 1961

Calvary Church, Pittsburgh, Pennsylvania. Boston: R. G. Badger, 1908

Carnprobst, John L., "A Federal Case". *The Gun Report,* vol. IX, no. 11-12, vol. X, no. 1-2, April-July, 1964

Catholic Pittsburgh's One Hundred Years. Chicago: Loyola University Press, 1943

Centennial Anniversary, Sewickley Presbyterian Church 1838-1938. Sewickley, Pa., 1947

Centennial History, Calvary Episcopal Church, 1855-1955. Pittsburgh, Pa., 1955

Centennial Volume of the First Presbyterian Church of Pittsburgh, Pa. 1784-1884. Pittsburgh, Wm. G. Johnston & Co., 1884

Chapman, Thomas Jefferson, *Old Pittsburgh Days.* Pittsburgh: J. R. Weldin Co., 1900

Charette. (Journal of Architecture) vols. 1-46, Pittsburgh, 1920 to date

Church, Samuel Harden, *Short History of Pittsburgh, 1758-1908.* New York: DeVinne Press, 1908

City Hall, Pittsburgh: cornerstone laid May 5, 1869; dedicated May 23, 1872 (Report of the Board of Commissioners for the erection of a City Hall in Pittsburgh, created by Act of Assembly, March 1, 1867, giving cost of building, description etc.). Pittsburgh, 1874

Collins, John F. S. Jr., "*Stringtown on the Pike*". *Tales and History of East Liberty and the East Liberty Valley,* Ann Arbor, Michigan: Edwards Brothers, Inc., 1967

Cloudsley, Donald Hugh, *Selected Annotated Bibliography of Materials Relating to the Fort Pitt Block House of Pittsburgh, Pennsylvania.* A study submitted in partial fulfillment of the requirements for the degree of M. L. S. Carnegie Library School, Pittsburgh, 1949

Craig, Neville B., *History of Pittsburgh: With a Brief Notice of its Facilities of Communication and Other Advantages for Commercial and Manufacturing Purposes. With Introduction and Notes by G. J. Fleming.* Pittsburgh: J. R. Weldin Co., 1917

Cram, Ralph Adams, *My Life in Architecture.* Boston: Little, Brown & Co., 1936

Creighton, Thomas H., *American Architecture.* Washington: R. B. Luce, c. 1964

Christner, Alice C., *Here's to Thornburg.* Pittsburgh: Davis & Warde, Inc., 1966

Dahlinger, Charles William, *Pittsburgh: A Sketch of its Early Social Life.* New York: G. P. Putnam, 1916

——————————, *Fort Pitt.* Pittsburgh: privately printed, 1922

Daller, Very Rev. Lambert, *History of St. Mary's Parish, North Side, Pittsburgh, Pennsylvania. The 100th Anniversary, December 8, 1948.* Pittsburgh, 1948

Davis (R. S. & Co.), *Souvenir of Pittsburgh: Photo-gravures,* Pittsburgh: R. S. Davis Co., 1910

Davison, E. M. and E. B. McKee, *Annals of Old Wilkinsburg and Vicinity: The Village, 1788-1888.* ed. Wilkinsburg: Group for Historical Research, 1940

Day, J. Ingersoll, comp., *A Few of the Buildings Constructed by William Miller & Sons Company, Pittsburgh, Pa.* Pittsburgh, n.d.

Dedicatory Services of the New Edifice of the Third Presbyterian Church of Pittsburgh, Penna. Pittsburgh: W. G. Johnston & Co., 1869

Demorest, Rose, *Pittsburgh: A Bicentennial Tribute 1758-1958.* Pittsburgh: Carnegie Library of Pittsburgh, 1958

——————————, *Pittsburgh, A Brief History.* Pittsburgh: Carnegie Library of Pittsburgh, 1944

A Descriptive Guide of Calvary Church, Pittsburgh, Pennsylvania. Pittsburgh, c. 1946

Desmond, Harry William and Herbert Croly, *Stately Homes in America.* New York: D. Appleton & Co., 1903

Dickson, Harold Edward, *A Hundred Pennsylvania Buildings.* State College, Pa.: Bald Eagle Press, 1954

Douglass, Harlan Paul, *The Metropolitan Pittsburgh Church Study, 1948.* Pittsburgh: Executive Committee of the Metropolitan Pittsburgh Church Study, 1948

The East Liberty Presbyterian Church. Pittsburgh, 1935

Edgell, George Harold, *The American Architecture of Today.* New York: C. Scribner's Sons, 1928

Ellis, Agnes L., *Lights and Shadows of Sewickley Life.* Philadelphia: J. B. Lippincott Co., 1893

Federation of School Agencies of Pittsburgh and Allegheny County, *Census Tract Index to Streets and House Numbers in Allegheny County Outside Pittsburgh.* Allegheny County Board of Assistance and Federation of Social Agencies of Pittsburgh and Allegheny County, 1939

——————————, *Place Name Directory for Allegheny County and Contiguous Territories.*

281

Allegheny County Board of Assistance and Federation of Social Agencies of Pittsburgh and Allegheny County, 1939

Ferree, Barr, *American Estates and Gardens.* New York: Munn & Co., 1904

The Fiftieth Anniversary Exercises of the Presbyterian Church, Sewickley, Pennsylvania, February 17th, 1888. Pittsburgh: W. W. Waters, 1888

The First Baptist Church of Pittsburgh. Boston: Merrymount Press, 1925

Fisher & Stewart, comp., *The Illustrated Guide and Handbook of Pittsburgh and Allegheny.* 1887

50th Anniversary Celebration. Swissvale Executive Committee, 1948

Fleming, George T., *Pittsburgh: How to See It.* Pittsburgh: William G. Johnston Co., 1916

——————————, comp., *Flem's Views of Old Pittsburgh.* Pittsburgh: Privately printed, 1905

——————————, comp., *Fleming's Views of Old Pittsburgh: A Portfolio of the Past.* (new ed.) Pittsburgh: Crescent Press, 1932

Fording, Arthur M., *Recollections and Reminiscences of West End, Pittsburgh.* Pittsburgh, 1926

Fort Pitt, Pittsburgh, Penna. Pittsburgh: Point Park Commission, 1942

Frey, Laura C., *The Land in the Fork: Pittsburgh 1753-1914.* Philadelphia: Dorrance, 1955

Gilchrist, Harry C., *History of Wilkinsburg, Pennsylvania.* Pittsburgh: Nicolson Printing Co., 1927

Gormly, Agnes M. Hays, *Old Penn Street.* (3rd edition), Sewickley, 1943

Greater Pittsburgh: A Religious Center. Pittsburgh: Philadelphia Co., 1926

Guidebook of the New St. Paul's Cathedral. Pittsburgh, 1906

Guide for the Pennsylvania Railroad. Philadelphia: J. K. & P. G. Collins, 1855

A Guide to the Heinz Memorial Chapel, University of Pittsburgh. Pittsburgh: University of Pittsburgh Press, 1938

Hamlin, Talbot Faulkner, *Benjamin Henry Latrobe.* New York: Oxford University Press, 1955

——————————, *Greek Revival Architecture in America.* New York: Oxford University Press, 1944

Hardy, Abbott Lawrence, *Story of Pittsburgh: A Series of Historical Sketches, Prepared From Newspaper Files.* Pittsburgh: Pittsburgh *Post*, 1910

Hare, John C., *The Presbyterian Church in Pittsburgh 1837-1870.* Pittsburgh: Ph. D. Thesis, University of Pittsburgh, 1951

Harper, Frank C., *Pittsburgh: Forge of the Universe.* New York: Comet Press Books, 1957

——————————, *Pittsburgh of Today, Its Resources and People.* New York: The American Historical Society, Inc., 1931-32

Harpster, John W., *Houses and Architecture in Western Pennsylvania, 1750-1815.* University of Pittsburgh in MS form

Hawkins, Glenn Baker, *A Critical Study of Pittsburgh As Seen By Travelers Before 1808.* Pittsburgh: M. A. thesis University of Pittsburgh, 1926

Heckler, Frank W., *Greentree Borough, Chartered 1885, 75th Anniversary.* Pittsburgh, 1960

Heissenbuttel, Ernest G., *Pittsburgh Synod Congregational Histories.* Warren, Ohio: Studio of Printcraft, Inc., 1959

History and Commerce of Pittsburgh and Environs: Consisting of Allegheny, McKeesport, Braddock and Homestead. New York: A. F. Parsons Publishing Co., 1893-4

Historic American Buildings Survey. Catalogue of the measured drawings and photographs of the survey in the Library of Congress March 1, 1941. Washington: U. S. Government Printing Office, 1941. Supplement 1958

Historical Sketch of St. Peter's Church 1850-1918. Pittsburgh: Nicholson Printing Co., 1918

History of Allegheny County, Pennsylvania. 2 vols. in 1, Chicago: A. Warner & Co., 1889

History of Allegheny County, Pennsylvania, 1753-1876. Philadelphia: L. H. Everts & Co., 1876

History of the Origin and a Description of Memorial Hall of Allegheny County. Pittsburgh, 1910

A History of the Presbyterian Church of Sewickley, Pennsylvania. New York: The Knickerbocker Press, 1914

History of the Presbyterian Church of Sewickley, Pennsylvania. Consisting of certain addresses delivered February 16-19, 1913, on the occasion of the 75th anniversary of the permanent organization of the church, together with a compendium of events, photographs and notes. Privately printed, 1914

The History of the First English Evangelical Lutheran Church in Pittsburgh, 1837-1900. Philadelphia: J. B. Lippincott Co., 1909

Hitchcock, Henry Russell, *The Architecture of H. H. Richardson and His Times.* New York: The Museum of Modern Art, 1936

——————————, *The Architecture of H. H. Richardson and His Times.* (rev. ed.) Hamden, Conn.: Archon Books, 1961

Holland, William Jacob, "Pittsburgh and Its Environs" (In Jenkins, H.M., ed.) *Pennsylvania, Colonial and Federal.* v. 2, pp. 529-618

Homewood (Pa.) Board of Trade *Official Souvenir Program, 1900-1941: 41 Years of Progress*. Pittsburgh ?, 1941?

A History of Homestead and Community. Homestead: Messenger Publishing Co., 1917

G. M. Hopkins Co., *Atlas of the Cities of Pittsburgh and Allegheny, From the Official Records, Private Plans and Actual Surveys*. Philadelphia, 1882

——————————, *Atlas of the City of Allegheny*. 2 vols., Philadelphia, 1891

——————————, *Atlas of the Cities of Pittsburgh, Allegheny, and the Adjoining Boroughs, From the Actual Surveys and Official Records*. Philadelphia, 1872

——————————, *Atlas of the City of Pittsburgh*. 5 vols., Philadelphia, 1889-90

——————————, *Atlas of Greater Pittsburgh*. Philadelphia, 1910

——————————, *Real Estate Plat-Book of the Vicinity of Pittsburgh, From Official Records, Private Plans and Actual Surveys*. Philadelphia, 1895, 1896, 1900, 1903, 1905, 1906, 1915

——————————, *Real Estate Plat-Book of the City of Pittsburgh*. Philadelphia, 1898-1903, 1904-1906, 1911-1914, 1916-1940, 1939

Howard, John Tasker, *Ethelbert Nevin*. New York: Crowell, c. 1935

——————————, *Stephen Foster, America's Troubadour*. (rev. ed.), New York: Crowell, 1954

Huff, William S., "Richardson's Jail". *Western Pennsylvania Historical Magazine*, vol. 41, no. 1 (spring, 1958) pp. 41-59

Inland Architect and News Record, Feb. 1883-Dec. 1908, vol. 1-52, no. 6, 1883-1908

James, Alfred Procter, and Charles Morse Stotz, *Drums in the Forest: Decision at the Forks, and Defense in the Wilderness*. Pittsburgh: Historical Society of Western Penna., 1958

Jenkinson, Mrs. Anna (Claney), *History of Bellevue*. Pittsburgh: Iron City Printing Co., 1927

Jones, Mrs. Ellen Campbell, *A Brief History of Pittsburgh, 1728-1927*. Privately published by Mrs. Edw. A. Jones, 1927

Kelly, George E., ed., *Allegheny County, a Sesqui-centennial Review, 1788-1938*. Pittsburgh: Allegheny County Sesqui-centennial Committee, c. 1938

Kelly, J. M., *Handbook of Greater Pittsburgh*. First annual edition 1895, Pittsburgh: J. M. Kelly, 1895

Killikelly, Sarah Hutchins, *History of Pittsburgh: Its Rise and Progress*. Pittsburgh: B. C. & Gordon Montgomery Co., 1906

Kimball, Sidney Fiske, *American Architecture*. Indianapolis & New York: The Bobbs-Merrill Co., 1928

——————————, *Domestic Architecture of the American Colonies and of the Early Republic*. New York: Charles Scribner's Sons, 1922

King, J. Trainer, editor, *Pittsburgh, Past and Present. Leisure Hours*. vol. 2, Pittsburgh: O'Dwyer & Co., 1868, pp. 113-144

Klauder, Charles Teller, *College Architecture in America*. New York: C. Scribner's Sons, 1929

Lambing, Andrew Arnold, *A History of the Catholic Church in the Dioceses of Pittsburgh and Allegheny from Its Establishment to the Present Time*. New York: Benziger Brothers, 1880

Lambing, Andrew Arnolds and J. W. F. White, *Allegheny County: Its Early History and Subsequent Development From the Earliest Period Till 1790* (in Allegheny County, Penna. Centennial Committee Souvenir)

Lee, Edward B., *City County Building, Pittsburgh*. Pittsburgh, n.d.

Lewis, Virginia E., *Russell Smith, Romantic Realist*. Pittsburgh: University of Pittsburgh Press, 1957

Long, Haniel, *Pittsburgh Memoranda*. Santa Fe: Writers' Editions, 1935

Lorant, Stefan, ed., *Pittsburgh: The Story of an American City*. Garden City, New York: Doubleday, 1964

Macartney, Clarence Edward Noble, *Right Here in Pittsburgh*. Pittsburgh: The Gibson Press, c. 1937

MacQueen, James M., *Backgrounds and Beginnings of Architecture in Western Pennsylvania*.

Major, Howard, *The Domestic Architecture of the Early American Republic: The Greek Revival*. Philadelphia, London: J. B. Lippincott Co., 1926

Map of the Cities of Pittsburgh and Allegheny and of the Boroughs of South Pittsburgh, Birmingham, East Birmingham, Lawrenceville, Duquesne, and Manchester, etc., Pittsburgh: Schuchman, Haulein, 1852

Map of the Original Grants of Land by the Commonwealth of Pennsylvania in Pittsburgh and Vicinity, plotted from the patents and surveys, by J. K. Cochran, Sharpsburg, Pa. 1906

Map of Pittsburgh and its Environs, surveyed and published by Jean Barbeau and Lewis Keyon, engraved by N. B. Molineaux. 1839

Maps of Pittsburgh and Environs, 1858-1860, 1876, 1888, 1897-1899, 1901-1908, 1916-1922, 1925-1943, 1947-1950, Pittsburgh.

Maps and Plans Related to Fort Pitt and Fort Duquesne. Pittsburgh: Point Park Commission, 1943

283

McKinney, William Wilson, *Early Pittsburgh Presbyterianism*. Pittsburgh: The Gibson Press, 1938

——————————, ed. *The Presbyterian Valley*. Pittsburgh: Davis & Warde, Inc., 1958

Memorial of the Celebration of the Carnegie Institute of Pittsburgh, Pa. April 11, 12, 13, 1907. New York: The De Vinne Press, 1907

Memories Commemorating Clairton's 25th Anniversary. Pittsburgh: Clairton Silver Jubilee, Inc., 1947

Memoirs of Allegheny County, Pennsylvania: Personal and Genealogical With Portraits. 2 vols., Madison: Northwestern Historical Association, 1903

Miller, Mrs. Annie Moorhead (Clark), *Chronicles of Families, Houses and Estates of Pittsburgh and its Environs*. Pittsburgh, 1927

Moore, Charles, *Daniel H. Burnham, Architect, Planner of Cities*. 2 vols., Boston & New York: Houghton Mifflin Co., 1921

Mount Lebanon Fiftieth Anniversary, 1912-1962. Pittsburgh: Mt. Lebanon *News*, 1962

Mulkearn, Lois and Edwin V. Pugh, *A Traveler's Guide to Historic Western Pennsylvania*. Pittsburgh: University of Pittsburgh Press, 1954

Mumford, Lewis, *Sticks and Stones: A Study of American Architecture and Civilization*. New York: Boni and Liveright, 1924. 2nd rev. ed. New York: Dover Publications, 1955

——————————, *The Brown Decades: A Study of the Arts in America 1865-1895*. New York: Harcourt, Brace & Co., 1930, 2nd rev. ed. New York: Dover Publications, 1955

Negley, Georgina G., comp., *East Liberty Presbyterian Church: With Historical Setting and a Narrative of the Centennial Celebration April 12-20, 1919*. Pittsburgh: Murdock-Kerr & Company Press, 1919

Nelson, L. H. Co., *Pittsburgh*. Portland: L. H. Nelson Co., 1905

——————————, *Allegheny*. Portland: "Published exclusively for J. G. McCrory & Co., c. 1904

Nevin, Franklin Taylor, *The Village of Sewickley*. Sewickley: Sewickley Printing Shop, 1929

Nichols, Lowell W., ed., *Alexander C. Robinson Collection of Western Pennsylvaniana: an Annotated Catalogue*. Sewickley: Library Society of Sewickley, 1940

North Braddock Golden Jubilee, 1897-1947. Pittsburgh, 1947

Oakmont Golden Anniversary, 1889-1939. Pittsburgh: Allegheny Valley Advance Leader, 1939

Official Municipal Program of the Sesqui-centennial Celebration of the City of Pittsburgh, September 27-October 3 and November 25, 1908. Pittsburgh, 1908

Official Report of the Dedicatory Exercises Held at the New Court House at the City of Pittsburgh, County of Allegheny, September 24, 1888. Pittsburgh: William G. Johnston & Co., 1889

Official Souvenir. Fourth Annual Convention National Association of Master Bakers . . . 1901. Pittsburgh: Eichbaum Press, 1901

Official Souvenir Program, 1900-1941: 41 Years of Progress. Pittsburgh: Homewood Board of Trade, 1941?

Olmsted, Frederick Law, *Pittsburgh Main Thoroughfares and the Downtown District: Improvements Necessary to Meet the City's Present and Future Needs*. Pittsburgh, c. 1911

100 Views of Pittsburgh. Pittsburgh: Hammond Hook & Co., 189?

Our Cities, Picturesque and Commercial: Pittsburgh, Allegheny and Vicinity. Pittsburgh: Pittsburgh Foundrymen's Association, 1899

Palmer, Robert M., pub., *Pictorial Pittsburgh and Prominent Pittsburghers Past and Present*. (with history of Pittsburgh by H. M. Phelps) Pittsburgh, 1905

——————————, *Views of Pittsburgh and Environs*. Pittsburgh, 1903

Parke, John E., *Recollections of Seventy Years and Historical Gleanings of Allegheny, Pennsylvania*. Boston: Rand, Avery & Company, 1886

Past and Present of Trinity Episcopal Church: Our Hundredth Anniversary. Pittsburgh, 1898

A Photographic Reproduction of the Original Map of Lawrenceville, surveyed by Rev. John Taylor and used by W. B. Foster for 20 years in the sale of his lots. 1815-16

Pittsburgh (an illustrated pamphlet descriptive of the city, its buildings and industries, issued for the tenth annual meeting of the American Street Railway Association in Pittsburgh, October 21-23, 1891). Pittsburgh, 1891

Pittsburgh, engraved from R. E. McGowen's map for George H. Thurston, Pittsburgh: Wm. Schuchman & Bro., 1856

Pittsburgh Architectural Club Yearbooks; Annual Exhibitions (1st-11th), 1900-16. 1900-17. 11 vols.

Pittsburgh and Allegheny. (Folder of photographs, continuous strip folded) Columbus: Ward Bros., c. 1900

Pittsburgh and Allegheny. (Folder of views). Witternan, c. 1885

Pittsburgh and Allegheny. Pittsburgh: Myers, Shinkle & Co., 1892

Pittsburgh and Allegheny Illustrated Review: Historical, Biographical, and Commercial. Pittsburgh: J. M. Eistner & Co., 1889

Pittsburgh and Its Exposition. Pittsburgh: Press of Pittsburgh Photo Engraving Co., 1889

Pittsburgh Art Commission, *Program of Competition: Entrance to Schenley Park*. Pittsburgh, 1914

284

_____, *Annual Reports 1911-12-1915* (In Pittsburgh Annual Reports of the Departments and Offices, 1911-12-1915)

_____, *Annual Report-Pittsburgh 1916-18*

"Pittsburgh as an Art Center", *Art and Archaeology, 1922*. Pittsburgh double number which appeared as vol. 14, no. 5-6, Nov.-Dec. 1922 of *Art and Archaeology*

"Pittsburgh as seen by early travelers; descriptions by those who visited it from 1783 to 1818." Reprints published in the *Monthly Bulletin* of the Carnegie Library of Pittsburgh. April 1902-June 1906

Pittsburgh at the Dawn of the 20th Century, the Busiest City in the World. Pittsburgh: Pittsburgh Photo Engraving Co. for the Pittsburgh *Leader*

Pittsburgh Blue Book, vol. 1, 1887, vol. 2-30, 1889, vol. 31, 1932, vol. 32-33, 1936, vol. 34, 1940, vol. 34a, 1942, vol. 35-39, 1944, vol. 40, 1954, vol. 41, 1956, vol. 42, 1958, vol. 43, 1960, vol. 44, 1962, vol. 45, 1964, vol. 46, 1966. Pittsburgh: Blue Book Publishing Co.

Pittsburgh, Commemorating the Fiftieth Anniversary of the Engineers' Society of Western Pennsylvania. Pittsburgh: Cramer Printing & Publishing Co., 1930

Pittsburgh: the Distributing Point for the West and South. Allegheny County Destined to be the Greatest Manufacturing Center of the World. Pittsburgh: Mercantile Illustrating Co., 1900

Pittsburgh District Survey, Russell Sage Foundation, 6 vols., Philadelphia: William F. Fell Co., 1914

Pittsburgh Illustrated (text by C. T. Dawson). Full page pictures of residences and public buildings with descriptive text. H. R. Page & Co., 1889

Pittsburgh in Ye Olden Time: a Pictorial and Chronological Review of the First Century of its History. "A souvenir of the Sesqui-centennial, 1758-1908". Pittsburgh: Benton, 1908

Pittsburgh Quote, vol. 1-3, no. 1, 1955-58, vol. 4-8, 1959-64. Pittsburgh: Herbick & Held Co.

Pittsburgh Strangers' City Guide. Pittsburgh: McFarland, 1871

Powell, Lyman P. (ed.), *Historic Tours of the Middle States*. New York and London: G. P. Putnam's Sons, 1899

Presbyterian Banner Special number on the history of Pittsburgh and Pittsburgh Churches, Pittsburgh, 1926, vol. 113, no. 17 (Oct. 28, 1926)

Removal of Present County Jail and Rebuilding of Same in Conjunction with New County Office Building and Power Plant. Pittsburgh: Department of Public Works, Allegheny County, 1925

Report of Point Park Commission. Pt. 1, Pittsburgh, c. 1944

Report on the Celebration of the Centennial of Allegheny County at Pittsburgh, September 24-26, 1888. Pittsburgh: Smith, 1899

Robb, Mary Cooper, *The Presbyterian Church of Sewickley, Pennsylvania, 1838-1963*. Pittsburgh: Davis & Warde, Inc., 1963

Ross Township Sesqui-centennial, September 8-19, 1959. Pittsburgh, 1959

Sacred Heart Church, Pittsburgh, Pa. Pittsburgh, 1945

Sacred Heart Church, Shady Avenue & Walnut Street Guide Book. Pittsburgh, 1927

Schoyer, William T., *A Century of Saving Dollars 1855-1955*. Pittsburgh: Davis & Warde, 1955

Schuyler, Montgomery, *American Architecture*. New York: Harper & Brothers, 1892

_____, *American Architecture and Other Writings*, ed. William H. Jordy and Ralph T. Coe. 2 vols. Cambridge, Mass., 1961

Building of Pittsburgh, 1911. Issued as the Pittsburgh number of the *Architectural Record*. vol. 30, no. 3, (September 1911)

Scott, Henry Brownfield, ed., *Sesqui-centennial and Historical Souvenir of the Greater Pittsburgh*. Pittsburgh: Davis & Mason, 1908

Seawright, Delmar Clarence, *The Effect of City Growth on the Homewood-Brushton District of Pittsburgh*. Pittsburgh: MA thesis University of Pittsburgh, 1932

Sesqui-centennial of the Plum Creek Presbyterian Church, New Texas, Pennsylvania 1802-1952

Sewickley Centennial: One Hundredth Anniversary of the Naming of the Town "Sewickleyville". 1940

Sexton, Randolph Williams, *American Apartment Houses, Hotels, and Apartment Hotels of Today*. New York: Architectural Book Publishing Co., Inc., 1929

Shields, Betty G. M., *A Short History of the Shields Presbyterian Church*. Pittsburgh: Chatham Associates, 1964

Shinn, Rev. George Wolfe, *King's Handbook of Notable Episcopal Churches*. Boston: Moses King Corp., 1889

Slattery, Charles Lewis, *Felix Reville Brunot, 1820-1898*. A civilian in the war for the Union, President of the first Board of Indian commissioners, 1901

Smith, Joseph, *Old Redstone* or *Historical Sketches of Western Presbyterianism*. Philadelphia: Lippincott, Granbo Co., 1854

Souvenir Program Celebrating 150 Years of Progress. County of Allegheny sesqui-centennial, 1788-1938, Pittsburgh, 1938

Stewart, Howard B., comp., *Historical Data, Pittsburgh's Public Parks*. Scrapbook (Carnegie Library of Pittsburgh).

Writer's program-Pennsylvania, *Story of Old Allegheny City.* (compiled by workers of the writer's program of the Works Projects Administration in . . . Pennsylvania), Pittsburgh: The Allegheny Centennial Committee. 1941

The Story of Pittsburgh and Vicinity, Illustrated. Pittsburgh: Pittsburgh *Gazette Times,* 1908

Stotz, Charles Morse, *The Architectural Heritage of Early Western Pennsylvania.* Pittsburgh: University of Pittsburgh Press, 1966

——————————, *Defense in the Wilderness.* Pittsburgh: Historical Society of Western Pennsylvania, 1958

——————————, *Bibliography of Books From Which Notes Have Been Taken for the Text of the Western Pennsylvania Architectural Survey.* Typewritten copy (Carnegie Library of Pittsburgh)

——————————, *The Early Architecture of Western Pennsylvania, a Record of Building Before 1860.* New York: published by W. Helburn, Inc. for the Buhl Foundation, 1936

Strassburger, William J., *Grant Building: Pittsburgh's Largest, Tallest and Most Modern Office Building.* Pittsburgh: Grant Building, Inc., 1928

Stryker, Roy Emerson, *A Pittsburgh Album 1758-1958.* Pittsburgh: Herbick & Held Printing Co., 1959

Sturgis, Russell, *A Review of the Work of George H. Post.* New York (?): Architectural Record Co., c. 1898

Swetnam, George, *Where Else But Pittsburgh!* Pittsburgh: Davis & Warde, 1958

——————————, *The Bi-Centennial History of Pittsburgh and Allegheny County.* Pittsburgh: Historical Record Assoc., 1955

Tallmadge, Thomas Eddy, *The Story of Architecture in America.* New York: W. W. Norton & Co., 1936

Taylor, George, Jr., *The Beulah Romance: History of the Beulah Presbyterian Church.* Pittsburgh, 1954

Thompson, Vance, *Ethelbert Nevin.* Boston: Boston Music Company, 1913

Thurston, George Henry, *Allegheny County's Hundred Years.* Pittsburgh: A. A. Anderson & Son, 1888

——————————, *Directory of the Monongahela and Youghiogheny Valleys.* Pittsburgh: A. A. Anderson & Co., 1859

——————————, *The Book of the Fair.* Pittsburgh: A. A. Anderson, 1860

——————————, *Pittsburgh and Allegheny in the Centennial Year.* Pittsburgh: A. A. Anderson, 1876

Union Arcade Building, Fifth Avenue, Grant Street, Oliver Avenue & William Penn Place. Pittsburgh (?), 1916

United States Treasury Department, *History of Public Buildings Under the Control of the Treasury Department, Exclusive of Marine Hospitals and Quarantine Stations.* Washington: Government Printing Office, 1901

Up-town, Greater Pittsburg's Classic Section. East End. The World's Most Beautiful Suburb. Pittsburgh: Stewart Brothers, 1907

Van Renssalaer, Mariana (Griswold), *Henry Hobson Richardson and His Works.* Boston and New York: Houghton, Mifflin & Co., 1888

Van Trump, James D., "An American Palace of Culture: The Architecture of the Carnegie Institute Building." *Carnegie Magazine* XXXII: 1 (January 1958) 21-30; 2 (February 1958) 51-61

——————————, *An Architectural Tour of Pittsburgh.* (rev. ed.) Pittsburgh: Pittsburgh History and Landmarks Foundation, 1965

——————————, *The Architecture of Frederick G. Scheibler, Jr.* (Catalogue of an exhibition). Pittsburgh: Carnegie Institute, 1962

——————————, "Castles on the Allegheny". (An architect's fantastic demesne near Pittsburgh). *Charette* 43: 2 (March 1963) 8-10

——————————, "The Church Beyond Fashion". (A discussion of Henry Hobson Richardson's Emmanuel Church) *Charette* XXXVIII: 4 (April 1958) 26-29

——————————, "Dramatic Prelude: The Rotunda of the Pennsylvania Station in Pittsburgh". *Carnegie Magazine* XXXI: 8 (October 1957) 266-267

——————————, *Evergreen Hamlet.* Pittsburgh: Pittsburgh History & Landmarks Foundation, 1967

——————————, "From Log Cabin to Cathedral: The Pittsburgh Church Building 1787-1960". *Charette* 41: 9 (September 1961) 2-13

——————————, "Gargoyles from Texas". (A study of the sculpture of Calvary Methodist Church) *Carnegie Magazine* XXX: 8 (October 1956) 275-279

——————————, "The Gothic Revival in Pittsburgh". *Charette* XXXVII: 3 (March 1957) 23-25, 30-32; 4 (April 1957) 15-17, 32-33; 5 (May 1957) 20-22, 27-30; 8 (August 1957) 14-18

——————————, "The Lamp of Demos: Some Pittsburgh Public School Buildings of the Past". *Charette* 42: 3 (March 1962) 17-20

——————————, *Legend in Modern Gothic: The Union Trust Building, Pittsburgh.* Pittsburgh: Pittsburgh History & Landmarks Foundation, 1966

286

_____, "Lions in the Streets: A Sculptural Hunting Party in Pittsburgh". *Carnegie Magazine* XXXIV: 2 (February 1960) 41-44, 52

_____ and Arthur P. Ziegler, Jr., *1300-1335 Liverpool Street, Manchester, Old Allegheny, Pittsburgh*. Pittsburgh: Pittsburgh History & Landmarks Foundation, 1965

_____, "The Mountain and the City: The History of Shadyside Presbyterian Church, Pittsburgh, as Seen Through its Architecture". *Western Pennsylvania Historical Magazine* 44: 1 (March 1961) 21-34

_____, "Of Footbridges and Preservation". *Western Pennsylvania Historical Magazine* 43: 1 (March 1960) 135-146

_____, "The Palace, the Loft and the Tower-Some Notes on the Development of the Urban Hotel in Pittsburgh". *Charette* 42: 11 (October 1962) 12-17

_____, "Pittsburgh's Church of the Ascension". *Charette* XXXVI: 6 (June 1956) 14-16, 29

_____, "A Pittsburgh Palazzo, The House of Arthur E. Braun". *Carnegie Magazine* XXXIII: 1 (January 1959) 23-30

_____, "A Pittsburgh Pantheon: Allegheny Cemetery". *Carnegie Magazine* XXXIII: 1 (January 1959) 271-273

_____, "Pittsburgh Railroad Stations Past and Present". *Charette* XXXVII: 12 (December 1957) 19-22, 35; XXXVIII: 1 (January 1958) 21-30; 2 (February 1958) 51-61

_____, "Project H. H. Richardson: The Allegheny Court House and Jail". *Charette* 42: 5 (May 1962) 4-5, 20

_____, "A Prophet of Modern Architecture in Pittsburgh: Frederick G. Scheibler, Jr." *Charette* 42: 10 (October 1962) 1-15

_____, *Railroad Stations of Pennsylvania. Their Architecture and History 1800-1964*. Pittsburgh, 1964

_____, "The Romanesque Revival in Pittsburgh". *Journal of the Society of Architectural Historians* XVI: 3 (October 1957) 23-29

_____, "St. Peter's Pittsburgh by John Notman". *Journal of the Society of Architectural Historians* XV: 2 (May 1956) 19-23

_____, "The Skyscraper as Monument". *Charette* 43: 4 (April 1963) 10-13, 21

_____ and Barry Hannegan, "King's Folly". *Western Pennsylvania Historical Magazine* 41: 1 (Spring 1958) 11-16

_____ and Barry Hannegan, "The Stones of Carnegie Tech". *Charette* XXXVIII: 9 (September 1958) 23-25, 27; 11 (November 1958) 25-29, 35

_____, "The Stones of Venice in Pittsburgh: The Pittsburgh Athletic Association Clubhouse". *Charette* XXXIX: 4 (April 1959) 24-27

_____, "Temples of Finance". *Charette* Part II (Pittsburgh) 44: 5 (May 1964) 31-35

_____, "This Great Hospital: Some Pennsylvania General Hospitals". *Charette* Part III, 45: 4 (April 1965) 10-15; Part IV, 46: 12 (December 1966) 6-11

_____, "The Tomb, the Temple and the Casts: The Hall of Architecture and Sculpture Court at Carnegie Institute". *Carnegie Magazine* XXXII: 5 (May 1958) 167-174

_____, "Towers for the Tycoons: Pittsburgh Industrialists and Their Monuments". *Pittsburgh Quote* (June 1960) 18-23

_____, "The Triumphant Stone: A Study of the Foyer at Carnegie Music Hall" *Carnegie Magazine* XXX: 5 (May 1957) 167-175

_____, "The Unsubmerged Cathedral-Trinity, Pittsburgh". *The Cathedral Age* XXXII: 3 (Autumn 1957) 10-13

_____, "The Urn and the Tree: A Commentary on the Early Days of Carnegie Museum". *Carnegie Magazine* XXXIII: 5 (May 1959) 169-174

Wagner's Complete Map of Pittsburgh and the Adjourning Boroughs. Pittsburgh: Wagner, 1920

Wainwright, Nicholas B., *George Groghan, Wilderness Diplomat*. Chapel Hill: University of North Carolina Press, 1959

Ward Maps of Pittsburgh as Redistricted in 1924. Pittsburgh: Lippincott & McNeil, 1924

Western Architect. 1908-March 1931, vol. 11-40

Western Pennsylvania Historical Magazine. (Quarterly) 1918, vol. 1 to date. Pittsburgh

WHARTON, ANNE HOLLINGSWORTH, *In Old Pennsylvania Towns*. Philadelphia: J. B. Lippincott Co., 1920

Whitaker, Charles Harris, ed., *Bertram Grosvenor Goodhue, Architect and Master of Many Arts*. New York: Press of the American Institute of Architects, 1925

WHITE, EDWARD, *150 Years of Unparalleled Thrift: Pittsburgh's Sesqui-centennial Chronicling a Development from a Frontier Camp to a Mighty City*. (Official history and programme) Pittsburgh: White, 1908

Wiley, Richard Taylor, *Monongahela, the River and its Region*. Butler: The Ziegler Co., c. 1937

Wilhelm, Carl, *Complete History of the City of Allegheny, 1740-1890*. 1890

The William Penn Snyder Home, 852 Ridge Avenue, Pittsburgh. American General Life Insurance Company of Delaware-Pittsburgh Regional Home Office. Pittsburgh, 1965

Wilmerding's 50th Anniversary Celebration. Wilmerding, 1940

Wilson, Erasmus, ed., *Standard History of Pittsburg, Pennsylvania.* Chicago: H. R. Cornell & Co., 1898

Withey, Henry F. and Elsie Rathburn, *Biographical Dictionary of American Architects (Deceased).* Los Angeles: New Age Publishing Co., 1956

The Work of Cram and Ferguson, Architects, Including Work by Cram, Goodhue and Ferguson. New York: The Pencil Points Press, Inc., 1929

Official Publication Commemorating McKeesport's "Old Homeweek Celebration", 1759-1960. Yount., B.A., ed., 1960

Yountz, Philip Newell, *American Life in Architecture.* Chicago: American Library Association, 1932

Ziegler, Arthur P., Jr., *Pittsburgh History & Landmarks Foundation: Our First Fifteen Months.* Pittsburgh: Pittsburgh History & Landmarks Foundation, 1966

INDEX

Architects

Areas

Structures

APARTMENTS

291

HOSPITALS

HOTELS

HOUSES

LIBRARIES

Miscellaneous